DISSENT—
The Dynamic
of Democracy

DISSENT—
The Dynamic
of Democracy

George S. Swope

A Division of American Management Association

TO
My Mother, My Father,
Mag, and Charlie

Preface

WE are in an age of disquiet, an age of dissent in which the most time-honored customs and traditions are under challenge. The leaders of institutions are questioned and confronted daily by restive members. Authority is openly resisted.

Such an age is not new in the world. A study of the eighteenth century reveals many of the characteristics—the same inquiring and dissenting attitudes, for example, that are found today. Much of our problem is caused by institutional lag. All too often, institutions have allowed their traditions, outlooks, and ways of life to depend upon the past and have failed to adjust their practices to the demands of a more informed and independent-minded group.

Today we are more aware and far less tolerant of the obedience demands of institutions. We want a greater voice and authority in matters affecting our welfare. These are the demands of the times, and intelligent leadership must meet them if its institutions are to survive in an effective way. This applies to all institutions, whether political, economic, religious, or educational.

One of the major challenges today is: What should leadership do to manage rightful dissent, to avoid having it turn into strikes and riots? And, should the break-up point be reached and riots occur, what steps ought to be taken?

Unfortunately, leadership of many of our institutions lacks the experience, particularly in the universities, to know what to do and what not to do when striking or rioting is either incipient or under way. Many times, appeasement has been used when a firm stand was in order. But appeasement leads only to more and more demands, until authority reaches the point of no return, has to stop and face the dissidents, or capitulates. Or it may return violent action with strong reaction, which only increases the fury.

The world of labor-management relations went through the violent period long ago, and in that arena, much has been learned about the causes of dissent, strikes, and rioting; how to resolve them; and, *more importantly,* how to prevent them from occurring in the first place.

Although there is still dissent between labor and management, the uproarious days have long since ended. Many problems are settled amicably between the two. The public, however, sees only the Titan disagreements and not the cooperative relationships.

It is in this field that we may look to find, in part, lessons about how to manage dissent. This book analyzes the forces at work that cause dissent and attempts to offer leadership guidelines for adjusting and managing our institutions during these tumultuous times.

Deciding who should be shown deserved appreciation in an acknowledgment is a difficult task, because I owe so many a debt for wise counsel and guidance. Space demands that I confine my expression of thanks to a few of those who have influenced my executive career or have been particularly helpful.

To the late Clarence B. Randall, who taught so many of us to sense the urgent need for executives to articulate the actions of management and take the initiative in exercising the public responsibility of business, I pay my deep respects. His foresight was so keen that only now—forty years later—are leaders coming to understand his sound principles for executive development in a space age.

For his wisdom I also offer my respects to F. E. Burgess, former chief executive officer of the Burgess-Norton Mfg. Company.

I would like to extend my appreciation to my partner, William L. Davidson, and to my associates, Dr. Philip Ash, John Magos, Robert Harschnek, and Cherry Smith.

To Elwyn Smith, Gordon Smith, and others so helpful during my tenure at the SCM Corporation, I give my regards.

For assistance and advice, I offer a thank you to William S. North, president of the Union Special Machine Company.

Also, I offer my appreciation to George C. McKann, Jr., executive vice-president of the Midwest Industrial Management Association.

I thank George S. Swope, Jr. for his assistance in writing this book.

George S. Swope

Contents

1

The Age of Dissent

IN this age of dissent, basic forces are at work in society causing discontent against the customary conformance demanded by our institutional traditions. Among these forces are technological acceleration, the educational boom, the growth of affluence, the shrinking of the world, ease of movement, and lack of stimulation on the job.

Technological Acceleration

This is a time of spectacular technological achievement and invention. It is reflected in the amount of capital we have employed in research and development. For example, more has been spent since the beginning of World War II than had ever been spent before that time. One may argue that we have channeled too much capital into technological research instead of using it to relieve poverty and suffering—but it remains a fact.

During these years the transistor, computer, inertial guidance systems, and atomic, rocket, and jet power have been invented. Without them flying to the moon would be impossible. Man, in less than a lifetime, has gone from Orville Wright's wobbly, twelve-second, one-hundred-and-twenty-foot flight to Neil Armstrong's giant step. This is one of the great technical advances of any age.

1

In the field of transportation, not only have we developed jet- and rocket-powered aircraft, but we have also produced advanced cars, arterial highways, radio, radar, and television.

Our achievements have not been in the physical sciences alone. Outstanding progress has been made in the behavioral sciences as well. Economists have refined techniques for predicting the course of the economy; we have better control over the direction it will take and have not had a deep depression for over thirty years. Psychologists are learning more about human behavior. Sociologists, in their study of societies, have contributed much to our understanding of human organization and of why social fabrics have come to be structured as they are.

The medical profession has reduced childbirth deaths to a minimal number and now seems to be on the threshold of conquering deadly cancer. The transplant of organs from one human to another is no longer a rare occurrence.

These are blessings indeed, but they have brought with them hard problems. The ease with which we can move about and communicate with each other tolls the end of a nationalistic era in which peoples could live in a state of independence. The world political and social structure is rapidly becoming less and less one of isolated nations with few metropolitan centers and many isolated towns and villages. Nations have become interdependent, metropolitan centers are growing, and towns and villages are connected to the centers and the world by transportation systems and communications.

This is at once a cause of conflict and the hope of the future. Developments are forcing nations with customs foreign to each other to learn to live together. Out of the learning rises the conflict. But as we learn, we increase the level of international understanding.

We have not solved the problems of poverty and pollution. Pollution is one that man's inventiveness will one day conquer. He simply needs to recognize the problem and turn his creative concentration to it. Poverty we may not ever eliminate, but we can at least alleviate it.

The Educational Boom

An abundant world has made it possible to realize our strong aspirations for more education. The widespread demand at the college level has created massive educational institutions—the multiversities.

The vast size of these institutions causes students to lose their sense of individual identity. The educational life of the young is long, and it keeps them removed from the responsibilities and actions of the adult world after they have matured. They are not allowed to function as grown-up individuals, but are compelled to remain in cloistered affluence. They say, "You demand that we act and be adults without the responsibility of an adult. This causes us to be frustrated." They want to be given responsibility, but the paternalistic system won't permit it, and they are rebelling.

The educational boom is not confined to the colleges and universities alone. Sources of information are more readily available to everyone. We learn through papers, periodicals, radio, and television. The ease with which we can travel about the world exposes us to the experiences and customs of others, increasing and broadening our knowledge. The result of this is a better educated, more aware, and more informed citizenry.

The Affluent Generation

Our children have been raised in an environment of affluence by a generation deprived of many advantages by a depression and a war. We know what want is; our children do not. Because we don't wish them to undergo what we did, and because we can afford it, we thrust material advantages on them and are permissive. At the same time that we have given them material comforts, which they accept as a matter of course, we have been less attentive to their psychological needs for understanding and assistance in coping with growing into mature individuals. As a result, our relationship with our children, instead of being a close one, has sometimes become sterile.

More than ever, our culture worships youth. We admire the freshness, the vitality, and the gaiety of the young—ours is not a society that reveres the aged. This attitude, together with the ability to provide financially, has increased our permissiveness toward our heirs.

Because we treat them with material abundance, what we expect them to appreciate they take for granted. But how can they, who have never undergone deprivation, understand want? Their needs are more psychological than material.

For these reasons, members of the younger generation are less economically oriented than we, and often, in our minds, unrealistically so. But they are more alert, more aware, and more concerned than we were at that age and do not see the world in the same material terms. Their scale of values is different, and, in terms of social concern, more real, even though their attempts to convert concern into action may be naive and ineffective.

They aren't really against the establishment so much as they are against the lack of understanding of their outlook by an unimaginative paternalistic system. We allow our children permissiveness when they are young, but at the threshold of maturity, thrust from unreality into the real world, we face them into a disciplined order and expect immediate, correct response.

So the stage is set and the field open for small, militant groups to arise—groups that deliberately and relentlessly play on their restiveness and discontent, causing rioting, disruption, injury, and even death. But these groups have been rejected. Other means to bring about change are sought.

We tend to underestimate the next generation. While they lack experience, they have improved knowledge, more knowledge than we at their age, and they have a fresh, creative, intelligent approach. With experience, they will bring constructive action.

What they do and become is our responsibility.

The Megalopolitan World

During this century we have seen the rise of political monoliths, huge government structures controlled by a few—sometimes by one man. As the world is drawn closer because of technological achievements as well as for other reasons, many of them economic, a massive ideological struggle has been taking place. The world is no longer a comfortable small town where the way of life is familiar and secure. It has become a vast and troubled one, reaching into the awesome vaults of black space.

Great metropolitan centers have grown, and continue to grow, into huge sprawling areas; some of them have become almost unmanageable. It has been estimated that, in the not too distant future, from north of Boston to south of Washington will be a completely populated area, and from the southern end of Lake Michigan through Chicago and Milwaukee and north to Green Bay will be another one.

The growth of metropolitan areas throughout the world, and the closing of what were once great distances into what are now only hours apart, are creating a megalopolitan world, bringing races, colors, and nationalities to an elbow-to-elbow closeness. We will soon be impelled to restructure our relationships to meet the international cooperation this will demand. Either we do this or destroy each other. We will do it. Man has not survived for hundreds of thousands of years by failing to meet the awful challenges he has had to face.

Amid this immensity each of us feels small and insignificant. We sense a loss of individual identity and, immersed in the swirls of change taking place, wonder about our purpose for being on earth. Rather than standing tall, we have a pygmy complex. This creates a wondering restiveness in all of us.

The Mobile Society

With the ideological struggle and the change from a national to an international age have come new social demands by members of institutions. This is a restless not a reflective age. It is an age of mobility and conflict. There is the constant, cacophonic din of war, the movement of whole peoples, and the rise of new nations. Every hour of every day sees an exchange between nationalities as intercontinental jets fly through crowded airways from one seething metropolis to another. Instant communication, visual and spoken, occurs between cities and nations not on a daily but an hourly schedule.

This is a mobile society, or, more aptly, a complex of international mobile societies. The social complexities developing out of the impact of these forces are intricate. They compel change. They press and strain against institutional structural fabrics keyed more to the past than the future. Members of institutions who are more informed and more economically independent are discontented with the institutional standards erected in the past to guide the course of institutional affairs for less informed, more docile groups. The result is confusion, dissent, and demand for change.

Because of the turmoil arising from these demands for change, leadership itself exhibits a lack of understanding and uncertainty about the forces at work that crunch against the structures of its institutions. Often leadership's only answer is to grip hard on the way things have been done. This only heightens the dissatisfaction and adds to a sense of insecurity as the lower echelons see evidence of unsure guidance.

The Monotonic Society

Our technological blessings have created problems in the working society. The organization of work has become so finely divided that the worker either confines himself to a single monotonous rhythm or simply tends a machine. Physical and mental demands are so simplified that less than human abilities are sometimes required. Many jobs pay well in money but, as far as human satisfaction is concerned, are barren.

Overdivision of work is also a problem, at higher as well as lower job levels; many executive and other salaried jobs are more specialized than need be. In this assembly-line society, the lack of work stimulation, the absence of the feeling that what one does is a real contribution to his daily life, has created dissatisfaction and restlessness. Work is boredom, and satisfaction must be sought outside the job world.

This monotonic tone contributes much to discontent and active dissent.

2

The Challenge to Established Authority

BECAUSE the traditional structure and authority of institutions, whether political, religious, educational, or economic, are being challenged by their members and other groups, an analysis of the nature of authority would seem to be in order.

The Need for Authority

Authority is a process inherent in any human organization, necessary to maintain the order and security which its members demand. It is a system erected for protection against disorder, violence, and anarchy.

The core of authority, however it is exercised in any institution, is the assent of the governed. This is so regardless of the form it may take: monarchical, patriarchal, communistic, or democratic. Ultimately, authority must meet their needs. If it does not, it must change—or fail and die in revolution. Authority is essentially a self-regulatory system, not one imposed solely by the will of the elite. History proves this principle.

There are four basic types of authority structure: political, religious, educational, and economic. The political structure is the most basic—the overall social framework within which the others are constructed. It sets the general order for a particular society, establishes public policy, sets up administrative agencies to conduct public affairs, and sees to law and order.

There is a difference between the other three in the degree of government control. Religious institutions are—as they should be —more immune than the others. They are controlled by their own constituted authority, which is sometimes exerted internationally from the religion's country of origin.

Private educational institutions are also less subject to control, but the opposite is the case with public educational institutions, which are under direct political control. Economic organizations are very much affected, not only through the legal system as such, but also by administrative agencies of the government, such as the Securities and Exchange Commission and the National Labor Relations Board.

Each of these four structures has arms, or control systems, for exercising authority to maintain order. For political and general control: the armed forces, the police, and the court system. For religious control: excommunication, censure, and the fear of God. For educational control: dismissal and social disapproval. For economic control: firing and the withdrawal of economic support.

These arms are the visible means of control, consciously built to meet the inherent demand for order in human organization to satisfy the instinctive awareness that order is basic both for survival and progress.

We run into trouble when the systems lag behind the changing sophistication and attitudes of the members. As the systems fail to adjust to these changes, they enter into difficult times—a revolutionary period, either mild or violent, depending upon how great the lag is. Individuals and groups come to believe that certain actions imposed by the traditional way are crude, unfair, or perhaps degrading and unacceptable. Then they want change, and more determination in bringing it about.

Organizations grow and age, not unlike human beings. Traditions become deeply ingrained and resist change, and the older the organization, the stronger the resistance. A heavy inertia develops which must be countered by a force great enough to move it.

When change is being demanded, authority must recognize dissension but resist destruction. More than that, it must be able to see the difference between the two. Dissension is orderly disagreement, acknowledged and permitted to assert its disapproval according to accepted legal procedures. Destruction is the course sought by those who believe that the solution to problems lies not in order but in demolition of order without regard for the law. Dissension is the protected right of minorities. Destruction is illegal action by irresponsibles, who arrogantly abuse the established order, using the right of dissent as a camouflage for anarchic behavior.

Positively put, authority, with its laws and rules governing reward and punishment, is necessary to preserve the order required to advance an institution's reason for being. While at times he may not appear to be so, man is a creature of order. Instinctively he organizes himself into groups to do that which he cannot do alone. It is this genius for organization that places him on the highest plane among other creatures and enables him to advance his lot.

The Limits of Authority

When an institution's authority structure ages and becomes rigid, unyielding, and clearly unfair in the hands of its leaders, when it lacks the imaginative perception to understand the impact of its clumsy actions, the group rebels as soon as it is able to mount enough power to do so. History is full of chronicles recording the downfall of organizations of all kinds, brought about when the authority system became unacceptable to the governed. As many of these are familiar to all of us, there is no need to repeat examples here. At some point in time, the authority of leadership diminishes to such a low level that it no longer has the strength to quell the rebellion, and the institution either goes out of existence, such as the Russian monarchy did, or it is taken over and reorganized, as happened in England. Our own economic structure, which once operated free of government intervention, has evolved into one regulated by a watchful government and an informed public.

These are the dramatic upheavals in the world. But the same result occurs in smaller organizations as well, following the same pattern of aging deterioration. This is often at the root of strikes and violence in an industrial organization.

An authority structure must have a system of appeal for the protection of the individual or group. The more informed the group, the more vocal the demand, and the system can be only as effective as the justice and dispatch with which answers are given to those demands. If those in control make a mockery of the right of appeal, if it is either obstructed or taken away, the system becomes weakened and obsolete, and the institution is in trouble. If a just appeal with a reply given in a reasonable time isn't possible, the system may be held together by force for a time, but it will eventually fail.

It is this very failure by leadership to see the justice of an appeal beyond the standards of the present system that causes hidden dissent to burst into outright resistance. The strikes and rioting that have been and are occurring have some base in such a failure to respond to legitimate demands, such as some say by students in how they should conduct themselves.

Authority should not be conceived only in the narrow sense, as a system for reward and punishment, but in the larger scope of leadership's invested right to make major decisions for the course of the organization, with accountability to the governed but with the ability to act without always having to get their immediate consent. Invested leadership authority is necessary in any institution so that there can be a point where the course of the body as a whole may be coordinated and unified. It is also necessary that authority be ready to act in times of crisis when there is not time to seek consent, as happened during the Cuban missile crisis when President Kennedy confronted Khrushchev and forced him to back down.

Where there is no unity of authority, the result is a Tower of Babel. Authority structures range from those which invest an absolute control in the power elite to those which place strict limits on its actions. The less sophisticated the group to be governed, the more absolute the authority complex; the more enlightened the group, the less likely it is to be absolute, with limitations held in the hands of the group itself.

In a less informed society there tends to be a Carlylean hero-worship of the more informed elite. This means that more authority is delegated to the elite than would be the case were the group itself as well informed as those to whom the authority is given, or were they to want more voice in and control over decisions that affect their well-being.

Authority must resist the waves of temporary emotionalism that occasionally sweep across an institution, but it must also recognize real needs, and respond to them. Abuse or clumsy use of authority is more often the result of not sensing the real needs of the group than it is a contrived malevolence on the part of the elite. It is not that students have no right to participate in determining the course of university affairs. In my opinion they do, within the limits of their experience. Nor should we simply huff and puff at a man who strikes to better his economic position for his family. Until we find a better means of settling such disagreements, he should have the right to strike as long as he does not inflict serious damage on the community. It is not so much willfulness on the part of leadership that is at the bottom of protests against the structure; more often, it is failure to see the need for adjustment to meet the changing character of the internal and external forces shaking the structure, including the attitudes of members.

This is especially true when the institution is an old one steeped in long traditions worshiped as timeless universalities. Leaders have been raised in and taught to respect these traditions until they have become so ingrained that they find it difficult, if not impossible, to change their behavior. To them the traditional administration of institutional affairs is inviolate, and this tends to narrow their view toward change. Except for a few farsighted individuals, they would be less than human if they reacted in any other way. Leadership is as subject to human frailties as the rest of us. There is also the point that, were the structure allowed to be altered and changed without careful regard for the consequences, the result could be chaotic. The wise move ahead with deliberate speed, and do not simply hold on.

As it is with society in general, so it is with institutions inside society's framework. They reflect the impact of the course of events in the larger unit.

Authority, to be successful, must serve its primary function of preserving order while not suppressing the aspirations of the membership through rigid adherence to worn-out customs. It is at its best when it encourages individual as well as group achievement and mobility—upward mobility from a lower to a higher status. Hope is a force inherent in man's nature, so powerful that it cannot be denied—the element that moves him to higher levels of civilization. Our own system provides for this, and we must not lose it.

The Right to Challenge

Traditional organizations, particularly those of long standing, are failing to adjust rapidly enough to the changing conditions and attitudes in a world that is undergoing one of its great periods of change and advance.

Because of the forces at work, a mobile and better informed institutional membership, with an increasingly independent-minded, individual outlook, is demanding more say in affairs that affect them. The traditional, rule-by-fear structures are being challenged. Resentment exists against authority that is in the hands of a few with a father-knows-best outlook who determine by themselves what the actions affecting the welfare of all will be. Paternalistic leadership is out. It had its place, but now belongs to the past.

Authority systems are lagging behind the changing sophistication and attitudes of individuals and groups belonging to them. The degree of lag and inertia in an institution can be measured by the intensity of the dissent with which the institution is confronted. And the dissent rises in proportion to the inflexibility of or time lag in leadership response.

This may be seen in the church, where there is resistance to the long, traditional policies against birth control in an age when many Catholics believe it is common sense under certain conditions—economic, for example. And there is also strong resistance to the tradition of celibacy. In economic organizations, too, there is a demand for more say in when and how their members work, and in how much they are paid. There is open protest and rioting against war and the draft, as there was during the Civil War. University authorities are besieged with protests of all kinds—some legitimate, others abortive.

Resistance has built against these structures. At times it is expressed in an evolutionary way, in seeking to change laws and policies, but often it is expressed in marches, strikes, riots, and outright anarchic behavior. Whatever form resistance takes, it is a protest against what the dissenters believe to be the inflexible "establishment."

Leaders are appalled and confused by what they see as irreverent attacks on sacred tradition. But today the more informed, independent members no longer stand in awe of their institutions' leaders or traditions. That there are extremists among these groups is obvious, but there are also those who are levelheaded dissenters. They are demanding more freedom to choose within the structure.

Resistance to attacks on authority has taken two extreme forms: rigid opposition and capitulation. Dissenters are either hit head-on with a negative stand or strong police authority, or their demands, often outlandish, are met with complete surrender.

Neither of these is the answer. Both lead to violence. The reactions to campus and street riots, because of both over-force and over-capitulation, have often caused further disruption and loss of control.

Over-capitulation has resulted in an erosion of authority, and further, in contempt for it. Blind force, on the other hand, only increases the anger of resistance. Both reduce the acceptance and effectiveness of authority and may lead to wanton destruction.

An example of utter capitulation took place some time ago in one of our old, revered universities, when the president not only conceded to rioters' demands but excused some who had carried weapons and ammunition in full view. They were excused because they explained that they had not really meant any harm. Carrying a dangerous weapon and ammunition under these circumstances is a dire threat, and those who did so in this riot should have been dismissed immediately.

When over-force is applied and individual dissenters are subjected to unnecessary, brutal beatings, this only increases the intensity of the reaction and gives rise to public indignation. Here we have a dilemma. Quelling an incipient or actual riot or strike demands stern, swift action, such as the use of tear gas and arrests. Otherwise, the injuries, death, and damage may far exceed any injuries the rioters might suffer as the situation is brought under control. Too often, however, this has been called brutality. Professional revolutionaries know only too well what can happen during the fever pitch of a riot, and they use it to point the finger of accusation at police authority with the hope that public accusation will be incited against the establishment. The Chicago riots in 1968 are a case in point. Slanted reporting, intended or otherwise, helped to raise public indignation.

Unfortunately, as has happened and will happen again, innocents on the fringes caught up in the rioting deliberately incited by others, suffer injury and death. But when a peaceful meeting is turned into a brutal mob, those who take part in or stand at the edge of a strike or brewing riot must understand that they run the risk of injury. They cannot blame others for what happens to them.

Some leaders fail to understand the need for change or how to change the authority structure without sacrificing its basic function: to maintain coordination and order within an organization. It does not include appeasement, conciliation, or compromise in the face of civil disobedience. It does include a more sensitive and efficient response to *legitimate* demands and appeals, however, and a conciliatory response may well be a good method of reacting to orderly dissent. How and when to use this will be discussed later.

Leadership by paternalism, by fear, fails today because the elite no longer have the same powerful authoritarian instruments for control that they have had in the past. In business organizations it is no longer possible to take away an employee's economic support by firing him or holding that threat over his head. In this age of affluence, unionization, and shortage of skills, the employee can bargain through his union and has the power of his skill. In fact, some believe the problem to be that, as a group, employees may have too much power through their unions, and that the unions, in turn, do not use their power wisely.

Economic organizations aren't the only ones where the paternalistic rule belongs to the past. Political, religious, and educational institutions are being attacked. Again, the mobility of, and the competition for, the membership weakens the governing grip of those in power. In the public sector, schoolteachers are organizing into unions to protect and promote their rights. And excommunication from the church isn't the same powerful deterrent it once was.

A typical youthful impatience is prevalent in society now. But the young adults lack the practical experience to enable them to bring about constructive change in a world full of faults and virtues; so do some of their more theoretical leaders. In the forefront of the youthful movement are the revolutionaries, violently attacking authority. Their actions obscure the more sensible, questioning attitudes of an alert and well-informed young adult generation seeking the answers to changes they believe are needed in our institutions and way of life.

Theirs is a healthy attitude, a necessary one, in fact, if we are to make the changes and improvements, both social and political, that are needed to overcome institutional lag and allow us to continue our democratic way of life. In a very few years it will become the responsibility of these young adults to bear the burden of leadership. And it is our duty to see that they come well prepared to do so.

Among us are those who seem to forget that the dissent of the past ten years is not something that suddenly arose in the 1960s. Today's indignant "hard hats" were the dissenters of the 1930s. And there were times when they, too, were brought to court charged with the destruction of private property. And there were those among us who were against war and the draft.

Dissent is not confined to youth alone. It is general. The

young are visibly dissatisfied and concerned—they have the time available—but so are elements within the older generation. They too are against war, pollution, and religious and economic practices they consider obsolete. They are for the Pill, and against corporate actions that provide the consumer with a less than satisfactory product and price. There is loudly expressed dissent at what usually are insufferably dull stockholder meetings. A more informed public sees sex as something more meaningful than a mechanical means of reproduction. A more independent distaff group are vociferously demanding a more equal role in affairs over and above the responsibility of housekeeping.

The Icon Breakers

Challenge is present in many forms throughout society, and most of it is peaceful. But it has also erupted in the form of extreme defiance by an exhibitionist, revolutionary minority and by misguided idealists, fostering intergroup friction and tension, manipulating youthful and emotional ideals and social problems for their own ends. These are the professional revolutionaries.

They assault the "establishment elite," using the old tactic of blaming and caricaturing less articulate leadership as pompous, unfeeling, and selfish. Railing against our economic leaders as crass, materialistic Philistines and unthinking, conformist Babbitts, they build mistrust among our young.

Their aim is iconoclastic—to knock over and pull down institutions and their symbols. Destructive acts are a favorite pastime. Knocking over and breaking the statue of a Chicago policeman standing in honor of those killed during the Haymarket Square Riot is one example. Another is the bombing of University of Wisconsin buildings where military research and development was taking place.

Their outlook is one of nihilism, "a doctrine or belief that conditions in the social organization are so bad as to make destruction desirable for its own sake independent of any constructive program or possibility." They are against and they destroy, but they have no creative construction to offer in place of what they knock down. When asked what program they have in mind, they become confused and speechless. There is none.

They march and march, and talk and talk. All is against and nothing for.

This is more a by-product of change than a general movement, and it is being indignantly rejected by the more levelheaded among our young adults.

Not a New Age

Because of the changing social standards and in order to meet the demands of a new era, confusion, tension, general disillusionment, and cynicism are attitudes that characterize the times. We are in one of those periods in history when man and his institutions are in conflict over the traditional outlooks, a time when we ask that our structures be changed to meet our changing needs.

Such an era is hardly new; it appears to run in cycles of two hundred years. A study of the fourteenth century, the age of Chaucer, reveals that similar attitudes were present. And a study of eighteenth-century revolutionary developments brings them to light again.

Every generation of young adults feels that the world isn't being run properly. This is a universal characteristic. The young aren't inhibited by experience or by the habits of conformance to past institutional standards. Today their complaint is that we have failed to eliminate poverty, ignorance, and war. We have. But those of us more battered by time remember having these same worthy ideals—before we developed the experience-leavened view that such complex problems should but can't be easily and quickly solved. We recognize that segregation of blacks, containing them at the lower strata of our social order, has to be overcome, but that superficial means such as busing are hardly the solution. To change the basic fabric and prejudices of centuries, while long overdue, needs education, time, and money. This is a major crisis of our times, but there are others of equal priority, such as metropolitan disintegration and abject poverty, and each must command the attention and allocation of resources it deserves. But all cannot be resolved at once. An order of priorities has to be set, with an understanding that long-range considerations and schedules are necessary for the ultimate resolution of these basic problems.

The intensity of youthful dissatisfaction is understandably greater than that of the previous generation, because our children are coming to adulthood in unusually turbulent times.

3

The Anatomy of Dissent

ALL dissent, whether internal, as occurs *within* an organization, or external, as occurs *between* organizations, can be labeled either vertical or lateral. A strike against an industrial firm or industry is vertical dissent. The whole union movement against management is lateral, as is a war between two countries. Political parties disagree with each other—a form of lateral dissent. Within church institutions the various forms of worship represent differences. The Church of England arose out of dissent against Catholicism. John Wesley and Martin Luther, founders of the Methodist and Lutheran churches, were dissenters. Our own country was founded on political as well as religious dissent. Some of our most successful corporations came into being because their founders disagreed with the way business was run in their previous firms.

Dissent ferments, rumbles, and boils over in direct proportion to leadership's failure to sense the need for change and to adjust to new attitudes and wants. At first passive, it moves to an active and finally to a violent form. The longer change is delayed, the greater the split between the leaders and members of an institution, or between institutions. The more insulated the leadership, the more violent the form of dissent will be, and the more difficult the resolution.

In this and following chapters lateral dissent will be discussed, but the primary emphasis will be on vertical dissent—the various forms it can take, how to recognize them for what they are, how to manage each form when confronted by it, and how to keep dissent from occurring at all.

Underlying Causes of Dissent

When dissent appears in an institution, it is a sign that the institution is suffering from decline, either temporary or permanent. A subtle loss of rapport—the harmonious relationship between the leaders and the members—has been taking place. The cause may lie in organizational structure or in inept leadership, or in both. Communication has degenerated to the point where only open dissent can call attention to the problem. Unawareness, or a miscalculation of the seriousness of the disagreement, has resulted in benign and inattentive complacency at the top, and no action through ordinary organization channels can be expected. It is not so much a question of whether the command group is decisive or dilatory as it is lack of perception of the problem and the need for a decision. It is a matter of misplaced executive emphasis on the relative seriousness of the numerous problems facing the institution.

Persistence in maintaining the traditional status quo by the executive group in an institution, despite insistent efforts from below and from the outside, causes dissent to break out into the open. The top believes that what has been best for the organization continues to be in its best interests, while those below are convinced that the leaders have fallen behind the times. Both are at least partially right. The leaders are right in maintaining that the course of the institution should not be allowed to be changed by the temporary waves of emotionalism and hysteria buffeting against it, but the members are right in their demand for changes to satisfy different attitudes and wants. Simply to insist upon standing on the past, or to take a negative approach to contemporary outlook, is to abdicate leadership responsibility and certain to unify and amplify the strength of dissent. On the other hand, running scared before the forces of dissent and giving in to them is to fail to meet leadership responsibility.

The nice problem that faces the top is when to flex and when to stand. To seek a change in the housing policies of a university is a legitimate demand and should be duly considered on its merits. Here the top may flex. But when the dissenters break the law and damage property, the demand should not be considered until the lawbreakers have been dealt with as lawbreakers, and not dissenters. This is the time to be forceful and decisive. The president of San Francisco State College understands this distinction very well. Unfortunately, some other presidents do not. When leading in the face of open dissent, turning the other cheek is not the answer. Neither is the rigid, unyielding position. In the face of a storm of protest the weak structure breaks apart and the rigid structure collapses. It is the flexible structure that stands.

This is the hard decision Governor Rockefeller had to make during the 1971 riots at Attica State Prison. He had tough alternatives: give in to all demands, including amnesty and firing the superintendent, or stand. Because hardened criminals were flouting authority, he elected to use force should the prisoners not meet a deadline to stop. They did not, leaving him no choice. He felt his decision was necessary to preserve the authority structure of the system. Otherwise, criminals in a high-security prison would have won a capitulated victory and the structure would have been seriously weakened. After-the-fact observers said that more negotiation should have been attempted. Perhaps. No one will ever really know. Further delay might also have brought more carnage than actually happened.

Lack of Action

This is the base of all dissent. No single thing contributes so much as does leadership inaction in the direction that members want for their benefit. To the outside world the top group may be doing a creditable job of administering the affairs of the organization, while the members may be disgruntled about lack of action in those matters which affect them.

In one university, a student request for a change in dormitory living arrangements lay on a vice-president's desk for eight months without so much as a partial answer being given. Is it any wonder that there was protest?

Physical Distance

The further the leaders are from their membership, the more difficult are the problems of communication. As executives lend their attention to matters immediately before them and relegate those at a distance to a lower priority, the frequency of face-to-face discussions tends to drop off sharply. In one case involving dissatisfied employees a long distance away from management, by the time the seriousness of the situation was brought to the top it was too late to prevent the group from unanimously accepting union leadership.

There is a tendency in organizations to put too much confidence in written bulletins and memorandums, the teletype, or the telephone. Dependence upon frequency reaches the point where it becomes burdensome to those on the receiving end. At best this is an inadequate substitute for on-the-spot seeing, listening, and answering. How well this problem is understood by executives in charge of outlying geographical units of the central organization. Politicians, too, clearly see that success depends upon and is directly related to the frequency of their appearances before the voters who elect them.

With physical distance may come a divergence of outlook, background, and objectives. This is what we face internationally. To be successful requires learning about and visiting other countries to develop an understanding about acceptable conduct in relationships with them. But this is also true in our own country. While we are basically the same, acceptable conduct differs from one metropolitan area to another. This is also true between north, south, east, and west. Politicians are well aware of this, too, and adjust their plans and actions accordingly.

Psychological Distance

Individuals and groups display different degrees of compatibility with each other in terms of their personality, temperament, and cultural backgrounds. Where they are too diverse, there is bound to be disagreement. This is especially true among groups with different ethnic backgrounds. Economic, social, and religious values also may differ quite widely. The most obvious economic example is the dissent between management and the unions over the sharing of the benefits of production—what constitutes a fair wage and a fair profit. The blacks are demanding a more equal status and more economic opportunity, and they are raising hell to win them.

When there is a high degree of incompatibility between the top and those below, or at the same level between organizations, dissent is almost inevitable. A chief executive officer was brought into a corporation from the outside. His temperament and background had suited the military very well, but the corporation's products were technically complicated and involved highly creative engineering skills. On the staff were a large number of creative professional engineers who were the technical superiors of the chief executive. He attempted to run a tight ship. This, of course, had an adverse affect on their creative work, and the result stopped just short of revolt. Engineers began resigning, as they found the environment stultifying and restrictive. The chief executive had to be replaced.

In another organization, a well-known one, the top and the group next in line were tradition-bound to a matter-of-fact view of company affairs during a period that demanded a more creative approach toward the future. Strikes began to occur. Expensively recruited young talent left in numbers after finding the environment incompatible with their hoped-for development. A change at the top had to be made before this deterioration could be stopped.

Sometimes dissent is aimed not at a system but at a personality. An old axiom in labor relations is: Where there is chronic trouble with employees in the form of grievances, work stoppages, and other forms of dissent, analyze not only the system but the leadership qualifications and personalities on both sides. Employee dissatisfaction may lie in the unacceptability of a supervisor's personality. In one manufacturing facility there was considerable disagreement, and employee relations problems were a compounded number of small complaints. When the situation was analyzed, it was discovered that the manager remained aloof and withdrawn, not only from his employees, but from his supervisory staff as well. He was neither close to the group nor sensitive to their needs. They felt he didn't care. He did, but it was not his nature to be outgoing in his relationships with others. His background was technically oriented.

Communication Factors in Dissent

The broad, underlying causes of dissent have been outlined, but so much of dissent is seeded in and grows out of interpersonal, interorganizational, and intraorganizational communications weaknesses that, as the very core of dissent, the subject warrants a more detailed analysis.

Misinformation

Whether intentionally or not, the passing of wrong information creates misunderstanding. At times it is a deliberate attempt by someone to foster misunderstanding. So often, however, it is situational rather than personal; that is, a faulty communications procedure causes the misunderstanding that generates the misinformation that creates an incident.

This cause-and-effect situation occurs frequently when there is too much reliance on oral instructions and notices in complex organization units. It has been proved time after time—and the simple game of "telephone" easily demonstrates this—how little correct information is passed orally through as few as six individuals. What is passed on by the first person to what is received by the sixth is often nearly unrecognizable when the two are compared.

In one organization, top management decided to give everyone a general pay increase in order to keep current with the increase in the cost of living. The increase was a fair one, and management made the right decision. But, as it turned out, there was considerable disgruntlement among the staff. Everyone was told or heard about the increase from someone else. Several months went by, and complaints about pay began to surface. One key individual was thinking about resigning. Investigation revealed that the increase was announced by word of mouth; when it was to take place and how it was to be applied was not explained at all. Naturally, members of the staff thought it was to come immediately, and when it didn't arrive in the paychecks of some, while it did in others, those who were left out felt they were being unfairly treated. What they weren't told was that the increases were to be given in stages throughout the year according to employment anniversary. Once discovered, this misleading information was quickly corrected in writing and the discontent was appeased.

How many times have employees been led to believe that a promotion is forthcoming, only to find later that it was only an inference or general comment and should not have been taken seriously.

Vague statements misinform because it is natural for the listener to interpret them in terms of his own best interests; what are intended as comments or possibilities may be interpreted as promises. This is often at the root of employee relations problems. That a pay raise *may* be given, depending upon business conditions, is soon interpreted as a guarantee. It is sound practice to word such announcements carefully and specifically in writing or in person. By doing so, much unrest and discontent may be avoided. By not doing so consistently is to invite a strike or another active form of dissent.

Announcements which may, even though inadvertently, contain an implicit promise should be consciously avoided unless that promise can be kept. Otherwise, they become a source of misleading information. This applies universally to all situations involving human relations. Politicians, because they are so widely exposed and quoted, have more than usual difficulty with this problem.

False Information

Giving out false information is a deliberate tactic used to smokescreen the real direction of an intended action. It has long been used in international affairs, but it may apply to local situations as well. It is a tactic of those who want to create and foment dissent and disruption.

Deliberately accusing police action necessary to maintain or restore civil order as being brutal is a form of false information. It is a conscious intent to discredit the forces of law and order by those whose single objective is to turn the full impact of public opinion against the established form of law and order. These are the ones who seek to destroy the political order, and they should be dealt with as such, and not as peaceful dissenters.

But the false-information tactic is used in less alarming situations as well. It has been used against management by the less ethical among union leadership to whip up and maintain strike enthusiasm among union members. Stated intentions by management are twisted for this purpose. A firm announcement that management intends to hold to its position in bargaining, and will take a strike to do so if necessary, may be turned by union leadership into the firm conviction that management is out to "bust the union." But this tactic is becoming a thing of the past as the unions and their leaders, as well as management's relationship with them, become more mature.

Misinterpreted Information

Often individuals and groups misunderstand or misinterpret the words, actions, expressions, gestures, and attitudes of others. Subordinates in organizations carefully watch the top group for these, and they draw conclusions from their observations. This is natural for them to do, because those at the top hold the employees' well-being in their hands. But because they are very sensitive, they often misinterpret what they see.

In a department store a saleswoman was very worried that she had done something wrong and thought that her job was at stake. When questioned, she admitted her feelings. Her post was behind a counter just inside the main entrance. Every morning the president came by on his way to his office, and in the past he had always said a cordial good morning to her. But lately he had been going by without a word, so she concluded that she must have done something to make him angry. The fact was that he was so preoccupied with a major problem facing the store that he hardly noticed anyone around him. But the employee didn't know this, and as a result, she was concerned, justifiably, about her welfare.

During riots or other situations in which individuals or groups face each other warily, a wave of the hand is often taken as a threatening gesture. How actions are interpreted depends upon the emotional and mental conditions of the interpreter at the time. Under stress, distortion of the words and actions of others is very likely to take place. During a negotiation between a union and management, which had been long and bitter, a member of the management team raised his hand to strike the table to emphasize a point he was trying to make. The union negotiator nearest to him took this to be a threat, and a fistfight broke out.

It is not unusual for disagreement between two individuals or groups to hinge on reading different meanings into one word, phrase, or sentence. In the Wagner Act, a basic federal law governing union-management relations, there is a statement which says that management cannot coerce employees from joining a union. What "coerce" means has been a long, bitter argument on all sides.

Swear words during an argument are often misinterpreted as being personally directed and may cause the heat of the disagreement to rise. For example, in a negotiation the question of the wage settlement was being discussed. This became lost in an argument over whether a swear word, used by a member of the management group to emphasize a point, was directed at the leading union negotiator. The meeting had to be adjourned temporarily until tempers cooled.

The settlement of a strike was delayed for three weeks primarily because of one sentence. The sentence read, "Employees may be transferred temporarily between jobs without regard for seniority." The intention here was to give management more flexibility in assigning employees to cover absenteeism or emergencies. That was the only intention. But, as it later turned out, both the employees and the union read this as a hidden threat to their jealously guarded seniority system. It was not until a guarantee that it would not affect their seniority was written into the statement that they would accept it.

Here, "seniority" is an example of an emotionally charged word. "Mother," "father," "alma mater," "our team," "the flag" —wherever the emotional attachment is deep—are other examples. Because in this context seniority meant security of job and pay to take home, any reference to it immediately raised defensive feelings and easily led to misunderstanding.

During the 1971 furor over the publication of the Pentagon Papers, an article appeared in a national magazine just when the debate over the freedom to divulge information affecting national security was at its most intense point. The article was full of such words as "lied," "liar," "crowed," "deceiver," and "deception." They struck with anger those against whom they were directed and only served to heat the debate.

Emotionally charged words, carelessly used, will intensify disagreement and widen dissent; they should be avoided wherever possible, particularly when feeling is running high. If they are necessary, then they should be thoughtfully explained and reexplained until everyone agrees to the meaning.

Information Shut-Off

Information shut-off is the denial of relevant information to those who want and need to know what is occurring within, or in other cases between, institutions. This is one of the most frequent causes of dissent and reflects insensitivity at the management level. When leaders do not speak out and explain their actions, they easily expose themselves to ridicule and caricature by others whose purpose is to generate dissent.

An accounting manager decided to change payday from once every two weeks to twice a month, which, of course, changed the amount in everyone's check. He did this without explaining to anyone what he intended to do. The first check under the new system happened to fall on the regular Friday of the old schedule, but the amounts were different. It took all of Friday and part of the next week to calm the uproar.

A complete section of a plant was rearranged over a weekend. The employees were not told that this was to happen. They arrived on Monday morning to face a totally new situation: their whole work and social pattern had been reorganized without their knowledge or any regard for their consent. They walked out. It was difficult to get them back, and the section had chronic grievances for months afterward.

It is not difficult to imagine the low esteem with which they regarded those responsible, and we can guess the ribald names they hung on them. For some time, they were easily aroused by almost any action that management took.

Making changes that affect individuals or groups without soundly designed, open, and well-executed communications is one of the most common errors that can lead to dissent. It raises fears, restlessness, and anger because no one knows what may happen next. The best way to make a change is not only to explain it beforehand to those affected but, if at all possible, to include them in its design stage.

Some of our more renowned universities are having very difficult problems with alumni relations and are suffering, financially and otherwise, from alumni alienation. Much of this is due to the lack of a contemporary and sophisticated system of communications. Instead, an occasional report or a hurried-up letter to explain a crisis already past is intended to mollify a smoldering alumni body. This is an outdated approach and as ineffective as it is naive. It is also a type of communications shut-off, since the alumni know very little about what is going on unless they read or hear about it from unofficial sources.

Our political leaders face a terrible dilemma here. Deciding when to shut off communications to protect national security, and when to reveal events as something the public has a right to know about, is an intricate and delicate question. The angry debate that flared up over *The New York Times*'s revealing the Vietnam War escalation is an unfortunate illustration, but it dramatically showed the difficulty of deciding what to release to the public, as well as the intensity of the public dissent if they feel that what they should have been told has been withheld. Rightly or wrongly, the withholders were labeled "liars" and "deceivers." Whether there was actual deception or whether it was an honest error was lost as emotions ran high and objectivity was swept away. The question of what is or is not top secret continues to strain relations between the press and the Nixon administration.

At times, a shut-off of information is deliberate and sensible. During major union-management negotiations, as they reach the critical point near settlement, both sides agree to maintain silence as far as the press is concerned. In this way, misunderstandings that might break up negotiations can be avoided.

Infrequent Information

When the frequency of communication is too low, it results in insufficient information for the needs and wants of those receiving it, who fill in the gaps with their own interpretations—and often misinterpretations—about what is happening.

Another result of a long time lapse is that much that was timely is forgotten or has become stale; the positive effect intended is lost. In fact, a negative effect may be the outcome: "So what else is new?" Or "Who wants to read last week's news?"

Infrequency in communications brings to mind the old adage, "Out of sight, out of mind." Sparseness of information from the top is a visible indication that management is out of touch with the institution's real world, and open dissent comes with a jarring shock. So infrequent was the flow of other than technical information from headquarters to a distant branch of an organization that by the time the top was alerted to what was going on in the region, the bet was that the union was a shoo-in. It was.

One management decided to play the game in low key, holding back the issuing of information during a union organization drive. Fortunately for them, several executives who had the confidence of the employees discovered that this was being interpreted to mean that management wanted a union. A well-planned, aimed, and paced informative campaign was launched in time for management to win the election by a good margin. The information given to employees was regular, concise, honest, and continuous, and it made use of headlines and summary paragraphs—all basics of good journalism.

Infrequency affects the relevance of information—either the sender or the receiver may forget what was previously said. The result is a loss of continuity, vital to developing an understanding of the past and current activities of the institution.

One corporation sent its employees information only when there was a crisis, such as an impending strike. Naturally, a feeling developed among the employees that they heard from management only when management wanted something. The reaction was of course negative. Having learned the hard way, that organization now has a well-organized and effective system of communications with its employees.

On the other side of infrequency is voluminous output. Overdone, this is just as bad. Volume requires that the sender find much to say that is of value to the reader or listener; in turn, the reader must spend a lot of time absorbing the information. Running out of meaningful information and not having the time to read it critically reduce the positive effect of communication at both ends. In the extreme, volume is reduced to "junk mail" which the reader puts aside "to be read later." Often that time never comes.

Fragmentary Information

This differs from infrequent information. It refers to incomplete information that is so general or so piecemeal that it creates confusion instead of the understanding it is intended to develop. Fragmentary information is communication taken out of context —information lifted out of its frame of reference so that it can be interpreted in any of several ways by the receiver. A speaker or writer quoted out of context is often subjected to unfair criticism because his meaning has been distorted.

One corporation was merged into another. Within the merged company little information was sent out to explain what life would be like under the new arrangement. What little information was transmitted—officially or by rumor—was understandably misread. A strong feeling developed that those in the merged company would lose their old identity and be completely dominated by the other corporation. This was far from the truth. Actually, the intention was to coordinate the activities of the two while definitely retaining much of the old identity because of, among other reasons, the fine reputation the merged organization enjoyed. But this was not realized and corrected in time to avoid a number of executive and other staff resignations.

In a plant, a raise was given to bring some men in line with others; a study had shown that some employees were being underpaid. In all fairness, but in innocence, the adjustment was put into effect, but it was announced that only certain employees would receive the raise. Nothing was explained about the reason for the increase for some while not for others. The result was a wholesale walkout at a time when the plant had to ship a new product to meet advertising and sales schedules. All this because of the interpretation by employees that the company was playing favorites.

Both of the above situations could have been avoided had the complete intent of management's actions been thoughtfully and carefully transmitted to those affected by them.

During the argument between the government and the press over the disclosure of the Vietnam reports, one of the points made by the government was that the information contained in them was narrow, selective, and out of context. In other words, the claim was that it was fragmentary—incomplete and misleading. The comment was also made that information such as this blurs the context, leads to mistaking the motive behind the action, and assigns too much or too little weight to individual responsibility for what actually happened. Surely this is a dramatic example of the effect that fragmentary information can have in raising dissent over a question of international magnitude.

Fragmentary information is frequently the basic cause of un-necessary dissent against actions with which the dissenters might agree, were they to be given a more complete explanation of the intent behind them.

Timing of Information

Proper timing is an essential of sound communications. Dis-sension may rise because leaders explain the purpose of an action just before or just after the fact—too late in either case. On the other hand, if the intention behind an act is transmitted too early to those concerned, it may be forgotten by the time the act occurs.

A lot of hubbub in the history of man has been caused by the poor timing of communications. The disagreement over the tim-ing of the flow of information from Washington to the army and navy in Manila at the time of Pearl Harbor will probably never be settled.

Change can, and frequently does, cause dissent in all forms, from verbal tangles to violent strikes. But the whole wage system in a sizable plant was changed with surprisingly little upset, and this is an area that is highly sensitive. The primary reason why there was so little difficulty lay in the communication approach. Before the change was undertaken, a communications procedure was designed and coordinated with each step in the technical procedure involved with the change. The whole program was care-fully explained beforehand by means of visual aids, face-to-face discussions, and letters. This was repeated at each step along the way, and disagreements and misunderstandings were therefore cleared as the program proceeded, not afterward. Very important to the success here was management's attitude. The top group faced the employees and told them they could make mistakes that might cause unfairness in the pay rate between two employees. That being the case, they offered to discuss rates before they were set, and to make corrections wherever employees could point out and convince them of unfairness. This was done, and corrections were made.

In this case, communications were timed to anticipate prob-lems or catch them quickly before they could build into a wave of dissent. Important too was the open, honest approach, which set a free-flowing tone. Arguments were free from fear, and discussion encouraged problems to be brought into the open.

Off-timing, as well as an error in approach, infuriated Presi-dent Kennedy when the steel industry announced a price increase just when the administration was attempting to hold the price line. The increase was announced without any warning; no one from the leading company that first launched the increase had conferred with the president. His reaction was one of blunt anger, and he condemned the industry publicly. The issue was settled only after the increase was "rolled back" by the industry.

Another instance of off-timing took place during the spring of 1971, when a peace march was organized to go to Washington. The marchers planned to camp on the Mall. When they announced their intention, the administration jumped into action and de-clared that camping on the Mall was illegal. Anyone caught camp-ing there, the attorney general said, would be dealt with severely according to the law. Because the marchers openly said that their intent was strictly peaceful—and there were many Vietnam veter-ans among them—public reaction turned against the Nixon ad-ministration. Other veterans among the public sympathized with those in the march. The negative response forced the government to back off.

Correct timing requires a knowledge of human behavior and a sure grasp of the attitudes of those who will respond to the com-munication. For example, to take a legalistic approach at a time when there is sympathy toward veterans, on top of a long and jealously guarded tradition of the right to assemble peacefully, is to misjudge the public temper.

Language Differences

Language poses communication problems, not only between different languages, but between dialects of the same language. Within our own country we have different ways of expressing ourselves. A Vermonter may use expressions quite different from a Texan's to label the same intent. More pronounced is the difference between the British and us. To them an automobile hood is a bonnet. A wrench is a spanner, and a butt does not refer to a cigarette.

It has been claimed that the misinterpretation of one word may have prolonged World War II for several months. The Japanese word *mokumatsu* has two meanings. One is that whatever is asked will be considered—taken under advisement; the other is that the request is refused. During 1945 the Allies sent a demand for surrender to the Japanese, and their reply contained the word *mokumatsu*. It was interpreted as a refusal of the demand, when its intent was that the demand would be taken under consideration.

The emotional impact of swear words has already been discussed, but they also are interpreted in different ways in different places. In some parts of the country swear words that invoke the Almighty or deride the origin of one's mother are taken as a matter of course and are descriptive, not personal. Elsewhere they may be taken as highly offensive, as they are in certain parts of the South.

Years ago I was stationed with the army in Egypt. While bargaining with an Egyptian who spoke excellent English, I referred to his price as being so high that it was "crazy," in the vernacular sense. We got into a heated wrangle. As we argued on, I discovered that he had interpreted the word "crazy" in its literal sense, had taken it personally, and was highly offended. He calmed down only after I had apologized and explained the meaning I had intended.

Assuming that others read into our words and phrases what *we* mean by them is often the cause of disagreement. Any one of us can recall such a disagreement from his own experience Many strikes and arbitrations between labor and management have resulted from language misinterpretation. Two words, "skill" and "ability," when used within the context of defining seniority rights, have been at the core of endless hassles. Ability is defined as "competence in doing: skill." Or "natural talent or acquired proficiency: aptitude." Skill is defined as "the ability to use one's

knowledge effectively and readily in execution: proficiency." Or
"a developed aptitude or ability." From these definitions it is
easy to see that careless use of words—in an incomplete or fragmentary way, for example—can readily stir up dissent in its various
forms. This is why, while seeking to reach or maintain accord
between parties, it is so essential to define intent carefully in
writing, to rewrite, and to discuss until the intention is clearly
understood by everyone concerned.

Shortly after a merger, executives of the two corportations met
to discuss what organization form the merged company should
take. The problem was a complicated one involving not only
national but international organizations. Consequently, a staff
study and recommendation was precisely prepared and presented
to the two groups for discussion purposes. For a long day, little
progress toward any agreement was achieved. The executives from
the merged corporation seemed very reluctant to agree to any
unified form of organization. Finally the cause of this reluctance
surfaced: to them the carefully prepared study had a conclusive
appearance. They saw it as an attempt to force them to accept the
plan as final, leaving them no opportunity to suggest changes or
modifications. When this was discovered, the other group set about
explaining that the study was for discussion only. They began to
make suggestions, some of them sound. When these were agreed
to, the group became convinced that the discussion approach was
sincere. By the middle of the third day a redrafted version was
cordially accepted by both groups.

Believability of Source

Believability, or the much bandied word "credibility," is the
acceptance of information by the receiver as real or not, depending
upon how well or how badly he regards the sender's integrity and
his reputation for reliability and accuracy. This reputation is hard
to win and easily lost. Opinion surveys of communications problems reveal that people see believability of source as a major
problem.

The believability of President Johnson was often questioned
while he was in office. His tendency to hold information tightly
and close to his vest made him an easy target for critics, who derided his credibility, often unfairly. Because of the exposure of
parts of the Pentagon Papers, the believability of his administration has been under heavy fire. Critics claimed that he had already
approved plans to escalate the war when he was saying that he knew

of no far-reaching strategy being suggested or promulgated. One reliable reporter observed that some of the newspaper accounts were biased. Another said that documents used to compile the report were largely personal papers and were incomplete. A large part of why a fury of dissent burst over the report may lie in the key word "incomplete." The information under scrutiny may have been too fragmentary to make an objective and fair judgment possible. Out of context, it could do little more than raise temperatures to the boiling point, raise suspicion about the believability of government spokesmen, and cause our allies to look upon us as untrustworthy.

A depth survey sharply profiled the believability of the chief executive of an organization. Members were voluntarily unanimous in their firm conviction about his integrity and reliability, and their belief was based on their observation that he kept nothing from them. "Tells us anything we want to know," and "He always does what he says he's going to do." Or "If something's wrong, it's because he doesn't know about it. As soon as he hears about it he'll straighten things out."

The converse of this is the kind of top executive who makes promises and doesn't keep them; or who commits himself and the organization to a course of action they believe to be right and then reneges on it; or who takes no action at all.

In one institution the chief executive allowed his believability to deteriorate to the critical point. Promises of action were made but not realized. Unrest and turnover mounted. He had to be forced to act to begin the hard task of restoring lost confidence. And this is very difficult to do.

Another executive was known for making promises and putting them into action, but subordinates put little faith in his promises because they never knew when, in an arbitrary mood, he would rescind them.

Institutional believability is being questioned from all points. Advertising for products and services is undergoing a severe challenge that it is glib and short of the truth. Claims are made that cannot be met—about quality, for example. Stockholder meetings are fraught with loud dissent. Dissidents are claiming that while the corporation publicly protests its concern for ecology and fair employment, it practices segregation and pollutes the environment. University boards and administrations are harassed by discontent among students, faculty, alumni, and the public. Even our churches are not free from clamor and complaint.

To be believable, institutional leadership must be honest in communications, and actions and words must support each other. Leaders must be able to "put their money where their mouths are."

Believability is, of course, affected by information shut-off. The dilemma this creates for government officials has already been discussed, but it also applies to other organizations as well. Every organization has its reasons for keeping some of its affairs secret. Leaders feel that revealing certain information to the public would be detrimental to the best interests of the organization and its members. This includes financial position, new idea or product research, changes in personnel, moving plans, mergers, and so on. The problem is what to release and what to hold privy, and the inclination is, when in doubt, hold it. This leads to retaining facts about the organization that aren't really classified information and which should be released to others who have a right to know. When it becomes apparent that leaders are jealously holding on to that information, which has no secrecy value, they begin to lose their believability and the regard of others. An extreme example of this is the case involving a large organization, one of whose divisions would not release officially to outsiders a statement on an employee relations policy that it had distributed to many thousands of insiders.

Generally, among institutions, the error is more on the side of withholding than of revealing information. This is why we are at times something less than believable in the eyes of those weighing the qualities of leaders to whom they look for acceptable direction.

Fear and Apprehension

The flow of communication can easily be smothered by fear of disapproval or reprisal against an individual or group for forwarding problems to management that it may not believe or want to hear. The fearful often prefer to remain silent and resentful until they are in a position to dissent. With this in mind, written into our national labor relations law is the statement that employees may not be offered "promies of benefit or threat of reprisal" at a time when a union is seeking to organize them.

This fear is not limited to reprisal. No one likes to be publicly castigated by an organization superior for an error, often minor, that he has made. This fear may take the form of timid indecisiveness or, among the stronger, rebellious resentment that will boil up into dissenting action in time. Then the top will have its hands full, with some members resigning and speaking out and others coming forth in solid array with demands for change.

A securely positioned executive who continues to use this wrong technique for reprimand may find comfort in no evidence of dissatisfaction among subordinate groups. The strong dissenters have left, and he is unaware that only the timorous remain with him. Nor does he know that, wherever possible, adverse reports from numerous small activities, each in itself of modest significance, but as a whole important, are being kept from him. Minor instances of product failure may also be hidden, even though they add up gradually to a loss of customer faith. That a subordinate for whom he has a particular regard is causing unrest may go unreported. Professional incompetence may not be brought to his attention. As a whole, fear leads to erosion of the organization's long-term strength. It may be subtle, unseen from the outside, but it is as real as taxes.

Certain threats, such as bodily harm, economic insecurity, or extradition may suppress dissent for a length of time, but at some point, it will surely break out.

Fear of leaders has a negative thrust in any organization. It may dampen communications or foster discord where reasonable harmony is demanded for effective action.

Technical Jargon

Where communications are concerned, technical jargon can be the bane of this technological world. The use of highly technical language by trained specialists, such as engineers, scientists, economists, and accountants, is an excellent way for one professional to communicate with another. It aids them in speaking tersely and accurately. But, when a professional tries to use it in talking with someone outside his field, there is trouble. He forgets that to the listener his is a foreign language. Sometimes he uses jargon because of inability to communicate beyond the range of his specialty. It may be simply to pat his ego; but far from being superior, he is merely a communications dolt.

For any of us who must use technical jargon, it takes discipline to resist the temptation to embroider rolling patterns of resounding phraseology that are impressive, but may contain more wind than meaning. It may sound great to those of us in the technical fraternity, but it can be extremely boring to those outside the lodge.

Here is an example: "Would you be kind enough to elevate and forward the ceramic disk containing the soft emulsion of fat globules, atmosphere, hydrogen, and oxygen (in a nonflammable state) emulsified to acceptable specifications by using a vertical rotational axis with fixed ovate planes attached at symmetric intervals applied to set into a rotational direction the optimum quality of a secreted fluid until it attains the acceptable state required?"

This means "Please pass the butter."

In situations where an attempt to reach an understanding is involved, the use of technical jargon by professionals among non-professionals may cause confusion, raise suspicion, and generally hamper the attempt to reach a settlement. It can be used successfully only where there are like professionals on both sides to read each other and to translate technical words and phrases for their colleagues. More than a few negotiations between management and unions have been obstructed by engineering, legal, and financial jargon foreign to the nonspecialists on both sides.

Avoiding technical terms is as important when speaking to people outside the organization as it is within. In this economic, corporate world, the top has found it extremely hard to explain to the public what the word "profit" means and why it is necessary in a capitalistic economy. To do so is difficult at best. But one element in the problem is the habitual use of financial and economic jargon—return on investment, the attraction of capital, depreciation allowance, quick ratios, and so on. If, for example, the jargon were minimized and, without talking down, converted into the household as part of a going business, that practical economist, the housewife, would quickly understand.

The problem of jargon exists not only in the corporate world but in other organizations as well. In communicating with those unfamiliar with the internal language that is used, it is essential to convert explanations of top objectives and actions into clear, concise terms understandable by anyone.

4

Institutional Causes
of Dissent

WHILE a central leadership figure or group may appear to be the target of dissenting groups, such as a chancellor or a chairman of the board, they are only symbols of a system. The basic causes of dissent are more organizational than personal. Dissent arises in situations where there are elements present that cause disintegration and decline. If the institution is suffering from lag in making changes to meet the demands of the members, internal unrest, submerged or overt, begins to grow.

Dissent does not appear overnight. It occurs over a period of time during which an accumulation of unsatisfied demands mounts to the breaking point. As leadership fails to see the changes needed —or misreads the demands—and continues to apply obsolete methods for resolving new problems, the dissenters come to feel that the organization is repressive.

Dissent ferments long before it becomes visible. It begins as a quiet restlessness, often unspoken. It is scarcely noticeable, because it has not yet taken any particular form. As the discontent increases, a leader or leadership appears around which the dissent may pole, and finally it takes form. The leaders organize the group and come forth with demands, much to the consternation of the institution caught unaware of what has been happening. How this actually works is described in the case study in Chapters 12 and 13.

What are the characteristics of an institution that will bring about dissent? What are the marks of an organization in decline?

Tradition Worship

Supreme confidence in the infallibility of the past is one. Leaders always turn to the past for solutions to problems of the present. They quote chapter and verse. We have always done it this way or that way. What's wrong with the way we've been doing it for fifty years? We know what works. We know what is sound practice.

The past is treated as inviolable. Traditions are to be stoutly upheld, not changed or modified. When leaders are confronted with suggestions or demands for change, either from within or outside the organization, the immediate reaction is always negative.

In one industry, traditional thinking confidently overrode the suggestion that substitute materials were a threat to the basic product. Now those materials have captured a major portion of the market. In another industry with a tight, paternalistic structure, a small new corporation with a new approach implemented a radical change in the basic product and moved steadily ahead to capture first place in the market by a wide margin, while the others stood still, confident that the old product was the best and would survive for a long time. The old product is steadily declining and accounts for only a negligible portion.

One church official issued public statements announcing the position of his charge on a problem of broad social concern. He did so in the traditional way—without conferring with any of his parishioners—completely unaware that many disagreed with his committing them without their consent. Today's parishes are composed of well-informed members, and he should have sounded out their opinions before committing them to a major position. Despite his intelligence and ability, he was caught in the habit of traditional practice. This will not do. A situation of dissent exists here, more subtle than disruptive, and its expression may take the form of members' losing interest in church activities or simply staying away entirely.

Aged Leadership

Aged leadership results from tradition-worship. It may be simply a matter of physical age, but it is more often a question of outdated attitude. A leader of this type is comfortable only with long-established ritual. This he knows and applies very well, but he lacks the sensitivity and imagination both to gauge the changes that confront him and to alter his actions to meet these changes. At the first suggestion, he becomes confused and negative and runs to the nearest ritualistic solution for the answer. Any new approach to solving problems is suspiciously viewed as impractical because it has not been tried before, and if the new approach involves a radical change, it is regarded as loony.

Chacteristically, the leader and his immediate assistants cling to the customary ways. They are not inventive, so they resist inventiveness. New ideas are studied not on the basis of their merit but by how well they fit within the framework of what has been. And because new ideas aren't congenial with the past, they are rejected.

When the Wright brothers first wobbled off the ground in their flimsy aircraft, the world took little notice. A year passed before their achievement was recognized in a scientific journal. Because they were hidebound in the tradition of the infallibility of the infantry and heavy artillery, government and military leaders failed to visualize the sweeping potential of the airplane. British and European leaders did, and World War I caught us woefully unprepared. We never did catch up. We read about the courageous deeds of our aces, not one of whom ever flew an American aircraft in combat. Our inefficiency in the production of aircraft is a black spot on our record. In fact, during an investigation following the war, one of our great jurists stated that he regretted that the provisions of criminal statutes did not reach inefficiency.

During the 1930s, a period of turbulence and strife between management and the worker in the industrial world, there were wild battles on the picket lines and hard struggles in the courts to determine whether the worker had the right to be represented by a union. The action was often bloody, as it was at the famous "Battle of the Bridge" at the Ford Motor Company plant, when the late Walter Reuther was decked during the fight. During the "Little Steel Strike," workers were killed on the lines at the

Republic Steel plant in Chicago. The struggle was violent, and the industrial world was engaged in a civil war.

Management firmly believed that unions were violating their right to own and protect property, and to manage it as they saw fit. The unions bitterly protested that they had a right in determining what their wages, hours, and working conditions were to be. The government sided with the unions. Management, raised in the laissez-faire economic tradition, a nineteenth-century economic concept, fought a losing battle against dissenting workers, failing to see that the paternalistic institution was subtly becoming obsolete in a new age.

Entrenched Leadership

Frequently, but not always, aged and entrenched leadership is present in the same institution. Entrenched leadership exists where the leading group represents a long line of successive groups that have jealously guarded standing traditions. Its members believe in the universal rightness of the old traditions to the extent that they have become overconfident and politely smug.

Within the group there is concern for its common security. When they feel a threat from below or without, they close into a tight phalanx to protect themselves while they chant the traditional answers to protests for change. A close fraternalistic bond exists. It is exclusive. Newcomers are coolly received, and if they win acceptance at all, it is only after a long time.

There is little question of their competence at applying the traditional approach, but when they apply it to new conditions a breakdown occurs.

There is a tendency among leaders to keep a firm grip on their positions beyond the age of productive contribution, and to keep subordinates waiting in the wings until they, too, reach an age where the time left for productive contribution is short. This protects the system until dissenting forces from below and outside become strong enough to force change.

Entrenched leaders, growing insulated from the realities of the world around them, remain innocent of the dissent fermenting about them.

They become victims of their own systems. Age, deep-seated tradition, habits, and insularity shield them from the realities of the forces of change. They cannot react resiliently. And the longer they persist against change, the more painfully evident the inadequacies of their decisions become. But they are appalled when their leadership judgments are openly questioned. Forceful and able subordinates who try to suggest change cannot survive within this environment and eventually leave, either by choice or mutual agreement.

One of our great political leaders, Winston Churchill, entrenched in his position, was convinced that he must stay on, and did so. When he left, his successor, Anthony Eden, came to the position unprepared to meet the critical world problems he faced. He had been subordinated for so long in a number-two spot that he was psychologically unfit for the top position. He was voted out.

Sewall Avery, as chief executive, led Montgomery Ward through difficult times. He stayed on, applying techniques and attitudes that belong to the past. Subordinates, by invitation or choice, left to become successful in competitive firms or elsewhere. When he retired, there was no legacy of strength in the executive ranks. While the firm has made an excellent comeback after a trying period, it is unlikely to catch the leading competitor.

Resistance to Change

An inflexible stance, repeated resistance to a change of position, and a strong defense of the status quo are characteristic of leadership that will give rise to dissent. They also cause decline.

These qualities may be seen in aged and entrenched leaders, but they may also be found in other leaders and leadership groups that are younger and less confirmed in their positions. While the leaders themselves look upon their approach as a defense of the basic goals of the institution, in action it has a negative effect. Again and again they say no to any suggestion for change or the proposal of a new idea. Suggestions that come from within are treated as though they were made out of ignorance or a lack of experience with the inner workings of the organization. Those that come from without are rejected because they are made by someone who does not understand how the organization operates.

After constant rebuttal, those who offer suggestions and ideas finally stop, and the flow dries up. The leaders go on, smugly protecting their inflexible course, heading in confident ignorance toward trouble.

In one of our railway systems, a conductor, by actual count, made 135 suggestions for improving service over a 20-year period. Not one of these was adopted. Understandably discouraged, he quit suggesting anything. Only a complete management upheaval and a rigorous attack against the old way of doing things saved this system from bankruptcy and turned it to profit.

An executive group in a firm cut off the flow of product ideas from those who sold the products. This was reversed by a change in management, but only after product leadership had been lost. It has not yet been regained.

Is it any wonder that, after being soaked many times by the cold water of rejection, those who suggest changes to an inflexible leader turn silent or look elsewhere for leadership?

Slackness in Attitude

Characteristic of an institution in dissent is an overdeliberate, slow, decision-making process. There is no sense of urgency, of the need for dispatch. Decisions are normally late and sometimes tabled for much too long, far beyond the time it takes to make them.

Often decision making requires the approval of too many executives. The process demands checks and rechecks: instead of the two or three who could ably make the decision, as many as ten persons may be involved. Or the problem may be referred to a committee, where it revolves in endless consideration, reconsideration, and argument.

Meanwhile, those wanting an answer wait and wait, becoming more restive and dissatisfied. Dissent begins to ferment.

In one organization an employee relations problem languished in a committee of sixteen executives for six months. In another, it rested with a committee of five for seven months. The employees' request was neither unreasonable nor difficult to resolve, and would have improved working conditions. While the committee deliberated, the employees waited and got the distinct impression that the committee didn't care. For the situation to be corrected required less committee deliberation and more individual action, and a forty-eight-hour limit was placed on answer time. But before this happened, the employees began to listen to union organizers, who had discovered their restlessness. Had the system not been changed, there is no question that the employees would have voted a union in.

Where slackness is present, the atmosphere is comfortable, easy, and unhurried. Time is not of the essence; urgent pressures for action are resisted and, if persistently pushed, resented. The leadership group cautiously ponders every problem placed before it. Questions waiting for answers pile up as each one is carefully considered, often without regard for the relative size of the problem. The minor and the major get the same deliberate treatment. A fear of mistakes is present.

In one organization, a program for studying the effectiveness of the communications systems took two and a half years to complete. This was praised. There was no concern that it should have been completed in six months, except by those further down in the organization who were directly responsible for the study. There, considerable dissatisfaction developed, and dissent took the form of asking for a transfer to another assignment or of resigning.

Slackness is evidence of complacency. The leading group is comfortable with the conviction that their slow pace is a sensible one. "Let's not rush into this" is the order of the day. And while they sit, conditions change. The leaders fall behind, and move only when they are obviously so far behind that they are forced into change—frequently too late.

When this kind of attitude leads to losses and omitted dividends in business institutions, stockholder suit after stockholder suit is brought as a result of dissatisfaction. Or they may result from a raid by an investor who sees the potential profit in a change of management leadership.

Business organizations aren't alone in their slack attitude. Any type of organization can and does fall into this bad habit—universities, churches, and city and national administrations are guilty.

Formalistic Outlook

The formalistic attitude is pragmatic, pedestrian—matter of fact and unimaginative. To those who uphold it, exact and unquestioning conformance to the institutional way of life is paramount. Subordinates must adhere to rigid standards of behavior or they cannot survive. Nonconformance is simply not present.

A formal attitude may be reflected in styles of dress. At lower levels in the organization, as well as at the top, types and colors of cloth, cut, cuffs, and shoes are punctiliously copied, and there is a military sameness throughout.

But, more importantly, it may be reflected in complete conformance with the way of thinking about problems of the institution. The matter-of-fact approach to directing organization affairs is religiously followed and rarely questioned. The way of leadership is the right way; to question is to be insubordinate.

There is an exclusive attitude among the leadership group. Subordinates are excluded from important decision making, and association between the group and others is limited to that necessary to conduct the affairs of the organization. Social intermixing is on a formal basis, and it is cool rather than gregarious. The group is self-contained and remains withdrawn from others, except for association with similar groups from like organizations.

Successful subordinates are of an obedient nature. Imitating the behavior patterns of their seniors, they feel secure, and they look forward to reaching the top where they may continue the past and present organizational way of life.

Leadership in this type of organization is usually entrenched and self-protective as well, shunning actions and individuals not wholly in sympathy with its conduct.

The formalistic pattern becomes so habitual that the leadership group is often naively unaware of the extent to which it exists, and, when questioned about it, denies that it exists at all. By itself a formalistic attitude is not bad. A certain degree of formalism is necessary to the orderly conduct of any organization. It is only when it becomes dominant in the affairs of the institution that it causes dissatisfaction within the ranks.

Dissent takes the form of protest by younger, less experienced members, who have not developed the conformance habit and find it frustrating. Those who cannot bring about changes or conform to the pattern leave. Evidence of this condition is the high turnover among the younger talent coming to and leaving the organization.

Insensitivity to Changing Conditions

Insensitivity refers to an unawareness of the direction and thrust of changing conditions that are affecting the course of affairs. The leading group may actually be aware of these conditions but inaccurately gauge their direction and force. Or they may simply refuse to accept them, displaying an attitude that the changes might affect others' way of life but not theirs.

Other factors may contribute to the problem, such as formalism, inflexibility, or entrenched and aged leadership, which insulate the leaders from the realities of daily life around them and cause them to become ingrown. Their outlook is a provincial one, and they are not tuned in to what is going on beyond the confines of their immediate affairs.

The explosion of antipollution forces is a case in point. Those organizations which have been attacked were often caught totally unprepared to meet the persuasive power of the dissenters. Consequently, their public stance has been one of fire and fall back. Glossy, after-the-fact advertisements extolling changes that were forced are not the answer. An informed public will not accept them. In fact, its reaction might be to question the honesty of such efforts, however well intended they may be. Admitting past errors and following up with a well-planned and explained course for corrective action would be more acceptable. To admit that he has made a mistake is the hallmark of an honest, mature man—a believable man.

In one corporation, a mistake in disciplining an employee was made. When it was discovered, management publicly admitted the error and corrected it. The reaction was positive. This action, instead of being criticized, was approved for its fairness and honesty.

It is when leaders publicly attempt to cover up or explain away errors as not being mistakes at all that they lose believability. This exposes them to the crossfire of the dissenting groups, who use the disclosure of a bad decision as a weapon for attack.

Those in power, insulated by tradition and layer upon layer of organization levels—twelve layers from top to bottom in one sizable institution—lose their sensitivity and continue applying old methods under new conditions of which they are unaware. In one of our major industries, now under constant attack, there were plenty of warning signs of dissatisfaction for a number of years. But, with some modification, the leaders continued to use past practices in their consumer relations, which were becoming increasingly unacceptable. Had they made broad consumer- and public-attitude studies, in depth and beyond the narrow question of which color do you like, certainly some of their present difficulties could have been anticipated and avoided.

And this is an industry which has been a basic constructive force in our society, has added to our mobility and geographic freedom, and has been a major element in our defense. But all this has been obscured by the antipollution and safety zealots who are attacking the industry leadership and forcing it to a defensive stand—in the courts, government investigations, the public forum, and stockholders' meetings.

In this age of dissent, attacking institutions is a popular pastime for some, a career for others. It is more than a fad. It is based on the causes which have already been discussed. Neither their past experience nor insular outlook has prepared many leaders to meet these attacks with skill and understanding. They are not at their best in public debate, which colors and downgrades their true capabilities in the eyes and ears of the viewers and listeners.

The late Clarence B. Randall warned repeatedly that leadership in all fields must become more responsive to public demands and be able to debate them articulately.

For too long the signs of dissatisfaction have been ignored or treated in an offhand fashion. Now we must understand their direction and force and adapt our institutions to meet them. We can no longer avoid the reality of dissent.

We have fallen into the trap of institutionalism in the sense that we allow ourselves to react within the confines of traditional organization response, failing to consider other factors with perception, such as the force of dissent against this institutional outlook. This is more likely to be confined to larger organizations. Simply to say that a man of the cloth cannot marry because it is against the time-honored tradition of his sect is an unacceptable answer. If it were not, why is it that this tradition is continually being defied, both within and outside the church?

And the traditional, highly formal, staid corporate shareholders' meeting can no longer be run as rigidly as it has been, permitting little that is not completely pertinent to be discussed. While the chairman cannot let it turn into a wild sideshow, certainly, with the deft and flexible use of the Rules of Order he can and should encourage debate of general questions, even though they may be only indirectly concerned with the immediate affairs of the meeting. The meeting should be structured to encourage reasonable debate. It can also be used as a platform for corporate leadership to explain its policies and actions, particularly in the area of civic affairs, to the shareholders and the public. An honest owning-up to shortcomings as well as accomplishments would win approval. There has been too much emphasis on the glowing report and the glib downplay of difficulties. Before an informed audience this fools no one.

Ineffective Communications

An essential element in leadership is decisiveness. In directing the affairs of an institution, a leader must make decisions and give orders to carry them out. But before orders are issued, he should give insightful consideration to the reactions of those affected by them, and with the orders should go a clear explanation of the reasons for them.

Too often we are so busy deciding and telling that we forget to consider and explain.

It is an axiom of sound communications that they are based upon careful listening. This is where we fall down. In our rush, we fail to listen. In discussions, for example, we are so busy figuring what we want to say next that we do not hear the arguments of the other side. By deciding to say nothing and listen for a single half hour, we could be amazed by how sensible and knowledgeable others are.

Face-to-face communications are difficult enough, but within the maze of an organization they become an intricate, hard task; communications with the outside are equally complex. As an organization grows, the number of relationships between individuals and groups, both inside and outside, mounts rapidly to a large number far beyond the comprehension of the few at the top. And it is when these few try to control those relationships as they have in the past that problems begin to form. Between an executive and one subordinate there is obviously one relationship. But when the number of executives reaches eleven, the relationships expand to 4,100. Is it any wonder that attempts break down when one man tries to exert personal control over this complex in the fashion he applied when the relationships—the communications—were few? Yet, in varying degrees, this is what happens, and communications become faulty and ineffective, to say the least. Imagine what happens to complicate this problem when layers are added within the organization between the top and the bottom. And this does not take into account those relationships with the outside world.

This burden of communications adds to the insensitivity of leaders to the problems that are smoldering beneath and around them; they see only those that flare up. As they sit in entrenched exclusion, only a tiny trickle of changing attitude and other festering conditions within the system filters through to them. They do not listen because they cannot. The traditional structure makes it impossible even when they sincerely try. There is no sensitive listening system present in the organization, no effective structure for resolving the complaints, grievances, or suggestions from others. In the case of extreme insensitivity and exclusiveness, there are no open, interpersonal relationships between the top and the next level, and a breakdown occurs there as well as below.

As a result, dissent emerges in the form of action groups clamoring in the dean's office, the bishop's office, the White House, the senator's office, the stockholders' meeting, and anywhere else the dissenters believe it worthwhile to raise a ruckus.

To meet this problem, two approaches are currently popular: the direct line and the ombudsman. The direct line allows an unsatisfied customer, for example, to call direct to the top with an appeal for resolution of his dissatisfaction. The ombudsman is a selected individual to whom those with a problem may go, chosen because he is supposed to have the background and skills to be able to mediate between the top and the dissenters. As a temporary stopgap these systems may be all right, but they are no long-term solution. They contain basic weaknesses. For one, they bypass all internal levels involved with the problems, and may, but also may not, correct the cause at its source. They are a substitute for an objective organization and communications analysis to find out the basic causes and the corrections needed. Until that is done and action taken, the old way drags on and a faulty system is prolonged.

Today an informed institutional membership will not accept direction by edict. Leaders can no longer assume that they may issue orders without explanation or as they always have in the past. Because of their insulation from others, they cannot assume to know the attitudes of the membership and how it will react. An official in a university town where there has been considerable dissension between town and gown assumed that there was high anti-university sentiment among his constituents, and he made a remark publicly against the university. He lost the next election. Had he taken the time to ask a number of his supporters what their opinion about the university was, he could have avoided making the remark and would still be in office.

Study upon study of organization and community-membership attitudes consistently shock leaders when they discover that there is strong disagreement with the way affairs are being run. No matter how large or small the organization or how well it is managed, be it church, university, business firm, or political group, it is a mistake for those at the top to believe they know all about their members' attitudes in this changing world.

In one corporation it took sixteen weeks of negotiation and strike before management uncovered an attitude among the striking employees that had enabled the union to keep them on strike for so long. When it was discovered that the men thought their seniority was being threatened because management had asked for more freedom to transfer them between jobs, corrective action was taken and the strike quickly settled. In addition, during the final discussions management learned about other attitudes among the men. They found talent in their ranks and later promoted two of the strike leaders. The strike was a difficult but healthy lesson on communications.

Absence of Leadership Succession

One of the characteristics of an institution facing serious problems is its lack of true leadership succession. Leaders claim that succession exists among the ranks, pointing proudly to one or several subordinates. But a closer examination of those likely to take over reveals that their talents lie more in an ability to conform than to lead. And, when they do succeed, a pattern of close conformance to the past is followed because of a lack of talent for, and training in, innovation. And all kinds of explanations are invented for their defense of the past.

But at least there is an earnest effort here. In other organizations, executives are so concerned with self-preservation that capabilities are deliberately snuffed. Subordinates simply aren't allowed to express themselves or exercise any independence of judgment. Those who persist in doing so leave or are gently eased out. Only those who passively submit remain. The successor is apt to be indecisive and vacillating, or sometimes overbearing in his attempt to camouflage his insecurity. When this happens, the only course left to arrest decline and turn the organization around is to go to the outside and bring in vigorous leadership.

In some organizations top executives are so immersed in daily operating detail that the vital question of succession is overlooked, lost, or only given lip service. When the time comes, and a decision has to be made, either because of age or death at the top, the most capable from a group untrained in top leadership is selected, sometimes too hurriedly. The chances of success for an individual appointed under these conditions are low.

Because the environment does not encourage self-expression and growth, young talent disagrees with the system and leaves. Or, worse than that, because of the organization's reputation as being no place for the young and able, they shy away from coming at all.

Where no leadership succession is consciously set up, other elements that foster decline and dissent, such as insensitivity and ineffective communications, are sure to be present.

However great he may be, a domineering leader usually fails, consciously or unconsciously, to provide a vigorous successor. He may do this unconsciously because he must domineer, or consciously for political reasons, or both. Look at the great political leaders of the past three decades, and see where this has happened.

When a successor comes to the top unprepared and without the practical skills and innovative talent necessary to meet the critical problems faced by institutions today, he has a hard time of it, and his efforts may be ineffective. This explains in part the difficulties in our universities. Presidents, selected because of academic achievements, are expected suddenly to understand the world of strife and become skillful negotiators with dissenting groups, strong commanders in quelling riots, and capable administrators of complex institutions suffering budgetary ague. Although some of them leave something to be desired, others have done well with little or no experience to help them.

Lack of Creative Adjustment

Leadership lacks inventiveness, not in the technical, but in the organizational, sense. There is too much reliance on the traditional way of running the affairs of the organization, and too little willingness to adopt new techniques. When faced with new conditions, the top falls back on traditional habits to solve problems. New concepts of planning, of plotting the future of the institution, are judged to be theory instead of a hard look into the future to see what its effect will be and to decide what adjustments should be made to meet the changes it will bring. No clear-cut objectives are spelled out for the organization or for the members of the staff leading it.

Membership attitudes are assumed instead of being independently surveyed to learn what they really are, to discover areas of discontent and correct them before they become an issue of open dissent.

The psychological and sociological disciplines have much to offer about what causes individuals and groups to act positively or negatively in response to executive action. We know that groups react positively to consideration of their welfare, that they show more will to do when they have a truly active role in deciding matters that affect their daily lives, and that openly or otherwise they reject direction by edict. This is the base of our political system, and yet, within our institutions, we do not practice it as much as we should.

As leaders we have not sufficiently sensed the impact that the changing attitudes of aware, well-informed members have on our institutional structures. Failing to do this, and using the old ways to meet new problems, we find ourselves caught up in open dissent.

Parishioners, customers, students, professors, stockholders, Democrats, Republicans, no longer bow to paternal direction. In this affluent world there is a strong feeling of independence, of the need for more individual expression, and it cannot be denied. We must allow more room for debate. We must do more listening before we act.

Much of our problem lies in faulty structures that cause communications distortions and shut-off; also to blame is a lack of skill in leadership by participation. Many of our present leaders have been raised in a disciplined, paternalistic environment, and some simply do not understand how to manage by participation. This applies not only to internal relationships, but to external as well. As an example, one top man in an organization that was characteristically paternalistic in attitude decided that there should be more management by participation. To do this he held periodic staff meetings in his office to discuss major problems. Executives were included from around the organization. To him this was participation; to the others it was not. They found themselves listening to hour-long monologues, and decisions were still made in which they had little part. Because the man at the top was not listening, he had no way of knowing how dissatisfied these executives were with this arrangement.

Because we have not truly read the trends of changing attitudes, we have been forced to the defensive in the area of corporate public responsibility, whether the concern has been about pollution, honesty in product or service promotion, the war, the underprivileged, or safety. An informed public wants straightforward, believable actions and explanations. Institutions need systems that will send to the top, from all points of the compass, accurate information on the wants and dissatisfactions of their various publics as well as their own membership. How to do this will be explained in more detail in a later chapter.

Failure to Meet Overexpansion Needs

When an institution expands at too rapid a rate in both size and diversity, problems develop, particularly if it is managed as it was when it was a smaller organization. The structure and the communications become inadequate for coordinating the differing patterns of behavior and the complex of relationships that arises. The old, less formal systems serve more as centers of confusion than a means for expediting the affairs of the institution or for solving questions of membership wants and demands.

Since World War II, institutions of all types have expanded in size rapidly and beyond all predictions. But we have not adjusted our institutions to meet their size or the changing conditions confronting them.

Consider the case of the ombudsman. As we have seen, this is, or should be, only a stopgap. For one individual to be able to serve the many needs of a large organization is too much to expect. An appeal system that moves with dispatch and fairness needs to be built into the structure, just as the world of union-management relations has developed its grievance and arbitration procedure. Although this can present problems, it works effectively in the hands of intelligent and fair-minded men on both sides.

Not only do we need appeal systems, but we need carefully constructed lines of communication that open up the way for and encourage others to suggest, recommend, and otherwise take part in the affairs of the organization. These lines must also serve the function of enabling leaders to prepare the way for and explain their actions.

There are two basic principles that must be applied if these systems are to be successful: The decision for solving a problem or acting on a recommendation should be made as close to the source as possible; and actions should be taken with reasonable dispatch. Nothing can cause disgruntlement more than undue delay in acting on a problem, or the decision's being made by someone so far from the source that it is apt to be unrealistic.

5

The Shape and Direction of Dissent

INSTITUTIONAL and communications problems that are at the core of dissent have been examined, and illustrations of causes and effects of dissent cited. It would seem appropriate now to look more closely at the shape of dissent as it exists today, the direction dissent may take in the future, and what to do about it.

Before discussing the actual forms of dissent, several remarks ought to be made.

Dissent centers on our right to speak out our grievances—imagined or real. When one group dissents from another, the believability of the group toward which the dissent is directed is impaired, and it must be repaired or reconstructed by that group. This requires an honest, candid approach. In this sophisticated world, glibness will only increase the degree of the unbelievability. Some leaders seem to have a horror of admitting to an honest error. Not only should it be admitted, but it should also be explained, along with plans for corrective action. This is not always possible, as in the case of a military error where disclosure would give aid and comfort to the enemy. But we can do more than we do.

We Americans are a fair-minded people, strongly believing in fair play. We are reasonable in our reactions if we understand what others are doing when we are involved. It is when we do not understand—when what is happening has not been clearly explained, or not explained at all—that we may seem to be unreasonable.

But this is a new age. The older among us have to adjust our habits of conformance, learned in a more conforming world, to the present, where unquestioning obedience is resisted. Some of us seem to have forgotten that this country was founded on dissent. As a nation, we have always been characterized as highly independent, bristling against overbearing direction. And now we are resisting institutional traditions that are thought to be sharply curbing our independence and well-being.

It has been said that the way to get an American to do what you want him to do is to tell him that you don't want him to do it. General Lafayette, after his experience with our army during the Revolutionary War, shrewdly observed that the strange genius of this people is that first you must explain, then give the order. We do not conform simply because we are told to do so. We want to know *why* we should do something. Basically, this is probably a universal trait of man, and not confined to any one nationality.

The Forms of Dissent

But what are the forms that dissent takes, and what should be done about them when they appear? There are essentially three varieties: passive, active, and violent.

Passive Form

This is a negative kind of dissent. Members of an institution, disagreeing with the actions of their leaders, lose interest and withdraw their support. They may refuse to participate in organization activities, such as serving on voluntary committees and attending meetings. Or they may discontinue their financial support or resign.

Today, this form exists among the alumni of many of our colleges and universities where the feeling of revolt is mild. Dissatisfaction with their alma mater's admission policies and its permissiveness toward faculty and student activists is widespread. Alumni think that their interests have been forgotten and lost, as university leaders rush to appease campus activists who disrupt the

And, when discipline is applied, it must be done carefully and not precipitously, to be sure that it is just and fair. In the heat of anger, unjust errors can be made, causing further unrest.

After the initial action has been calmed, meetings with responsible representatives from the dissenters should be held to find out what the cause, the real cause, is. On the surface, it may be the dismissal of a professor, thought to be unjust. But the actual cause may be an insufficient or unacceptable explanation of the reasons for letting him go. More than that, it may lie in a general sluggishness in communicative response to the needs of students and professors.

In the church, as well as in the academic world, there is considerable unrest. Parishioners are not always in accord with what the elders and the clerics decide or follow. Clergymen are speaking out against what in their opinion are obsolete traditions. They are resigning in protest. They are rebelling against the strict paternalism of their orders, which they consider to be medieval in outlook. They want to be less withdrawn and more involved in ordinary, daily living. They no longer feel that an inviolable rule that they cannot marry should be placed on them. They are defying it, leaving the church, and marrying.

The answer here is for church leaders to examine their structures and traditions in terms of contemporary life to find out what it is that they must do to adjust to the world of today and tomorrow. The strict canon law of yesterday, demanding unquestioning obedience, is not and will not be accepted in many instances, by either clerics or parishioners. They want some say in the governing of the church, and not simply to be told by a higher body withdrawn from today's living.

Church leaders face problems similar to those that concern the top executives of other kinds of institutions. They too must probe the attitudes and dissatisfactions of their members, decide where their structures and traditions are more related to the past than to the present, and make adjustments—an extremely difficult task—without sacrificing those traditions that come from within man. Much of their problem stems from an age-old fatherly outlook, reflected in what today is considered a rigid structure. Too many decisions are made at the top, but the top remains withdrawn, and pronounces when it should listen. Adjustments need to be made in the structure and in communications to allow more representation from an enlightened membership. This has to be done if the religious leadership so vital to human society is to be maintained. It is encouraging to see religious leaders, obviously well aware of the problems they face, acting in this direction.

Economic institutions are being hit by dissent from all sides. Stockholder meetings used to be formal and stiff, with very little occurring to upset the dry routine. Now meetings are frequently disrupted by shouting dissenters debating everything from product quality to pollution. Instead of being routine and briskly adjourned, meetings may run for six or seven hours. In addition to noisy and disruptive hecklers, there are also present those who are concerned about practices in customer relations that to them fall short of what they should be, hurting the corporation's image and long-range profitability.

For the most part, stockholders have been a silent group. When they did not agree with the direction of the corporation, they simply sold out. They still do this. But stockholders are no longer so silent as they were, and they are aided by the increasing professional dissidence they see around them.

It would seem that the old form of stockholder meeting is slipping into the past. The strict procedures, the glib or inarticulate explanations of corporate affairs playing down difficulties, will no longer do. More perceptive managements are realizing what is going on, and they are changing the structure of their meetings to meet the need.

Management can adjust and successfully turn dissent to an advantage for all. First, without revealing competitive secrets, it must be willing to take a forthright approach in explaining its actions. Along with the good, the unobscured bad should be described. This will increase believability. Currently, many annual reports sound as though the same public relations staff wrote them all. Common phrases such as "your strong management team" thread throughout the texts. While well done in many ways, one senses from them that there must be more difficulties than they disclose. Fortunately, a move toward the good seems to be taking place.

Secondly, the form of the meeting needs to be restructured to include scheduled time for open debate following the rules of order. This should be encouraged. Where management lacks debating skills, it should develop them. An open forum structure will provide management with an excellent platform for exchanging views with stockholders, as well as an excellent opportunity to explain its past and intended actions not only to the stockholders but to the press and the public as well.

A less obvious type of dissent occurs in corporations in the form of disagreement from the subordinate executive ranks. They, too, may have their quarrel with the top. How dissatisfied such executives are may be gauged by the rate of turnover among the group. There is normal turnover in any organization—retiring, leaving for better opportunities, moving away—but this is relatively infrequent. However, when executives come and go regularly, there must be unusual dissatisfaction with leadership.

They leave not so much for more money as for more opportunity for professional growth. Some of the immediate reasons may be dictatorial supervision, too narrow or too little real respnsibility for decisions, little room for or too slow development, little actual participation in management decisions, or unfair compensation. What to do about this will be outlined later. The solution lies in changing top attitudes to recognize the need for enlarging subordinate opportunity for constructive contribution and growth. Training disciplines will have to be broader, with more emphasis on skills in organizing and delegating.

Our political system, the party system, is based on the right to dissent, but it seems to be extraordinarily wracked by turmoil these days. Much of the discontent rises out of the belief that our administration and party leaderships are too full of too many men with obsolete views, attitudes, and neckties. The young believe they are out of tune with the contemporary world, that they are callous about war and poverty. This is true among both nonprofessional and professional members.

Politicians are by training and ability astute at sizing up the attitudes of constituents, and most of us could learn much from them. But today a number of political leaders seem to be listening more to the past than to tomorrow. Some should orate less and listen more in an attempt to develop an accurate grasp of the forces at work in our society.

The problems in the political system are no different in substance from those troubling other organizations. Parts of the structure are for a smaller country and for the past, not the late twentieth century. The seniority practices of political parties and legislatures are an example. Present seniority traditions protect the old and discourage the young. The "turks," the younger politicians, find themselves in an uphill battle when they buck the system.

Because of our bureaucratic way of life, it is not easy to attract young talent to a government career, except for the more romantic occupations, such as the Peace Corps or the FBI. The federal administrative process is fraught with an overstuffing of departmentation, fragmentation, and duplication. This leads to interunit conflict, inefficiency, and slowness of action, causing not only internal unrest but public disapproval. Any institution is difficult to reorganize, but because of the power structure, political ones are about the hardest. Progress is slow, but both our parties are working constantly to improve the process and reduce the bureaucratic proliferation.

Our armed services have suffered a battering of dissent from all sides. There is public disapproval of their actions in Vietnam, widespread draft dodging, and resentment of the rigid orthodoxy of the services themselves. Those raised in a more permissive environment are rebelling against the hard military discipline. Officers are resigning. Enlisted men are "fragging" their officers. Returned veterans march in protest.

Much of this turning against the services has been unearned. They have been fighting because of a political decision that they do so. The killing of civilians may occur in any war, but where it is sometimes impossible to distinguish civilian from soldier, the chances are that it will happen.

In an attempt to improve the serviceman's morale, top commands are issuing orders for actions intended to take some of the drabness and monotony out of military life. Hair may be grown longer, barracks may be decorated with more than pinups, and clubs now have floor shows with dancers.

This type of change helps, but the services are hampered by the general disenchantment with the war. They are unpopular because the war is unpopular.

The services, too, must examine their basic doctrines and ways of life in light of tomorrow's world; they, too, must adjust to the trends of the future. Technological developments and changing public attitudes are having a profound impact on the traditions and organization of the services, and these cannot be escaped if they are to carry out their mission of protecting the peace successfully.

Active Form

Dissent may move from a passive to an active form. It becomes active when passive steps fail to gain desired action. Dissenting individuals and groups may take action in a number of ways to call attention to their wants. Failing to win satisfaction by appeal, the dissenters may turn to the courts to gain their demands, or seek to have laws passed that prohibit actions with which they disagree.

When an organization is faced with active dissent, it has only two courses of action: to resolve the issue through the courts or to settle outside. What to do depends upon the nature of the complaint. The seriousness of the legal question may have to be weighed against that of public reaction in the form of approval or disapproval. This is the kind of complicated problem facing the leaders of the automotive and steel industries when dissenters cry out that the products they make are unsafe or pollute the air and water. With little or no knowledge of the intricate steps and burdensome costs involved in the corrections demanded, it is easy for those who point a scolding finger at corporations to thunder righteously. In turn, it is difficult for corporate leaders to speak of their problems without appearing reluctant to make changes in the public interest.

At times the demands are so unrealistic—quick correction of a complicated steel mill pollution action, for example—that the companies have no recourse but to take legal action.

On the other hand, corporations and other sources of pollution need to gauge the temper of the times more realistically, examine their practices within the framework of this temper, plan changes, inform the public of their intentions, and act before public censure forces them to move. Planned obsolescence, a long-standing practice in the automotive world, is being forced out of existence by public dissatisfaction. Here dissent may take the form of public outcry, or the more direct one of purchasing a foreign car.

Peaceful picketing is a common form of dissent. A group forms a file and marches up and down before the site of those against whom they have a complaint. The pickets usually carry signs of protest. The White House, the Capitol or other government offices, and corporation headquarters are favorite picketing grounds.

As a means of expressing dissent, peaceful picketing is surely lawful. The problem is that it may be inherently dangerous, because it can be, and often is, tripped into violence. The pickets may taunt or be taunted by others disagreeing with them. Taunting leads to pushing and shoving, followed by a breakout of physical violence. This is what happened when "hard hats" and pickets confronted each other in New York. The reaction of the "hard hats" was direct—and violent.

Being a lawful means of assembly, peaceful picketing has to be allowed, but because it can turn into violence, it should be patrolled by police or any other force delegated the responsibility for maintaining law and order. Patrolling should take place in the background as much as possible, because the taunting of pickets and bystanders might turn on the police. But on the slightest sign of trouble, the police should move in quickly to prevent any possible violence before it occurs. In the interest of public safety, they may have to order the meeting to disband, even though they may be accused of interfering with the right to assemble.

Dissent may be expressed through a meeting called for that purpose. Again, the right of peaceful assembly is involved and such a meeting must be permitted, unless the intent of the gathering is to commit an unlawful act. Most of the time, meetings by dissenters involve much argument and many resolutions and are not patrolled unless by request. Employees may meet with the idea of forming themselves into a union. Others may do so to form a church more to their own liking, or to draw up a proclamation against some one person or group with which they are dissatisfied —for the war to be stopped, polluters to be punished, or police brutality to be put to an end.

But, as with peaceful picketing, lawful assembly in meetings may turn to violence. This happened to an apparently peaceful meeting in Haymarket Square in Chicago on the evening of Tuesday, May 4, 1886. Anarchists called a meeting to denounce the latest atrocious acts of the police—the shooting of workingmen before the McCormick Works the day before while attempting to stop a riot. The meeting began peacefully. On the fringe of the crowd was Mayor Carter Harrison, and after listening to the early speeches, he went to the police station a block away where several hundred men were at the ready. He said that the meeting was orderly and that as long as it remained so, he had no right to interfere. He and the chief of police left after placing an inspector of police in charge. Without telling his superiors, the inspector made his own preparations. Detectives who were spread throughout the meeting brought reports back to the inspector. They reported that an anarchist speaker was saying that the law must be throttled, killed, and stabbed. The inspector lost his temper and marched his men toward the meeting. Rain had begun to fall, and the meeting was beginning to break up when the police arrived in such a way that the crowd was pushed back together. A captain in the front ranks ordered the meeting to break up. A bomb was thrown and exploded among the police, shots were fired from both sides. In five minutes it was over. Seven police officers were killed and sixty injured, and crowd casualties were high. So it was that a peaceful meeting, which could have ended quietly and never been heard of again, turned into a bloody fight that is history in Chicago.

The Haymarket Riot is a dramatic illustration, but it serves to demonstrate the inherent danger in a meeting called to express strong dissent. Most of the time this danger isn't present, but leaders of meetings and public authorities should be aware of the possibility that it might be. In this event, they should make careful and calm plans to meet the danger in case it begins to develop. Here the action is to move in quickly, divide the crowd, and remove the instigators.

Much of the recent student unrest has been expressed at meetings to decry the Vietnam War, to deplore the tragedy at Kent State, or to censure university leaders. Some of these meetings, intended to be peaceful, have ended up tragically. Often this has happened because those crowding into a meeting charged with emotion, with the exception of professional agitators, have failed to realize the potential explosiveness of the gathering. And, on the other side, the policing forces have lacked the training and skills to know how to handle meetings that could turn into rioting.

The inherent problem here is that, in meetings held for dissent, there are those who disagree with the dissenters present, and when emotions run high, normal heckling or filibustering may turn into an outbreak.

Pamphleteering is another way of expressing dissent. Handbills, letters, and pamphlets are given or mailed to those whom the dissenters wish to persuade to support the dissent. Today this may also take the form of spot notices or comments on radio and television, as well as ads in the newspapers. Pamphleteering was a customary means for Yankee dissenters when they began to resist taxation without representation. Thomas Paine's *Common Sense* had a tremendous effect on bringing about the Declaration of Independence.

Handbills and letters are commonly used by unions and managements, when the union is trying to organize employees or when a strike is about to happen or is actually going on. Each side is, of course, arguing the sense of its position. Recently the arguments have concentrated more on wages than they sometimes do. To management the demands are excessive and inflationary. To the union they are not, but are their just share of productive efforts. This may be seen in newspaper accounts reporting what the official spokesmen for each side have to say.

The effectiveness of using the various written techniques varies from being completely ineffective to having a persuasive impact in convincing others that the opposition's position is unfair. Letters to employees who are threatening to strike are least effective when they are hurriedly put together and poorly written under the pressure of a crisis. In fact, if they are used during a crisis period only, the reaction may be negative. The employees feel that management speaks to them only when they are in trouble, and discount what they have to say. They are most effective when issued as part of a well-planned, articulate, continuing flow of communications of interest and concern to employees. The best technique is to follow the time-tested practices of journalism, using headlines and summary paragraphs that are terse and clear, hold reader interest, and end before his attention drops off.

The value of newspaper ads and radio and television spots is not easy to determine. They have a place, particularly when the issues are cloudy or when the public is insufficiently aware of what is taking place. Thoughtfully planned, well-constructed, and carefully timed communications have a positive impact on public reaction when the reason for them is explained.

One word of caution is appropriate here. Care should be taken to avoid allowing the negotiations between the dissident parties to be drawn into public media. Arguments become influenced by the media, and attempts to reach a settlement are often obstructed.

Exposing unacceptable actions of leaders through the public media is a favorite technique of dissenters. Nader is a case in point. His exposure of what in his opinion are unsafe designs in cars has been a major factor in automotive design change.

This technique is a good one as long as those involved in it are sensible and fair, but in the hands of impractical busybodies it can be dangerous. Attempts by these people to interfere should be deftly turned aside and occasionally ignored, as their lopsidedness becomes quite evident in time.

The answer to an exposé is to meet it forthrightly, not defensively. The more defensive the reaction appears to be, the more the public will suspect that all is not well and that the claims of the exposer are true—even though they may be quite inaccurate. The best method of handling exposure is to anticipate it—to study trends in attitudes and dissatisfactions, and plan actions accordingly.

Boycotting is another form of active dissent. The name came into use in the late nineteenth century, when a land agent in Ireland by the name of Boycott was ostracized for refusing to reduce land rents. Now it means refusing—or getting others to refuse— to do business with someone in protest against his actions. A good example was the boycott launched against the grape growers in California by the grape pickers under the leadership of César Chavez. Chavez instigated a widespread campaign to convince customers to strike grapes from their shopping lists. This is known as a secondary boycott because the attempt is to persuade customers of a store not to buy grapes. The grievance is not against the store but against the growers who sell to the store. Were the store itself the target, the boycott would be a primary one.

When students decide not to go to class as an expression of disagreement, they are boycotting. Whether this should be permitted is an open question. In fact, students aside, there has been much argument over the years about the legality of the boycott— the secondary boycott in particular. The point in question is that an innocent third party suffers injury during a secondary boycott. But legal or not, the boycott continues to be used as a weapon by dissenters.

The counteraction to boycotting may be to seek legal restraint or to speak out publicly against the boycott, defending the position that caused it.

A form of dissent that could involve violence is the strike—an active withdrawal of support or a refusal to work or engage in a normal activity. Strikes are usually accompanied by picketing. Here, too, the problem is the danger that picketing will break into violence, so, as in the case of any type of picketing, it has to be patrolled carefully.

Picketing during a strike may take the form of walking up and down before a building of the institution against which the strike is directed, or the strikers may sit down in front of or inside the building to block anyone from going in or coming out.

The days of turning over cars, throwing bricks, clubbing heads, and shooting are largely past. Only rarely does strike violence occur before the gates of an industrial plant. Such action is considered to be futile as well as wasteful. Violence does happen, but it is relatively rare. Through law and practice, Queensbury-like rules have long since been established. The violence of the thirties has turned into casual walking up and down. The rule is that no one charges the pickets or crosses the line—except for the management group—and this has become a formality to be observed. The sit-down strike, the center of much violence and legal controversy during the thirties, is an infrequently used tactic today. The legality has long since been settled, and because of the union's established power position, this type of action is no longer necessary.

The recent strikes in the educational world are somewhat reminiscent of the thirties. Students and professors were green freshmen; so were the university officials. Neither knew quite what to do with this weapon in their hands. Once a strike had started, more often than not it led to violence and accomplished very little except to interrupt the educational process and destroy property. Harried officials, educators with little or no strike experience, reacted in a way opposite from the way they should have. They turned the other cheek when a firm stand should have been taken, and lost their position of leadership and respect. In too many instances, when striking students occupied offices destructively, they bent to their outlandish demands and capitulated. Under these conditions, direct action should be taken. The strikers should be asked to leave after a promise to meet and discuss their grievances with them has been given. If they choose not to leave, no further talk is in order and no further promises should be made. Forcible action is the only course to be taken. Giving in will only lead them to believe that, in the future, such action will gain their ends. There are courageous exceptions to this course of capitulation, but they have been few. For the most part, students were allowed to go on playing with fire. There are no gentle means for settling a destructive strike—they only worsen the situation.

Marching demonstrations are another active form of dissent. When they are peaceful, there is no recourse but to permit them as a lawful means of assembly. But, as with other active forms of expressing disagreement, marching contains the seeds of violence. The marches led by Martin Luther King were to be peaceful demonstrations, but violence followed in their wake, plaguing him to his death. Marches through the southern states were running fights. Demonstrations of this sort have to be carefully patrolled wherever crowds gather to stare curiously or jeer disapproval.

Small incidents must be quickly quelled before they swell into uncontrollable size. Although this itself may cause a melee, at times it can't be helped, and may forestall a rampage.

Violent Form

Dissent may reach a pitch where, intentionally or not, it breaks into violence. Rioting, breaking the law, or deliberate anarchic destruction may broil up. Violent dissent ranges from local incidents to widespread civil war. This is the form favored by the revolutionary, who cares little about property or the rights of others when they don't serve his ends.

We have seen much of this in recent years. There have been the Berkeley, Watts, Chicago, Detroit, Cleveland, and Newark riots, to name a few. A survey of the damage in the aftermath of such violence shocks the senses. Stark and mute, the charred and shattered buildings stand as evidence of the brute rage of a mob out of control.

Violent dissent occurs for a number of different reasons, but the primary one is an unsatisfied grievance that has been smoldering for a long time. Where other means used to resolve that grievance have met with failure—when direct appeal, laws, and court action fail to produce visible results—it is understandable that the grieved can be led into violent action to vent their suppressed frustration. Such a group may take action on its own, or it may be the perfect tool for professional revolutionaries.

Some years ago the rage was among the "hard hats." Now they have income, property, and status. The low-wage sweatshop is, with some exceptions, a condition of the past. The case of the transient agricultural worker is being fought out between the union and management today, but this is an unusual situation. The minority groups are the cause today. Years ago they had little or no status and no power to resist or actively dissent. Even the law offered little sympathy for their demands. They suffered from disinterest and neglect and were trapped at the lower end of the status scale, nursing long-festering grievances.

Now, with some help from the law through reform groups and agencies of the government such as the Equal Employment Opportunity Commission, and with leadership rising among them, they are openly, often violently, demanding satisfaction. Because of long neglect and deeply ingrained prejudices, to change their position upward on the scale is incredibly difficult, and violence is an unfortunate but inevitable consequence. Change cannot be forced into being overnight by passing laws, expecting that the statute itself will correct the problems. But neither can the change be denied, nor can it wait through long delay. This can only lead to further violence. Standing institutions are intricate patterns of customary relationships and habits that resist hurry-up schemes for fashioning a new institutional way of life. We are too prone to devise quick programs as solutions to difficult, long-range problems. What we need are well-planned programs, designed intelligently and calmly, for steady, not headlong, action to bring about change.

Quick solutions usually end in disruption and failure. This is a fact of life that the impetuous reformer seems unable to grasp. Deliberately favoring minority groups in the universities is a case in point. Minority-group students come wholly unprepared, academically and socially, for campus life. But jumping or rushing hurriedly onto the minority-group bandwagon with programs that are more emotional than realistic is not the answer. It creates inequities against other groups, does little for many of the badly prepared students themselves, and creates more dissent than it solves. Such approaches will have to be replaced with planned gradualness. Patience with impatient dissenters will be necessary, but the long-term results will be more sound and productive. What is needed is a comprehensive, carefully designed series of plans for upgrading the whole educational structure where a minority or the underprivileged are involved. And to these must be attached a realistic time schedule for execution.

Neglect—as we sat comfortable with our belief that the minority person knew his place and kept it—has been the real cause of violence. Now we are paying for being blinded too long by that traditional belief as upheaval explodes around us.

We are making progress, but it is slow and difficult, and it will take years to adjust our complicated system of institutions to meet the wants of the minorities and the underprivileged. Because this is so, we can expect more violence. The pace of adjustment will be too slow for those who would resolve the problem now, and they will erupt in dissent. But it will be essential that those among us responsible for leading our institutions, to paraphrase Rudyard Kipling, keep our heads while those around us are losing theirs and blaming it on us.

What the leader should do to manage the various forms of dissent, particularly during strikes and riots, will be discussed in later chapters in more detail.

This raises the question: During this age of dissent, where do we stand today and what does the future hold for us?

Where We Are

The sixties, as we all know, were turbulent times. Violence was rampant in our colleges and universities, towns and cities. Rioting embroiled Berkeley, Mississippi State, Columbia. Burning and destruction struck Chicago, Cleveland, and many other cities and towns. There were the King and the Abernathy marches, the peace demonstrations in Washington. The climax arrived when innocents fell dead on the campus at Kent State. This, the Wisconsin bombing, and other incidents where innocent and guilty alike were maimed and killed brought home the seriousness of the more violent forms of dissent. They were negative, nihilistic. They sought only to destroy and offered nothing constructive to replace. At the peak, toward the end of the sixties, negative activism reached a point of unbridled hysteria.

Now we seem to have entered a period of relative calm. Some of it is reaction; calm and rest follow the exhaustion sustained hysteria brings. But this is only one among a number of causes. Destruction accomplishes nothing and stiffens resistance. Students and others began to see that their high hopes for turning over the system now, through demonstrations, strikes, and rioting, were sadly misplaced. They see the futility of the more violent forms of dissent, are disillusioned, and for the moment at least, have rejected them. But because they want no part of violence does not mean that they have given up their desire for eliminating poverty, war, and discrimination. Quite the contrary. They mean to continue their drive for social improvement—and more power to them. Their calm seems to be a period of recovery and reflection about how to "have a go at it" in the future. They are considering that perhaps the best way to accomplish their aims is by working for change from within the system.

And where are the revolutionaries, so much in arrogant evidence during the destructive phase? The misled pseudorevolutionary has moved back into the system to some degree, at least, as have many of our dissenters of the thirties. But where are the dedicated revolutionaries? They have gone underground, as revolutionaries always have when the bristling arm of authority reaches too close. They are busy camouflaging and planning future action.

A hard fact has hit the state of dissent. For the first time since 1958, the economy has suffered from an extended recession. This has not been what the Eisenhower administration labeled euphemistically a "rolling readjustment," but a serious downturn as the administration applies the economic brakes to inflation. Jobs for the unemployed worker and manager are difficult to locate. The college graduate, so vigorously courted during recent years, can no longer pick and choose from many offers handed to him. He has to look for a job, an experience new to this generation.

Consumers have been in a saving mood from which they are only now emerging. The money is simply not available to support those who would spend their full time on dissent. Many of the students who were involved in demonstrations and other dissent actions have now graduated into the world where it becomes essential to earn a living, a pursuit which is a full-time occupation, particularly when the inspiration is to raise children and meet mortgage payments.

Many of the organizations—the bands—devoted to violent action overreached themselves with their effrontery and their disdain for authority and the rights of others. Whatever public tolerance and sympathy they may have had has turned against them. Their leaders have fled into exile, leaving them in a disorganized state. Once arrogant, they now wander as aimlessly as exiles. The militancy may be there, but the organization is gone.

Within the university complex the students may be calm, but the alumni are not. They are moving from the more passive, but effective, role of withdrawing financial support to forming organizations to express their dissatisfaction with official permissiveness in a more active way.

What We Can Expect

There is much that is puzzling about the calmness that seems to have settled over the universities and other institutions. Is it real, or is it deceptive? It is both—and bothers those who would forecast the future.

It is real in the sense that campus violence is unlikely to reach the extremes of the past five years; nor will militant bands be allowed to flout the law or disregard the public safety and the rights of others. Public patience has run out.

But the calmness is deceptive too. We cannot relax and say to ourselves that we are glad it is all over. It is not. Dissatisfactions are everywhere, and dissent will continue in its various forms, but with a shift in emphasis and direction to meet changing conditions.

The events of the sixties were shocking in the real meaning of the word. Our leaders fell assassinated; other public officials were harassed or injured. Court trials were uproarious. Mobs ran in unbridled fury, and demonstrations were countless. The White House became a favorite picketing ground. They were violent years full of clash and discord. But the tragedies of these years, hard blows that stunned us at first, shook us into realizing that we had neither understood nor comprehended the complexity and fierceness of the dissatisfaction with our institutions' ability to meet our changing desires. At first we panicked, reaching nervously for quick solutions, for panaceas. Now that the hysteria has lessened, we are taking a more objective approach. In this sense, these troubled years had the constructive result of forcing leadership to adjust to meet the challenges of a new age.

While demonstrations, strikes, and riots will be present, their number and intensity will be diminished. Leaders of movements will not use these techniques willy-nilly. Experience has increased their skills of organization, some of which were learned in the services against which they protest. This is also true of the other side—the police authorities whose job it is to control. Through experience and training, they are better able to handle demonstrations, or to dissipate them when strife breaks out.

Leaders of institutions are learning that the tough stance is the wise course—that much has been lost by capitulation and little gained save further disorder. But the hard approach should not be confused with a rigid one. That, too, as we have learned, only encourages further dissent. The courageous stand implies a willingness to listen and take action on those demands that are justifiable while refusing to give in to those that are not. An example of a just demand is the request by students and professors for more say in the community affairs of the university. An unjust one might be that they should determine whether classes are to be held, or what the curriculum ought to be. It is only right that their recommendations be honestly heard and considered as valuable. But students and professors are in no position to have an overview of all the problems of general administration of the university; they are limited by lack of experience.

In the coming years the blacks will want more. The problems of the ghetto are still there waiting to be solved. Other minority groups are stirring, beginning to assert their demands, and among them there will be restiveness and discontent, striking and rioting. We will need to give much attention to them and provide courses of action that are productive, not superficial. In the ghettos, for example, present plans for improvement are often more socially than economically oriented. Social agencies, according to Benjamin Duster, the perceptive chairman of the Illinois Commission on Human Relations, are not prepared, either in outlook or in program, to develop and initiate sound economic aid. He argues that what is needed is a sound approach that will build a going business structure in the ghettos, and that it needs the backing, both in money and know-how, of the business community. Some efforts in this direction have been made but are not nearly effective enough.

The minority-group problem is a difficult, long-range one that demands immediate attention and innovative action. Meanwhile, we shall have to suffer dissent in its active and violent forms, anticipating and curbing incidents while we work on change.

The fact has to be faced that minorities are not about to settle for anything less than equal opportunity, and the law and the courts are backing them. Many of us have to be forced to provide that equality. We must shift our attitudes and act to help bring it about, not resist it.

Dissenters of all sorts are beginning to work within the system to bring about the achievement of their aims. One of the techniques they have turned to is exposure. First, an investigation is made, followed by reporting to the proper government agency, if one is involved, and handing over the information to radio, television, and the newspapers. This is the Nader technique, and whether one agrees or not, it has been and is exposing questionable practices. One of the problems is that it attracts the reformer personality, who, in his ardor to straighten out the world this morning, is apt to magnify a minor malpractice into a major one. Another problem is the demand for immediate correction in complex activities.

Daniel Ellsberg, in handing over the Pentagon Papers, took it upon himself to expose political and military practices which, in his opinion, were and are deceptive. Many people feel that in doing so he betrayed a high trust, but he sincerely believed he had no other choice.

Government agencies, particularly the Food and Drug Administration, use the exposure method. A number of evaluations have been issued by them that reveal the danger to health of various food products. The surgeon general has warned that cigarettes may be a cause of cancer. Warn he may, but in our human contrariness, we appear to be going on happily puffing away.

Today and tomorrow we shall see more, not less, of the exposé form of dissent. The answer is to be honest and forceful when the spotlight is turned on. More than that, to counteract exposure demands an aggressive, imaginative approach. Leaders of institutions must carefully audit their practices to reveal inconsistencies and dissatisfactions with traditional ways, and then make their own adjustments. One approach is that an association should be formed to represent any institutional community for the purpose, among other reasons, of self-auditing ethical practices. Many such organizations exist today, but the self-auditing function is frequently weak or narrow in view. They need an injection of authority and ability.

The drive against pollution will continue unabated. It is a serious condition, although it would seem that the world is not to be choked tomorrow, as the alarmists predict. Active dissent in all its forms, including legislation, is and will be applied as pressure for polluters to cease and desist. There are also politicians who will use dissent against pollution as a political bandwagon step to more power.

Because of the rumpus raised, much positive action has already been taken to remove pollution from our streams, fields, and from the air. There is little disagreement over pollution itself—who can argue that destroying nature is desirable? The argument is about how and how soon pollution can be eliminated.

Pollution will be overcome, but countermeasures require technological developments and large sums of capital investment. Eventually, in one form or another, the public will have to pay for them, whether by taxes or through increased prices. This is a fact that those trying to solve problems of pollution must communicate clearly to the public, particularly to the zealots who are demanding that everything to remove pollution be done now.

This means that an industry, such as the paper industry, for example, must organize and execute a well-planned, straightforward campaign to inform the public about the complexities of the problems and what it intends to do about them. There is already a strong move in this direction.

What will happen to dissent in the university community in the coming years? With the students turning away from the more violent forms of protest, dissent on the campus will be less destructive than in the past ten years. The rising cost of education and the disenchantment of money-giving alumni will force university leadership to take a more hardnosed look at the conduct of its affairs. This will force trustees and presidents to take a less idealistic approach in determining policies for the universities. Available funds will not permit them to continue taking a disproportionate number of students from minority and underprivileged groups. The professor who would use the classroom as a platform to persuade students to his own political beliefs will not be tolerated. Nor will the myth be accepted that those who do so are only expressing their right to freedom of thought and speech.

Universities will return to their basic role of education. This is not to infer that stately calm will prevail. Activism and movements in less extreme form will be seen on the campus, and an alert and well-informed student body will still want more say in the affairs of the university. Intelligent presidents will construct a forum for hearing them out and acting on their suggestions. But act they must, or undergo more restless discord. Constructing a forum for discussion does not include placing barefoot smart alecs on the board, but it could, for example, mean having a responsible student committee report to the board as a means of bringing their recommendations directly to the trustees' attention.

The religious world faces a restless period. The various orders and sects are pressed to examine doctrines that may have been established during the Reformation to see whether adjustments are needed. Whatever they may do about them, the fact remains that the era of fatherly pronouncements from withdrawn seats of religious power will find it hard to survive in contemporary times. Parishes, dioceses, and the clergy itself have very independent-minded members. Church leaders need to find out more about the lay outlook toward the conduct of church activities, in addition to debating questions among themselves.

Religious institutions are universal in nature. Obviously, there is no question about their survival. But if they are to continue to exert a strong, and necessary, moral influence on our daily lives, adjustments to the changing attitudes of their members will have to be made. Otherwise, their influence will be weaker than it should be. Not to recognize the differences between the social conditions of today and those of the past can only lead to decline.

Our political system will be no less immune from discontent in the coming years. Attacks against entrenched leadership on the Senate and House seniority structures can be expected, even though they have failed before. The young politician believes that party leadership cannot flex its traditional behavior—its "establishment" outlook—sufficiently to meet the forces of social change with innovative programs. Although much of this criticism is unwarranted, there seems to be little question that it is partly true. Because political leaders have so much control over the careers of others, change is difficult to bring about, but it has to be done. All the way from municipalities to the federal government, we operate old systems that were adequate for more simple times but are obsolete, as well as wasteful, in today's megalopolis.

At the municipal level, this need is recognized and is being met by hiring administrators, professionally trained, to manage the day-to-day affairs of communities under the watchful eyes of the elected officials. The growth of public administration into a profession is encouraging. Professionals will bring badly needed organization into municipal affairs. There is one danger. Unless their authority is clearly limited, the more ambitious can gather for themselves considerable political power.

Each of our political parties should evaluate the party system to see whether the structure is as effective as it should be or too cumbersome, to see if party-member wants are being truly represented, and to determine how the young view the party platform and its actions.

The federal complex has been subjected to an organization evaluation, and though many changes have been made, many more are needed.

Dissatisfaction in public organizations is evidenced by the strong move to allow employees to join unions and strike under certain conditions. Some are already organized and do strike. Others express dissent by staying home with the "blue sickness," a substitute for striking where striking is not permitted—by policemen, for example. Also included in this group are the public school teachers. They will continue to organize and strike, and this will be accompanied by considerable confusion, because neither the teachers nor the administrators have much, if any, experience in the complex field of employee-management relations.

Laws are being considered by various legislatures that would set down the rules for public employee representation. In the rush to do something, the danger is that some bad law may be passed. To bring reasonable order into employee-management relations in the public field, either in negotiations or legislation, experienced negotiators from the industrial world should be brought in to advise and assist. Their considerable skill and knowledge can be of great benefit in dispelling the present confusion.

The military services are being battered with severe criticism from all points. Congress, the public, officers, and the men themselves are hammering at the military about expenditures for weapons systems research, too many and overstaffed overseas operations, the conduct of the war in Vietnam, the ethics of search and destroy, and civilian and top-level adherence to traditional doctrines and orthodoxy that are obsolete in a space-oriented world. Violent disagreement with strategy, such as all-out bombing, has been a page-one argument. The men at war believe it to be futile and openly disobey and dissent. Disenchantment with the services has sunk to a low equaled only by that preceding World War II. Officers on trial for killings in combat have been accused of murder. Others are resigning in protest over the conduct of their superiors. Fingers are pointing at supply officers, accusing them of the misuse of supply authority for personal gain.

The Pentagon Papers, incomplete at best, were smuggled to the press. Statements, some of which must surely be out of context, were cited to prove that our political and military leaders were less than honest about disclosing their real intentions. Officials and commanders were damned for using secrecy to hide mistakes.

Much of this damnation is downright unfair. Managing worldwide diplomatic and military affairs is an incredibly intricate business. To decide what can and what cannot be told to the public without endangering national security is an awesome responsibility that can be fully appreciated only by those who have had to bear it.

This is a dangerous mood. Our emotional disillusionment may lead us to be overzealous in cutting down the services—to a point where we are so weak in leadership and systems that our security can be critically exposed. We must not let the heat of reaction ignore cool advice and weaken that which may save us from another war. To do this would be playing into the hands of those who would destroy our democratic system.

It seems obvious that military thought needs a fresh and innovative review to change old-line orthodoxy into doctrine designed to meet the megalopolitan world of tomorrow. Such basic questions cannot be solved overnight, but research is already under way in the "tank," the room where top leaders study and project strategy for the future. And as younger leaders, less wed to tradition, succeed to the top, the task will become easier.

Modifying regulations to remove some of the monastic drabness of military life is healthy, but to relax discipline in a wave of permissiveness is not. A unit that is relaxed will suffer the highest casualties.

This is where dissent against the military is pushing us. With all the communications media available to it, the military must explain its aims and actions as honestly as safety allows. And we, as citizens, through our elected representatives, must insist that, though corrections are in order, the services' present unpopularity cannot be used by ambitious politicians to stampede us into foolish acts that will dismantle our security to an alarming point.

In the economic sector, stockholders' meetings may expect continued dissent and, as pointed out earlier, will become forums for reasonable debate. But a problem of a far more serious nature is wracking our economic world—the question of the balance of power between management and the unions. Our industrial union complex has become large and very powerful, too powerful. Unions have reached for and attained the power to enforce their demands on management. Management now gains little from strikes except to put the brakes on exorbitant demands. The level of settlements in wage increases is squeezing profit margins seriously, forcing price increases that encourage foreign competition. To compete, manufacturing operations of our corporations are being driven abroad, taking jobs with them. As for its impact on imports, one has only to count the number of foreign cars passing by on our highways.

This is a union-dominated economy. Unions, not the free market, are determining wage costs by winning their demands. Wages, as we all know, have a substantial effect on price levels, and indirectly, unions are driving up prices. As an example, the railway unions are insisting on hamstringing the railroads with costly work practices that are foolish. To cause deterioration at a time when the railroads are suffering from competition and other economic ills is willful blindness.

Experts in the field of labor-management relations have hoped, not too optimistically, that as our modern industrial unions grow and mature, their leaders will also develop a more statesmanlike attitude. A study of the union top command, however, is discouraging. Where among them is the labor statesman? Do they

worry about foreign competition, about losing jobs to European
countries or Japan? It seems that if there is any concern in their
minds, it is only superficial head burying. While voicing concern
out of one side of their mouth, they are busy threatening long
strikes out of the other. Publicly and to members, leaders boast
that the next settlement will be better than the last. And the
brute fact, as one wise economics professor put it, is that this
crowing is not an idle one. They *are* winning bigger settlements.
The leaders vie to outdo each other, with the top command of a
few big unions setting the pace—known economically as an oligop-
olistic structure.

This is not to condemn unions, but to say that today's top
leaders appear to show an inability to meet the far-reaching responsibilities thrust upon them. No innovation is present, only
adherence to the traditions and orthodoxy of past trade unionism.

Strikes seem to end up in favor of the union time after time.
Management has only two alternatives: better methods, which
means doing more work with the same number of jobs or the
same work with fewer jobs, and higher prices. Both are used by
management, but there are limits to how far they can be applied.
Profits are squeezed and jobs move abroad. The strike as an economic weapon has, in the past, been a hard but effective means for
settling disagreements. Now there is some question about its usefulness. With so much of the balance of power favoring unions,
the strike may have become more of a symbolic ritual than an
economic tool for determining wage levels. Actually, among the
more thoughtful leaders in both management and the unions,
there is concern about whether the strike is obsolete. But no one
seems to be able to create an innovative alternative other than
compulsory arbitration. Johnsonian "jawboning" has been tried,
achieving only modest success at best. Wage and price guidelines have been set by the government, only to be broken through
by the pressures of competitive wage settlements. Heated arguments over the efficiency of government wage and price controls
as a solution are endless. A wage settlement review board, using
past settlements as a guideline, has been set up as a compromise
between no control and complete control. What results it will
bring remain to be seen. At most it can be only a partial answer,
because its scope of authority and the area of the economic sector
within its reach are limited.

The administration's philosophy is to impose fewer, not more,
economic controls on unions and management. Any step taken

in that direction is a reluctant one. But lack of restraint in the use of power by union leaders may force more laws, just as laws were forced on corporate leaders for their lack of restraint in questionable, monopolistic practices. Misconduct in the administration of the huge welfare funds that have accumulated brought on the Landrum-Griffin Act, which obligates management, as well as unions, to disclose details about the management of welfare funds. Unions are at the peak of their power. Two obvious courses are open to them. Either union leaders must exercise more restraint in wage demands and in disruptive strikes or public indignation will result in laws that will impose more regulation on them. Meanwhile, a losing battle with foreign competition will continue.

President Nixon was forced to place controls on wages and prices, and, for the reasons already given, they will continue into the future. This was his answer to protests by an alarmed public against the rising cost of living.

Violent dissent has turned up in our penal system after a period of quiet. The underlying causes here are the rigid systems run by white overseers where the prisoners are predominately blacks and Chicanos. Unrest and violence will blaze wherever minorities are contained by institutions believed too repressive, whether they actually are or not. Paradoxically, observers of the situation believe that prison reforms have fed the fires of unrest by allowing more freedom of communication with the outside and raising hopes for improvement inside.

6

The Leader's Role
in a Climate of Dissent

MUCH has been said about dissent, its causes, forms, and direction. Now it would seem appropriate to examine the leadership qualifications necessary to carry an institution through troubled times. What are the personality and temperament characteristics we should look for in a man who is to lead an organization where dissent is boiling?

There are a number—self-possession, conviction, firmness, empathy, integrity, persuasion, confidence and boldness, emotional experience and maturity, and leadership action.

Self-Possession

Essential to the leader is self-possession and self-control. He must be able to discipline his emotions and remain objectively calm during a time of crisis. If he is to control the dissent fuming about him, he must first control himself. Increasing emotional tension will focus the pressures on him, subjecting him to the push and pull of the discord ripping the peace, and he will be damned for all that is happening.

During times of intense disagreement, when the internal security of an organization is in jeopardy, its members become excitable and are not always rational. Opinions and positions are based more on emotion than reason. As was mentioned earlier, this happened in the case of the Pentagon Papers, when emotionally charged words were leveled mercilessly upon the leaders involved. During the heat raised by the shock of exposure, little cool thought was given to the questions of Ellsberg's self-determined right to expose, or whether the facts were incomplete or taken out of context and distorted, or of the conditions that existed when the decisions were made. Much of the criticism of the administration was of the I-told-you-so, hindsight variety, and came from those outside the circle of conflict, with no accountability for the results of sweeping and critical decisions.

A leader must understand that when an event such as this occurs, the initial reaction of high emotion is a very human feeling and is to be expected. After all, while man is distinguished as a rational being, he is equally an emotional one. Understanding this, the leader has to exercise self-control and patiently withstand the pressures of crisis, playing for the time necessary to allow emotions to calm down to a rational level. Only then will he be able to argue for reasonable, not foolish, action.

The quality of self-possession is a function of temperament and of experience. Watch the man who has it. As the crisis deepens, he becomes not less steady and calm, but more so. It is his insight into the need for calm and his innate ability to control himself that sets him apart from other men. Add experience in dealing with conflict—an absolute must—and he has the skills and confidence to bring about a successful solution.

If such a man is not present when upheaval occurs, he had better be brought into it. Otherwise, under excitable and inexperienced leadership, the tension can only worsen into deeper conflict more difficult to resolve later.

Conviction

An unshakable belief in the rightness of the course set for the institution is a quality of strength demanded of a leader during a crisis. Conviction gives him the courage to decide and act. He knows that vacillation is the hallmark of the weak leader, of the one who will lose control of himself. Conviction helps him to move steadily through change, upheaval, and even violence, confident that time will prove his decisions to be right. If he is not convinced, he tends to ponder and hesitate at a time when action is vital.

Conviction should not be confused with overconfidence, pigheadedness, or unwillingness to listen. Quite the contrary, the strong leader has heard out the views of others, those who do not agree as well as those who do. He has the ability to develop an understanding of the problems he faces. The overconfident or pigheaded man lacks perceptive powers, blocking out understanding as he seeks only to impose his will against the advice of others.

After he has listened, the convinced leader may decide on a course of action opposed by the majority. He does this because, from his position, he believes that he has a better long-range perception of what is right for the institution. But his decision is made only after careful consideration of what his advisors propose. This takes courage.

No one could listen to Winston Churchill without being inspired by his deep conviction.

Firmness

To be resolute is basic to the nature of a leader during trying times. Firmness is neither arbitrary nor rigid. The leader who is firm is flexible and supple, adapting his actions to the needs of the moment. He uses his authority lightly but surely, without being heavy-handed. Members of the institution realize that when there is a trouble spot, he will not hesitate to move into it, consider the problem, and take thoughtful action. There is no hesitancy, no backing away.

If, for example, dissent occurs in the form of a strike, the firm leader will move immediately to the scene, observe what is happening, discuss what to do with others, decide what to do, and do it. If in his opinion the strike is illegal, he will say so to the strikers and tell them that if they do not disperse, he will bring in the police. Should they decide not to break up, he will do so, and the strikers will have to leave or be forcibly removed. He does not lose his nerve at the last minute and back away from his decision. This makes him believable, and those he leads, and others as well, soon learn that he means what he says and that he follows through. Whether others agree with him or not, his resolute decisions and actions win respect.

During times of crisis, followers look instinctively for this kind of leadership. What they want is a man with nerve, not nervousness. To some this is the quality of fortitude, the ability to see it through. A university president on the West Coast once displayed this quality admirably. When confronted with striking, threatening students and professors, he simply would not back down. Again and again they tried to intimidate him, but he met each such move with firm counteraction, including the use of police to quell rioting. Because he did this during a period when college presidents were prone to take the soft approach, to turn the other cheek, in attempting to settle student unrest, he was severely criticized. Time has proven that his actions were the right ones.

A resolute man is admired even by those who may disagree with his actions. A police captain in Chicago was this kind of man. He had charge of the Labor Detail, whose mission was to preserve order on the picket line during strikes. The captain won respect from both management and the unions because he treated each side alike and dealt with them firmly when they got out of line. In fact, one hot July afternoon a powerful union leader chose to give the captain some back talk after he had been told not to. He soon found himself steaming in the paddy wagon, where he was allowed to sit for the better part of an hour before being driven off to the police station. Had he been a management executive, he would have been given the same treatment. Chicago picket lines have long since been relatively peaceful.

Empathy

This is the ability to project oneself into the feelings and ideas of others. An empathic person sees all sides of a problem in human relationships even though he may disagree with some of the points of view. Within empathy is objectivity. This is the ability mentally to stand aside and look not only at others but at oneself as well. Many of us have this quality to a degree, but only a few are endowed with an acute sense of empathy.

An empathic man has a listener's ear. Most of us hear what others are saying, but we do not listen. To listen is to concentrate completely and to sense the real meaning behind the words. So often what we say is not what we really mean. This is frequently true when our sense of status in a group is affected. When arranging meetings within the official halls of a corporation, a subordinate quickly learns that when one executive says that a meeting should not be held up because of him, he really means that the meeting should be changed to meet his convenience.

Listening sensitively also includes hearing what another does *not* say, and surmising what he means. For example, when two people are talking about the actions of others, it may become apparent to the listener that one of a group of individuals discussed is not mentioned at any time, or only slightly. This may mean that the speaker doesn't like, or disapproves of the actions of, that particular person. Or he may be jealous of him. The exclusion is a signal to seek out why it is so.

It is this ability to see a dispute from the position of others, to assess its causes and weigh the various positions with objectivity that enables a leader to determine what has to be done to bring about accord.

Integrity

If a leader is to have the confidence of those he leads, or of others for whom he represents the organization, he must be trustworthy in their eyes. Particularly where dissent is involved, experience in all kinds of negotiations demonstrates the importance of personal integrity. If there are problems blocking progress, it is not unusual to find the cause in a lack of trust between the negotiators. Where there is trust, usually a workable relationship exists.

In one union-management relationship there were lots of fireworks and plenty of disagreement, but on the whole it worked very well. Both the union and the management negotiators were known as men who couldn't be bought. Each trusted the other. Disagreements were confined to the issues and never became personal. As a result, bargained solutions were found, and strikes, which at an earlier date had been frequent, became rare. The relationship was a healthy one.

The opposite, of course, is the case in which there is no mutual trust, where the integrity of those doing the negotiating is open to question. Here the situation is fraught with suspicion, and every move is looked on with a jaundiced eye. Progress is slow; sometimes none is made. In one industry-union relationship the climate for years was an unhealthy one. At the center of the trouble was one personality. The professional union representative developed a reputation as a manipulator, out more for the glory of the union and himself than the interests of the members. This, to be fair, was not quite true, but, nevertheless, this is the image he managed to win for himself.

As a result, a running battle between him and the industry grew, and it lasted until he was replaced. Strikes and unfair labor practice hearings were common. Corporations not organized by him worked vigorously to avoid becoming involved with his union. Constant disruption was costly to both the companies and the employees involved.

Attacks on the integrity of our political leaders are a common occurrence today. President Johnson and others were accused of escalating the war in Vietnam while telling the public they were not. What the accusers were saying is that investigation revealed that certain administration officials did not act in a trustworthy way. Apparently, to some this seems to have been an extremely unfair indictment, but because the question of personal integrity was a central issue, this is an argument that will be with us for some time.

Suspicion is the very core of the problem in the negotiations between the United States and North Vietnam. Each side believes the other to be negotiating in bad faith, and no progress can be made with suspicion present to the degree that exists so strongly now. Mutual accusations by each about the lack of sincerity in the other are hurled across the table. This is caused not only by enmity but by sharply contrasting beliefs and customs that make it difficult for us to understand each other.

Persuasion

It almost goes without saying that a leader confronted with the turmoil of dissent has to be persuasive. He cannot be the type of person who has trouble expressing his thoughts and ideas to others. Where discord is present, inarticulate leadership cannot be tolerated. A leader must be provocative in the sense that he can stimulate others to accept his requests and do as he asks, while at the same time exhibiting a personal magnetism that is cohesive and will draw others to him.

Whether or not anyone agreed with him, President Roosevelt had this provocative magnetism and drew a large devoted following during the troubled years of the thirties and early forties.

Winston Churchill, one of the great men of history, displayed this quality magnificently. He united the British people into a determined phalanx that would not be defeated. Very few men have had this quality as he did.

The ability to persuade is a characteristic commonly found in leaders of institutions, and though it is always an important one, during troubled times it is vital. To be able to face an aroused group and dissuade them from committing destructive acts, or to follow a course of action that may later prove to have been a mistake, calls for persuasion of the highest order. Many times groups on the verge of turning into rioting mobs have been turned back peacefully by a persuasive leader. Many times they have not. When union leaders have been successful in their pleas to keep strikers from being destructive, it is because they have had the persuasive magnetism to calm the group.

Presidents of the United States have not been above using their personal charm, as well as the power of their office, to convince others to act as they would like. President Eisenhower did this remarkably well, and few were those who refused him. Within 36 hours of his request to both union and management that a strike in a major industry be settled, accord was reached.

Mayor Daley of Chicago, while not to be classed as highly articulate, surely gets his point across to others. Unions and management, among others, have conceded to his wishes. One of our outstanding mediators in the labor-management field, the late Cyrus Ching, settled many complex disagreements because he had this ability developed to a high skill by experience.

Persuasion is not glibness. Glibness, in the sense of being superficially smooth, is exactly what is not needed. Persuasion coupled with sincerity is. Glibness in the absence of sincerity or integrity will eventually be taken for what it is, and it will be ineffective. In one series of negotiations, progress was slow because a glib negotiator wasn't quite trusted by the other side, which spent much time looking for hidden maneuvers in each stage of the bargaining. Negotiations dragged until he was replaced by a less spectacular but more sincere one.

Confidence and Boldness

Confidence and boldness are qualities a leader must possess to gain the confidence of others. They are even more important during periods of stress, when the institution is strained with dissension. At times boldness demands courage—not just moral courage, but physical courage as well. When a leader appears before a line of strikers or rioters or a group on the verge of an outbreak, his actions display courage and a risk of personal safety that will win a grudging respect and may well calm the mounting of anger before it breaks into mob destruction.

From time immemorial military leaders have taken risks to hold the line or stem retreat. Lee, Jackson, and Patton were known for their disdain of personal safety during the height of battle. The point here is that the risk is not an empty one. It is not game playing. Everyone involved knows that, and the leader draws respect because the risk is real. As the old saw goes, this is a job for men, not boys.

These two qualities are also related to self-possession. Bold may be the action to appear before a crowd headed toward a riot, but to show confidence as well requires considerable self-possession. It is the confident, in-control-of-the-situation attitude that may make the difference between stopping riotous action and having a breakout. Nervousness reveals a loss of confidence and self-possession, and a dissenting group will sense it and may lose its own control.

A milling group of pickets was seething restlessly and rapidly reaching the point of riot. Their complaints were over living and working conditions. It was an intensely hot summer afternoon, and the heat was oppressive—ideal conditions for the goading leaders to fan tempers into active anger. Top leadership recognized that some of the complaints were justified. One of the leaders, because of his reputation for calmness under stress, was selected to try to forestall the rising violence. He went before the group, asked for their attention, and proposed that if they would disperse, meetings with representatives would be held to hear complaints and make changes that were reasonable. Having had his say, he stood before them for some minutes, answering questions and taunts. As the group began to calm, he asked them to consider his proposal, then turned and walked away, hoping he wouldn't be bashed with a brick. He wasn't. Later, the group accepted the proposal and scattered toward home.

This, of course, is the dramatic incident where dissent reaches the violent stage. But boldness and confidence are just as necessary in less eruptive situations, such as when the chairman of a meeting must contain dissident factions.

Emotional Maturity

The leader needs to be an emotionally mature man, who can control his emotions during times of stress. The quality of maturity is related to confidence and self-possession, and without it he cannot have the other two. Working steadily to accomplish the aims of the organization, the leader is not disturbed by the fact that everyone will not always react rationally toward what he does, nor that within an institution there is a natural inertia, a resistance to change by individuals and groups. He is not put off by the knowledge that the more foreign an innovation is to customary behavior patterns, the stronger the reaction against it will be. But he does work to avoid abrupt moves that will cause upset or an outburst of violence.

On the whole, an emotionally secure person is well balanced; his reactions are seldom rash. Rashness is characteristic of the immature individual, and cannot be tolerated where active dissent is present. In the more highly charged forms of dissent, such as striking or rioting, the higher the emotional pitch, the greater the chances are of rash moves being made. And if the leader is rash by nature, his reaction to them will be even more extreme, and control may be completely lost.

A rash action may turn a peaceful demonstration into a riot. Even when demonstrators are orderly, any sudden move to advance and deal with one or several of them harshly in the hope of dispersing them may have the opposite effect and turn the incident into a mob action. Unfortunately, this has happened over the past few years during some of our antiwar and other confrontations.

Recently, in a huge industrial plant, an executive made a rash move in disciplining two employees severely before he had thoroughly investigated the reasons why they acted as they had. What should have been a minor disciplinary case turned into a strike involving thousands of employees. Neither management nor the union wanted the strike, but control was lost. Even though the two worked together to bring the strike to a quick conclusion, it was difficult to do so.

Perhaps it can be said that the emotionally mature man is one who accepts the world as it is and people for what they are, but who nevertheless keeps his eye on his more idealistic goals and continues to work toward them.

Experience

No matter how mature or self-possessed an individual may be, to be successful as a leader of an organization in times of dissent he must have had experience, a great deal of experience. What is needed in such a man is a working knowledge of the causes of active dissent so that he can see it rising and stop it by quick action or be ready to meet the situation when the crisis comes.

On a humid Thursday a group of employees, without warning, walked out of a plant. Because of the suddenness of the walkout, the local management, having no prior experience with this form of disagreement, was perplexed and at a loss about what should be done to meet the problem. The top executive and his staff were able at their jobs and fair to employees, but they lacked the know-how to meet such an outbreak. A call to corporate headquarters brought an employee relations expert immediately to the plant.

He arrived to find employees milling around in the street outside the plant. Their actions were not threatening, nor did there seem to be evidence that violence might erupt. In fact, the group appeared to be loosely organized and aimless. Several informal leaders were trying to form them into an orderly picket line and urging early night-shift workers to join the walkout.

The group was calm. But to sit by idly, hoping that the picketing would dissipate because of its formlessness, would have been foolish. Violence is always latent in active forms of dissent. A sudden, unexpected, usually small incident can trip the calm into brutal action. Control is lost. Damage and injury result.

The expert met immediately with the top staff to make an estimate of the situation and get to the core of the problem. They were not sure what the cause was, so the decision was made to bring in the informal leaders for a discussion of their grievance.

Two men, long-service employees, were asked to join a meeting with management. In came a tall man and a fat one. The meeting began uncomfortably. After some casual conversation about the unusually humid weather, the corporate executive explained that the purpose of the meeting was not to criticize or condemn but to find the cause of the grievance and correct it. He added also the promise that no one would be disciplined for any act committed or anything said on that day. By doing so, the fear of reprisal was removed. In a friendly and candid way he questioned the two about why they had decided to walk out. Throughout the discussion he stressed that management wanted to be fair—if the complaint was just, management had made a mistake and wanted to correct it. His manner continued to be conciliatory and respectful.

The cause finally came to the surface. The tall man said everyone was angry over the firing of an employee the day before. They understood that the reason for the discharge was lack of performance on the job. Employees who knew him said that he was a good worker, although somewhat loud and apt to beef openly about management actions. In their minds, said the two men, the real reason was that the foreman didn't like him.

In reply, the management spokesman said that should a thorough investigation of the discharge reveal this to be so, the man would be rehired, given lost pay, and placed in another department. He said further, that the company needed the production badly, that everyone would be losing pay needlessly, and asked everyone to go back to work. If they would do this, he promised, management would bind itself to meet with representatives of the group on Monday, and continue to do so until the question was resolved to the satisfaction of everyone.

On Monday afternoon the meeting was held, and the situation was thoroughly aired. The facts indicated that, as so frequently happens, the man was partly wrong, but so was his boss. He had been somewhat insubordinate, but not to the extent that so severe a penalty as a discharge was warranted. It was agreed that a three-day disciplinary layoff with loss of pay was fair. It was also agreed that except for such extreme and obvious acts as threatening with a firearm, no employee would be given a layoff or discharged unless a thorough investigation of the facts of the case revealed it to be justified.

Throughout this incident, the executive from the corporate offices displayed the calm judgment and sure hand that come only with experience. His open manner and respect for the thought of others had much to do with his skill in bringing the situation back to order. What could have turned into a costly strike was averted.

Leadership in Action

Where dissent is boiling to the crisis point, an executive leader must apply his skills with virtuosity, using the techniques of command, conciliation, and discipline in concert to help control and improve the situation. During a crisis, as discussed before, he has to be quick but not rash.

No one technique, such as conciliation, is adequate. Nor is severe enforcement. University presidents have tried conciliation during demonstrations, strikes, and riots in recent years, and the record has been one of consistent failure. On the other side, overreaction in bringing police force to bear has brought public charges of brutality. Some of these charges have had a basis in fact, but many feel that most of them have been either purely emotional or deliberately intended to turn the public against establishment enforcement. The injury of a student, unavoidable at times during rioting, can be used to play on the public's emotions and bring condemnation down on police action. In any event, overreaction has also failed.

There is a time for command, for conciliation, and for firm discipline. When dissenters come forward peaceably, conciliation is in order. If a riot is breaking out, decisive command and firm action are in order—arresting action, if necessary. This is not the time for mollifying or conciliating; that comes later. Unfortunately there have been incidents where conciliation was applied, not out of ignorance, but to screen a lack of courage.

In action, the responsible leader should project himself as a calm, sensible, and approachable man who will listen and act but will not hesitate to be firm when events demand a strong hand. Such an image will command respect, even grudging respect. The reverse will happen if the man at the top exhibits nervousness, timidity, and a tendency to freeze indecisively or jump rashly.

Actions ought to be planned deliberately, not impulsively. This does not rule out the use of intuitiveness, of sensing what is happening based on the acuity that develops from long experience in institutional relationships. For example, when a signal of rising dissent, such as an announced demonstration, appears, police action may or may not be necessary at the demonstration, but plans for its use should be made. A center for command and communication to coordinate the force ought to be set up. Procedures for action, including alternatives, should be clearly defined. The force to be assigned to the task should be carefully reviewed to be sure that less stable individuals, inclined to be rash, are not in the group; if they are, that they be reassigned. The plans and procedures should be acted out in drill, hard drill, to reveal any weaknesses and to make certain that everyone understands his task thoroughly.

It is not always possible to do this as nicely as would be desirable, but it ought to be done to the extent that time allows.

Because dissenting groups are prone to list their demands as they come from the members, they may range all the way from real, basic issues to the utterly ridiculous. Leaders must have the ability to distinguish between them and to establish a priority order within the legitimate list. An extreme example of this was the inexperienced student demonstrators who demanded every-thing from dismantling research and development facilities to the president's hat. Some of these, unfortunately, were taken seriously, and concessions were made. Should an international crisis arise, conceding to the demand that reserve officer training be discon-tinued will prove to have been a silly decision.

On the other hand, among the great majority of students, of whom we can be justly proud, there are true grievances. One of these is that officials either pay lip service to student suggestions or are extremely slow to act. Any experienced and intelligent execu-tive would sympathize with the students on issues such as this.

To be able to sort out and distinguish the true grievances from those that are really no issue at all requires intent, sensitive listen-ing. All too often, it seems, the tendency is for a top executive to override the discussion of subordinates, to cut others off before they have finished. The result is that he has only his own thinking and fragmentary impressions of that of others on which to base his judgments, and if it happens too frequently, he blacks out informa-tion he should have in order to make a fair decision.

To safeguard against this, an executive should mentally log, after a meeting, for example, how much time he preempted for himself. Startling is the discovery that his time "on the air" has been no less than 80 and often more than 90 percent. So it is, when surveys reveal the opinions of members, that the top people are shocked to find that their feel for members' thinking is far less accurate than they confidently believed it to be.

The intent here is not to condemn corporation executives or college and university administrators. Their responsibilities are many and heavy and their tasks hard, sometimes almost impossible. They are intelligent and dedicated. The point here is only to illustrate the need for a leader of any type of institution to exer-cise sensitivity and discretion in dealing with the demands of dissenting members.

7

Withstanding
the Pressures of Dissent

AS dissent increases, the pressures against the top mount sharply. An executive who must cope with such problems should recognize them for what they are and know what to do when confronted with them. The dissent environment is one filled with keyed-up emotions, nervousness, and, at some point, fatigue. If it is not already present, anger lies just beneath the surface, ready to rise up in a more active form, such as marches, picketing, and strikes, and, when control is lost, to spread out into the more rampant form of rioting, often tripped by a minor incident.

There are a number of techniques that can be used to keep actions under reasonable control and prevent the situation from exploding into active and destructive dissent.

Insist on Cooling Off

During meetings between responsible officials and dissenting groups, because the purpose of the meeting is to discuss points at issue, disagreement is there and, along with it, tension. As the meeting progresses, an issue may come up over which there is a wide divergence of opinion. If the meeting is a long one, or one in a series of long ones, tension will become more taut and angry blasts between negotiators will flame up. When this happens, the issue should be tabled and the meeting adjourned before anger takes over and the meeting deteriorates into a series of personal vendettas. A time lapse should be allowed to let tempers cool before the meeting is reconvened. How much time should be taken depends upon the urgency of the need to settle the issues and the width of the breach caused by the conflict. Time lapses normally range from several hours to one or more days. If the meeting has been held toward the end of the week, a common practice is to adjourn until the following week, with the intervening weekend providing a change of pace and a cooling-off period for the negotiators. Deft use of this technique can help avoid anger deepening into bitterness, which can only make the negotiations more difficult and prolonged.

In one meeting, part of a long and complex series, the management negotiator, suffering from strain and fatigue, was badly in need of rest. He opened the day with a pithy tirade, generously laced with obscenities, aimed directly at the union's lead negotiator. The latter shot back with his own brand of well-chosen and colorful epithets about his opponent, including his forebears. The meeting broke into an uproarious clamor. Control was lost. Within 15 minutes both sides stood up, glared, and stomped silently from the room. It took a week to calm everyone to the point where another meeting could be held—and only after a mediator was brought in to assist. Two and a half weeks elapsed before the two groups were brought face-to-face again.

In another series of negotiations, tension began to increase one warm June morning. Both lead negotiators saw the danger signals and, with the insight that comes with experience, mutually agreed to adjourn until the next day. This action avoided deterioration into bitterness, and on the following morning negotiations continued on course. They were successfully concluded without further dispute.

Require Rest Periods

Where dissent exists between two groups over issues that cannot be easily resolved, and when negotiations become long and involved, a sensible practice is to schedule periods of rest for those in the heat of bargaining. It must be remembered that disagreement is the basic reason for the meetings, and when that element is present, the situation is delicate. Even experienced people can easily trip over an issue and turn it into active or violent dissent.

As the time spent in resolving differences becomes more prolonged, objectivity of outlook lessens and emotional involvement deepens. With this condition facing negotiators, wise is the executive who will insist on pulling his representatives out of the meeting, to rest and do something entirely removed from the problems at hand. If he does not insist, the meeting will continue, with the men becoming more and more intense. The result of this may be that a few of the many issues involved are blown out of all proportion to their relationship with the whole package; so, too, with small personal differences. This leads to overemphasis on minor points, petty bickering, and very little or no progress.

This is where round-the-clock bargaining falls down. This sort of meeting, which lasts for 24 hours or more without any real rest, is intended to keep bargainers at work until they tire and begin to give under pressure. They do. But the danger is that bad agreements for the long term may result. They often do. After the conflict has died down and the agreement is read calmly, it is easy to see which parts were hammered out toward the end of round-the-clock negotiating—they read as though the intent of the bargainers had been to obscure what they actually agreed on.

Toward the end of one negotiation, the sides worked long into the dawn to conclude the agreement. After it was done, everyone shook hands and went off wearily to bed. Later, while reviewing the contract, one of the negotiators looked at one section in disbelief. He read it again, still unconvinced. But there it was. The oral agreement had been that a certain group of employees was, under certain conditions, to receive a 7 percent an hour raise. But as it read, the agreement badly stated that, under those same conditions, the group's wages were to be reduced by 7 percent an hour. A hurried meeting was called, and the embarrassed sides made the correction before the mistake could leak out and live to harass their dignity.

In another lengthy and complicated series of sessions, an extraordinarily skillful negotiator was suffering from a temporary attack of the flu. Normally composed and agreeable, he became stubborn and fractious. He demanded that the meetings continue because negotiations were going well and reaching the critical point where settlement could be made and a strike avoided. After trying to persuade him otherwise and failing to do so, his senior, for the first time in their mutually respectful relationship, ordered a halt in the meetings for 24 hours.

During the break, the tactics for the final meetings were deliberately not discussed, nor was anything that was connected with the bargaining. Fortunately, the meetings were being held in a historic city with an equally historic town nearby, and as the member with the flu was deeply interested in history, the group spent the day leisurely visiting eighteenth-century sites. This and a long night's rest were enough to bring him back to his equable composure. Negotiations proceeded to a successful conclusion under his able guidance.

Guard Against Fatigue

Guarding against fatigue is really an extension of the insistence on rest at certain times, but its importance warrants special attention. Fatigue is more than being tired. It is bone-aching weariness. Anyone who has ever been fatigued, and that group includes most of us, knows that as it creeps over an individual or group, it causes a type of mental and emotional distortion, which, in turn, magnifies irrelevancies. Decisions made in the face of fatigue are likely to be hasty and ill-conceived.

When tension is high and fatigue sets in, little progress can be made. What is likely to happen is that attempts to resolve differences will deteriorate into wrangling over relatively insignificant points that loom way out of proportion to their true weight. Progress slides backward.

In a collective bargaining meeting, an argument arose one morning over whether a notice to work overtime should be given 48 or 60 hours in advance. By one-thirty the next morning the question was still unsettled, with nothing accomplished except a lot of petty resentment, and the meeting broke up on that tone. Meanwhile, more important issues lay to the side. The difference was actually a minor one, but it had consumed a whole day, a day that added to the length of the strike.

Time off to rest the weary negotiators would have avoided this wasted day, and progress would have been much more rapid during the week than it was. In fact, additional time had to be taken to mollify the resentment that arose between members of the two sides.

During times of tension and strife between groups, anxiety develops among those involved, and there is pressure from all points to get the matter settled and come to an agreement. When the negotiations stretch over a long period, the pressure becomes intense. Representatives of both sides tire to the point of fatigue. Someone with the authority to call a halt must be able to recognize this condition, see the danger of backsliding because of it, and order a rest period.

Develop Facts

When active dissent exists, emotion tends to dominate; the more active the form of dissent, the more this is so. What is actually, or has been, taking place may be distorted while being reported by some person or group deeply involved in the act.

If a leader is trying to stabilize a dissent action, he has to be careful to screen out the actual facts from information reported through the distorted eyes of those emotionally charged up. Otherwise, he may move on the basis of wrong or defective information and make a mistake that would not only not settle the critical situation but make it worse.

In one incident where dissent was mounting rapidly, or appeared to be, the basic reason given for it by those whose emotions were running high was that a change in the wage payment practice had created pockets of inequities. These pockets were supposedly the source of unrest. Instead of planning moves to counteract and correct the dissatisfaction on the basis of these criticisms alone, management requested a factual analysis of the results of the change. The analysis revealed that the criticisms had no basis in fact. The reverse was true. Substantial corrections had been made by changing the practice, and inequities that existed prior to the change had been fairly adjusted. The unrest, it was discovered, rose from other sources, such as too long a time being taken by those in charge to give satisfactory answers to grievances forwarded by the group. Subsequent action was planned on the basis of this analysis. A positive approach to the wage change, in the form of a careful explanation of what its advantages were, was directed at the group. The system for processing grievances was streamlined, clearly explained, and immediately put into active practice. It proved to be valid, and the unrest subsided.

Had the factual analysis not been made, the whole direction of the action planned to correct the causes of dissent would have been based on an emotional miscalculation, badly aimed and unsuccessful. Had the other course been followed, suspicion that wage inequities actually did exist would have developed.

The higher emotions run, the more difficult it is to uncover the true causes of active disagreement. And to get to the causes of what trips a peaceful demonstration into a rioting mob scene is often impossible. Analysis upon analysis of the Chicago riots of 1968 has been reported officially and in the press. There seems to be some argument that the actions of the Chicago police force were distorted in news media reports at the height of the rioting. Beatings were thought to be distorted out of proportion, and perhaps too little was said about the abuse and injury suffered by policemen. The point here is not to accuse either the press, generally fairminded, or the police. It is to illustrate how incredibly hard it can be to analyze such a rampant event and to separate fact from emotion. Whether it is possible ever to make a cool, comprehensive evaluation of what happened is questionable. It is also probable that all the factors that contributed to Chicago and other major riots throughout the country and the relative force of their contributory effect can never be fully appraised. How much was the result of action planned by groups whose objective was to disrupt and how much was the result of incidents that happened during the fury of the rioting was obscured behind the emotions of those involved in or observing the action.

Much of the time, where emotions run so high that physical conflict—fighting—breaks out, finding the cause is far from easy, even in less spectacular events than the Chicago riots. One day a fight broke out between two groups that had been mutually antagonistic for several years. After it had been quelled, the cause was sought. The decision was that the leader of one group had started the melee by aiming a piece of wood at the head of the other. He missed, but then the fight began. The man who had thrown the wood was severely disciplined. The other got off with a light penalty. But a more thorough investigation revealed that the man at whom the wood was thrown had been taunting the other one continually for months, and those working around the two wondered why he hadn't lost his temper long before he did. On the basis of this analysis, a more just judgment was made.

Take Firm Action

Vacillation in decision making will always cause concern and dissatisfaction among those affected by it. Directions are never explicit, and the group finds actions—or decisions preceding them —confusing, because seldom are they handed down as a firm yes or no. A decision forwarded as a qualified yes and no is no decision at all.

If a top executive vacillates in deciding what direction to take for an organization, this not only causes unrest among those affected whether inside or outside the institution, but increases the intensity of dissent where it already exists. The lack of decision, or confusing decisions, slows action to a creeping pace and raises consternation among those who want to meet their personal goals and who want the organization to move ahead toward its goals. When these goals are not met, or when answers are far too slow in coming from the top, dissent will rise in active form.

While they may not agree with every decision, members prefer firm action to little or no action at all. This may seem to be an obvious statement, but often the top may be unaware of the effect a faulty decision-making process can have throughout the organization and of the degree to which its impact on individual and group attitudes is negative. This is most frequently true if the approaches to resolving problems are long-standing traditional ones.

Study after study of member attitudes toward an organization has established the fact that the height of dissatisfaction in a group is directly related to the decisiveness of leadership. The ones who win approval are the executives who get things done. Held in low opinion are those who "don't take hold" or "won't get answers for us."

When a single member or a group comes forward with an appeal that something be done about dissatisfaction with an organization's actions, firm moves should be made to answer them. Hesitancy, overdeliberation, or lack of resolution will force the individual or group to turn to a more active form of dissent— striking, for instance. This is not the time to be timid and motionless. Constructive movement before the eyes of the dissenters has to take place if more critical problems are to be avoided. The tendency to turn away and hope that the unpleasant problem will disappear must be resisted. This is a characteristic found in administrators who are more skillful technically than they are in interpersonal relationships.

At the base of the minority-group upheavals—the demonstrations, strikes, riots, and boycotts—is frustration with the lack of visible or foreseeable progress in improvement of their economic and social status within the structure of our society. Progress in the past has been either painfully slow or not made at all. Because the problems are intricate, progress, even with active attention being given to it, can't be made in a jump from what was to what should be. Economic assistance in the form of self-help to these groups means some restructuring of attitudes and approaches in the world of business. Improvement in education requires some overhauling of the system from the entry grades through the university structure.

Minority groups will continue to express dissent openly, but, as more firm action is taken to answer their needs, the severity of their protest will decrease proportionately.

Resist Hasty Action

During times when disagreement runs high and dissent appears in active form, pressures against the top demand immediate response, and the result of this strain may be hasty, ill-conceived action. Advice given to the top man may be based more on nervousness and fear than on sound thinking, more on a desire to avoid any unpleasantness than doing what is right for the long run. Taking correct but difficult action after calm consideration, which is likely to be criticized by those with less fortitude, requires courage and leadership of the highest quality.

Before World War II, Mussolini and Hitler were feared. Fear of war is natural. But when men are guided more by fear than sound judgment, their decisions may lead to results far more disastrous than a tougher course would bring. Neville Chamberlain, prime minister of Great Britain, chose to appease Hitler in 1938 and got him to agree that Germany would not overrun any more territory. When he arrived home, the agreement was hailed as a great move for peace. The world looked hopefully to Chamberlain while the dire warnings of such men as Churchill were ignored. That the warnings were ominously right and the agreement not worth the paper it was written on is history.

In less grand arenas, the same mistake occurs. Hasty appeasement is attempted where firm action ought to be applied. Gangs have been treated like spoiled children, and students have been granted outlandish privileges, sometimes simply by being noisy enough. Some university administrators and public officials have allowed themselves to be crowded into hasty, bad decisions. The decision of one top official to sit until after midnight, waiting at the convenience of a representation from the Chicago Seven, was surely a very questionable judgment. That he should have waited at a regular time of day may have been right, but that he should have inconvenienced himself to listen to a group whose actions were reprehensible, while turning his ear away from those with more legitimate requests, was a mistake. Long-run relationships with important segments of the institution were damaged by his behavior.

It is not always clear what a leader's course of action should be while undergoing the pressures of turbulent dissent, but a hasty move designed to cool down the immediate crisis is more often a mistake than a sound move.

In labor-management relations it is a long-established practice not to agree to the demands of, or even meet with, a group that has walked out despite its agreement not to do so. If management were to give in hastily, long-term relationships would suffer in terms of respect for any mutual agreement. It is a hard decision to stand firm when profits and wages are being lost, when pressures to settle push against the stand, but as severe lessons have taught, to give in means short-term gains taken from far greater long-term losses.

In one case, a young, inexperienced executive, when faced with a wildcat strike one morning, advised his general manager to meet with employee representatives. The strike was in violation of an agreement not to walk out. Lacking technical know-how and the levelheadedness that comes with experience, the executive gave hasty, ill-considered advice. Fortunately, his senior had the good sense to refer the problem to a higher-level professional with long experience. No meeting was held, and the management sat out the wildcat strike for ten days before the men finally came back to work. Time and money were lost in this situation, but the integrity of the agreement was preserved and a lengthy, far more costly strike, which would have been inevitable when the agreement was up for renewal, was avoided.

Take Appropriate Action

Action taken to resolve conflict must not only be sound and deliberate, but appropriate as well. It is a mistake to assume that an approach that has been successful in one situation will apply equally to all. The conditions surrounding restive dissent vary considerably and require different techniques to reach satisfactory solutions.

One top executive succeeded in persuading a small powerless group to accept a wage reduction in an economically distressed area where jobs were at a premium. The community was not large, and intracommunity job mobility, even in prosperous times, was low. Later, in a large unit, which was located in a dynamic metropolitan area and organized by a formidable union under a strong leader, the executive tried to apply the same approach. His attempt was so inappropriate that knowledgeable people involved laughed, believing him to be joking. Fortunately, he did not insist that this tactic be tried.

In the industrial world, a widely known approach to negotiating differences between employees and management is "Boulware-ism." The label refers to the man who developed this technique, Lemuel Boulware, when he was the vice-president in charge of employee relations for the General Electric Company. His approach involved taking a firm stand at the beginning of negotiating a new contract and, with very little variation, staying with it until the union accepted the offer, even to the point of taking a long strike if necessary. Boulware knew what he was doing for General Electric. Manufacturing units of the company were widely dispersed, and the principal union representing employees, the International Union of Electrical Workers, was not militantly standing solid behind an erratic leader. As a result, local units were inclined to go their own way when it suited them. For General Electric the technique has been successful.

The steel industry watched Boulware succeed while its own relationships were strained and strike-ridden. One year, against the advice of professional negotiators, several top executives decided to take over and adopt Boulware's strategy, demanding a long-term agreement and fixing the industry's final offer in a take-it-or-leave-it way. The attempt was an outstanding failure and ended in defeat.

This is a dramatic illustration of inappropriate action. Conditions in the steel industry are quite different from those at

General Electric. Operating units in steel are large and are concentrated in a few geographical areas. Shutting down a complicated steel mill, with its seven-day-a-week, fiery processes, is far more costly than closing a medium-size plant where there are few, if any, complicated, continuous operations. Also, the steelworkers stood militantly behind a strong and revered leader, Philip Murray. The strategy was too abrupt a change in the traditional bargaining pattern, which, until then, had been one of give-and-take. Bargaining began with Murray presenting a long list of demands to the industry. Trading point for point started from there, and this continued until an agreement was signed.

The strategy was abandoned.

Appropriate action can be determined only by a thorough study of all the facets of a given situation. This was done in the case cited earlier in which it was thought that pockets of inequity were the source of the dissatisfaction—a case in point that impulsive moves should be resisted.

Display Confidence

When dissenters press their leaders with grievances, the leaders have to meet them with confidence. Reacting to pressures with visible nervousness and lack of confidence may result in loss of control. Those who look to the top for strong guidance are quick to recognize these symptoms, and they react by moving more boldly to gain whatever they want for themselves. If confident leaders are absent, the boldness may lead to rash acts, and, in the extreme, to destruction and violence. This was the case in some of the university and community riots. What began as demonstrations ended in rioting, because the firm confidence to take appropriate action during the early stages was lacking. When students enter the president's office, sit with feet on his desk, and upset furniture, this is no time to hesitate. Prompt and forcible removal is the right action to take. Attempting persuasion and appealing to reason are inappropriate before such brash arrogance. Such a move is interpreted as a sign of weakness, of nervousness, and leads to more irresponsible acts. Dignity and respect are lost.

Had confident, direct action been taken in the early years of the rioting of the sixties, certainly much of the widespread and wanton destruction would have been nipped in the bud.

A confident man will, on the average, follow the correct course,

and the unsure one will more often vacillate into the wrong decision. Confidence in the top man fits him to stand his ground in the
face of severe pressures against which he should hold firm.

Exert Patience and Control

When an institution undergoes turbulent times, all the tensions and pressures focus on the leader. The discontented blame
him for their dissatisfactions. During periods of worldwide social
upheaval, which are accompanied by demands for change in institutional leadership behavior, confusion develops over which past
standards to discard and which new ones to adopt. Long-held concepts of political belief, of marriage and sex, of religion, of the
distribution of wealth, are suddenly under fire. But what the direction and extent of changes in belief ought to be is not clear, and
attitudes and thoughts are confused. A feeling of general insecurity develops, leading individuals and groups into an emotional
state that at times causes them to act irrationally. Present locally
as well as generally, it affects members of parishes, employees in
plants and offices, educators and students, nurses and doctors in
hospitals—wherever we may go about our daily living. It resides
just beneath the surface and has much to do with the cause and
tumult of dissent. A feeling of restlessness permeates our whole
society.

Because of this, the leaders of our institutions are likely to be
blamed unfairly for events which they have not brought about or
over which they have had little control. Leaders must understand,
however, that as we undergo this trial of change, such reactions
are normal, and they must discipline themselves to act with unusual patience. Otherwise, the relationship between those in
charge and those who are dissenting deteriorates into personal
spats, and leadership control is lost.

Understanding that this is so, and keeping it in mind when
confronted with dissent, will help leaders to keep a balanced per-
spective toward meeting and resolving dissatisfactions and enable
them to maintain patience and control through periods of strife.

No matter how exalted a position a man may hold, he is no
more or no less human than anyone else. Under sustained, re-
lentless, and extremely trying stress, even the most imperturbable
leader will lose his temper and make public statements he will
later regret. This is a sign of mental and emotional fatigue and

illustrates why it is so important to insist on rest periods for those subjected to severe strains under pressure.

Not only has the president been faced with the problem, but the mayors of our great metropolitan centers have also been subjected to a maze of incredible pressures, dissent in all its forms, and criticism from loyal citizens as well as opponents. Small wonder that occasionally one of them explodes in bitter denunciation of what he considers unjust criticism by troublemakers. It is a tribute to their firm control that such outbreaks do not happen more frequently. Such incidents may serve as a lesson for any in responsible positions who are confronted with dissent. When a leader becomes deeply involved and feels his patience being sorely tried, this should alert him that perhaps the time has come to back off for a rest and a change of pace.

Consider Long-Range Effects

Actions proposed to satisfy dissent should always be evaluated in terms of their future impact. Will an action taken today be good or bad for the long-term interest? This consideration bears hard on the leader. The long-range course may not be the easy course but the hard one, and unpopular at the moment. The tough decision can demand laying a career on the line, and it requires the qualities of conviction and courage.

General William Mitchell disagreed adamantly with the course the services were following during the 1920s. He proved the effectiveness of aerial bombing; he predicted Pearl Harbor. But his impatience with traditional military doctrine and his outspoken castigation of the navy and the failure of our generals and admirals to see the future of air power brought his suspension from the service. He knew he was risking his career, but that did not stop him. As the future unfolded into World War II, his convictions became bare realities. Only after his death was he reinstated with full honors.

The Mitchell case is a dramatic illustration, but the need to measure the correctness of action for the future as well as the present is seen daily in all kinds of organizations. It is natural to want to give in to the easier, more expedient way, and the tendency is not an easy one to resist. This is particularly true when the decision maker is under heavy strain from dissent racking his organization.

A saying in the world of labor-management relations is that you may buy labor peace now but pay dearly for it later. This came out of the cauldron of experience, where dismaying lessons were learned from actions based on too little consideration of the future. Institutions of all kinds are learning it the hard way.

One case from which we all learned out of their unfortunate loss was the Studebaker Corporation. During World War II and for a number of years afterward, Studebaker enjoyed profitable prosperity unhampered by strikes. Then came more difficult times. Eventually the company went out of the car-making business entirely. A number of factors contributed to the downfall of this firm, one of the oldest manufacturers of fine carriages and automobiles. For example, Studebaker had an agreement with the union on wages and work practices that worked when production was high and jobs plentiful. Layoff was no problem at all. But when hard years fell on the company, practices to which they had agreed to keep labor peace rose to haunt them. One of these was the layoff system, which, simply put, was so cumbersome and impractical that employees sat for weeks beyond their turn to be laid off before the procedure caught up with them. Much more was involved that created costly difficulties, but this would seem to be sufficient to illustrate the point.

As we know, today the railroads are suffering from work practices that have been in existence since World War I, when the government operated them. Management is required to maintain jobs for which there is no longer any need. Pay is structured on standards long since obsolete—a day's pay for each hundred miles of travel. Sharp criticism is leveled at past and present railroad management, and though some of it may be justified, much of it is certainly unfair. At any rate, to force management to continue these outworn practices, by permitting unions to continue them, may drive railroads from private to public ownership and further inefficiency, with jobs kept in existence only by public support. This is against the public interest, and if it happens, the public will have only itself to blame for being so apathetic now. Here is a unique case where we have not only failed to foresee consequences but are not learning from hindsight as well.

In an eastern city known as a center for the manufacture of ceramic ware, the wage structure was tradition-ridden, keyed to potter skills practiced way in the past. Modern methods changed the skill requirements and increased the number of units able to be produced during a day. Costs were soaring. To stay competitive, one company had to improve methods substantially and increase the daily production figure. The union resisted, then struck. Management stood fast, and the strike lasted for 26 weeks. Management won, not all, but much of what was needed to remain competitive. Later, after a comparatively short walkout and further negotiations, the union agreed to what management said was necessary. This made it possible for the operation to stay in business and keep the jobs in the community. Because management was willing to withstand the hardship of a long strike in order to shake the union loose from the past and move it into the realities of today, the operation and the employees continued to work. Had the stand not been taken, the plants would have gone out of business within a few years.

In a similar strike situation in a large midwestern city, management stood its ground against strong criticism. Critics complained that its position was rigid, that it was callous toward its employees by keeping them out of work for so long. Because management stood firm, thousands of jobs were saved and the company continues to be competitive. It would have been easy to give in and pass the problem to the future, which would have forced the company to close down and sell the real estate and buildings.

To take a stance in opposition to the SST, the space program, and anything to do with weaponry is popular today, but it weakens us for the future, perhaps to a dangerous point. It would seem to be vital that we stand up to the hue and cry of critics in order to protect our long-term interests.

8

Authority and
Conciliatory Techniques

WHILE attempting to reconcile differences between dissenting groups, it is necessary to understand when and how to use authority and when to apply conciliatory techniques. Under the tensions that grow taut as hostility increases, when those in command lack an understanding of the relationship between authority and conciliatory methods, the chances are that they will be misapplied. A settlement may be reached, but under conditions that will cause difficulties in the relationship in the future.

Four techniques are used to assist in bringing dissenting groups together: compromise, conciliation, mediation, and arbitration. All are designed to persuade sides with strong positions of difference to concede to each other so that agreement can be reached. Essentially, the four are means to the same end, differing only in approach.

Basic in the application of these is to avoid using them in a way that will sap the strength of authority. This is a danger inherent in all of them unless skillful and experienced hands are in charge when one of the four is needed. It is one thing to compromise a position and another to compromise authority. The former implies modifying a stand while retaining authority, whereas to compromise authority means that responsibility for decisions is given up to others who would take it away.

As an example of giving up authority in the guise of compromise, a group of dissenting students demanded that the top officials allow them to vote and decide university housing policy. The students had neither the experience, a broad understanding of the problem, nor the maturity of judgment to make decisions of this magnitude. Yet the officials conceded. Their authority was compromised and weakened. Had they agreed to take the student group's recommendations under consideration, seriously reviewed what they contained, adopted the useful ones, and refused those judged to be impractical, authority would have been retained. Only the position would have been modified.

Over the past 35 years, the authority of management to direct our industrial corporations has seriously eroded. This is singularly so in basic industries. Because any disruption in very large firms tends to discommode the public and upset the economy, political action is demanded, and as the effects of a strike spread, or a major strike becomes imminent, political pressure is brought to bear heavily from the White House. In fact, under the direction of the president, mediation and conciliation are deftly but firmly inserted into the relationship between the union and management. And it is only fair to say that the score of these settlements is far in favor of the unions. There is little question that this pattern has been compromising the authority of management in the areas of wage and price determination. Stripped of economic jargon, the bare fact is that under this system unions are setting wages, leaving management only the automatic recourse of raising prices. Each time this happens, foreign goods become more competitive, and more manufacturing operations are driven abroad, taking American jobs with them. Unions are forcing the loss of that which they claim to protect—jobs. The relationship has been compromised out of balance and is in serious trouble.

Should we let this state of affairs continue, the strike, as a form of dissent, may become obsolete for settling major disputes. The government will continue forcible mediation, and standard guidelines for wage and price increases will be maintained in an attempt to control inflationary pressures. During the closing phases of major negotiations, the government will be an ever-present third party. Actually, this prediction is only an extension of what is already taking place.

The government may not wish to be driven into this position, but the failure of the leaders of dominant unions to exercise restraint as they compete with each other to win ever higher settlements leaves the president only this option. Unions have more power than they should to damage the public interest, and unless more legal restraint is placed on their right to upset the economy, what alternate course of action is left?

Before further discussion of authority and conciliatory techniques, a definition of the four would seem to be in order.

Compromise

Compromise is "the process or a result of settlement by arbitration or by consent reached by mutual concessions." Emphasis should be placed on "mutual concessions." The word *compromise* is often misunderstood in the sense being used here because of another meaning, "to surrender," or "to make a shameful or disreputable concession." Unfortunately, in the course of settling disagreements, those without strength of conviction may do exactly that, and within this context compromise means weakness. But, as a conciliatory technique in the hands of a skillful leader, it is a basic tool for bringing dissenters from strife to accord. In the history of our country, one of the most outstanding figures to apply the art of compromise was Henry Clay. He earned the label "Great Pacificator" because during his career, using compromise and persuasion, he was instrumental in resolving national crises. Two of these, as we know, were the Missouri Compromise and the Compromise of 1850. He accomplished this by persuading a divided congress to accept mutual concessions.

Conciliation

Conciliate means "to gain (as goodwill) by pleasing acts, to make compatible: reconcile, to gain the goodwill or favor of." The key words of this definition are "by pleasing acts." When a leader is conciliating, his actions and attitudes are consciously designed to please those he is attempting to persuade. Here, too, misunderstanding can take place. A conciliatory manner is often confused with a subservient one, a bowing and scraping before another to gain approval. This is not the connotation meant when conciliation is used as a technique for seeking a basis for settling disagreements.

The phrase "by pleasing acts" does not imply actions bringing enjoyment to some person or group or bringing smiles to their faces. What it does imply is approval of an approach to solving differences extended with sincere goodwill.

During a crisis, an act of conciliation to show goodwill is to suggest meeting with the leaders of the opposing side in their own surroundings. This was the intention behind President Kennedy's trip to see Nikita Khrushchev and one of the reasons President Nixon visited Peking and Moscow. These actions were intended to introduce a degree of cordiality into a hostile relationship and open the way to eventual accord. A gesture of conciliation by itself does not usually settle issues between disputing parties, but is used primarily to seek a break through the invisible but hard wall of hostility between opposing sides. It is an opening gesture.

An excellent example of conciliation involved a temporary impasse in a union-management negotiation. Because the union was hung up by internal disagreement, three of its leaders asked for a private meeting with management. Not only did the chief negotiator agree readily, but he invited them to lunch at a private club. Nothing was said, but the implication was that management was meeting with the union as it would with any other business group. This happened at a time when union professionals were only beginning to win any status security in the community. The subtle gesture of acceptance pleased them, and the meeting was relatively cordial and constructive. Although nothing was settled then and there, the groundwork was laid for reaching agreement in several days.

Mediation

Whereas conciliation is a face-to-face technique for setting the stage to reach accord, in mediation an intermediary is asked to act as a go-between for the two sides.

To mediate is "to interpose between parties as the equal friend of each, especially to effect a reconciliation." Mediation is "intercession of one power between other powers on their invitation or consent to arrange amicably differences between them."

A mediator is selected to intercede, by mutual consent, between sides so far at odds that nothing effective can be accomplished in joint meetings. Mediation is applied at a point where personal frictions and animosities, as well as disagreement over issues, are so high that any meeting together can only result in a widening of the breach. Positions harden and appeals for concessions fall on deaf ears.

Normally, the mediator is brought in by request of both parties, but in union-management negotiations in major industries, a high representative is brought in from the Federal Mediation and Conciliation Service. This is done on strong urging from the White House, even though the government administration prefers to project the image of maintaining a hands-off, free, collective bargaining policy. But this is only a wish. Inevitably, the government is present as a third party. Actually, because of the impact of industry disruption on the economy at large, the mediator from the service represents the public interest. He is under as much pressure to bring agreement as the union and management are. The danger here is that the severe strain involved in the mediation process may force an expedient agreement not in the long-term interest of either the industry or the public.

Figuratively speaking, an increasing number of major negotiations are ending up in Washington. When differences are wide between management and the union, the union stands on its position, knowing that when the crisis point is reached, the White House will intervene. From experience, union leaders know that they are likely to fare better than management because of their unlimited authority to call a disruptive strike. Management has economic power, but it is not so infinite as it used to be or as some theoretical economists conceive that it is. Management is caught in a dilemma: Intense foreign competition places it in a position where neither long strikes nor high wage settlements can be afforded. Authority to make wise economic decisions has been greatly reduced, while responsibility for them has not. The problem is a serious one and concerns us all.

Under these conditions, mediation is not mediation in its true sense. The concessions demanded are too one-sided. This is not the fault of any one individual, but the result of traditional thinking. It is unquestionably true that, years ago, enormous economic power was held in the hands of a few while the workingman had little, if any. But this has long since ceased to be a fact. Through his union the worker now has the power that management has. Yet we continue to accept the premise that he still does not.

Balance will have to be restored through legislation or a government agency that will set limits on a union's right to strike against the public interest, or to ask for and get wage increases so large that they force wages and prices out of competition. If this is not done, we will suffer serious economic trouble.

How mediation works at its best is described in Chapter 13, "Return to Accord."

Mediation Skills

When a serious rupture in the negotiation of differences between groups becomes irreconcilable, or apparently so, the techniques of conciliation and mediation offer excellent means for repairing the break. Because hostilities and tensions have developed which, temporarily at least, slow further progress by direct negotiation to a dribble, a mediator is interposed between the two sides, and, working back and forth from one to the other, he begins the sensitive job of bringing them back to accord. To serve as a successful mediator requires unusual skills in human relations.

If mediation is to be proficient as a technique for coaxing divided groups back together, everyone concerned must thoroughly understand the mediator's role. His position is an impartial one. He has to balance the fairness of the points at issue. He must have the fortitude not to accede to the blandishments of the more powerful or attractive side. Nor should he try to exercise power by maneuvering one side against the other. His job is to maintain objectivity. There are times when human nature tempts him to partiality, and it is difficult not to woo him with engaging cordiality. Some degree of such interaction is inevitable, but if it is allowed to get out of hand, the results won't be healthy for anyone.

One of the obvious qualities that an effective mediator ought to have is insight, an above-average understanding of human behavior. Very important is the ability to comprehend how individuals and groups react under sustained stress. More than that, he has to have the skill to do something to change or modify reactions. For example, he may know that anger stems more from a personality clash than a disagreement over issues, or that stubbornness has been exaggerated by fatigue. Having uncovered these problems, he moves to keep the clashing personalities apart and calls for rest periods to overcome fatigue.

Patient tolerance is a virtue in a mediator. He moves in the center of a maze of relationships that are in disorder. Observing and assessing the maze demands not only insight but patience as well. Many times the basic causes are not so obvious as they may appear to be. There is no easy, patent-medicine solution for repairing a discordant complex of human relationships. Patience with anger, curtness, and accusations is demanded of him, and he must discipline himself not to be caught up in the swirl of high emotions.

Personal integrity and a sound sense of fairness are an absolute must. Parties to disputes are willing to overlook other shortcomings in a mediator, and they will place their faith in him if they know him to be a man with a sense of fair play who cannot be bought. Of all the qualities needed in a mediator, these are the two most important.

A mediator needs easy confidence of manner and a degree of affability, but pleasant traits cannot be allowed to turn into overfriendliness with one side or the other. This reduces his effectiveness as an impartial go-between.

And, of course, experience in the field is necessary. Natural talent is desirable, but, without experience, it is not enough. To be a top mediator, a man must be mature and urbane—he must have been involved in the world of affairs throughout his career so that he can be practical in his approach as well as insightful. It is a form of diplomacy, and as David Bruce, a highly skilled and experienced diplomat, has said, "Diplomacy is not a system of moral philosophy, and, when negotiations are begun, with either hostile or friendly powers, the moral sphere gives way to the tactical implementation of policy."

An experienced mediator will also develop the self-control to withstand the pressures generated during a difficult period so that he will not be upset by them. If he loses his self-control—his temper—his usefulness is lost.

Mediation Procedures

One of the first procedures in beginning a successful mediation is to separate the sides physically to avoid direct conflict between them. This means actually placing them in separate rooms or quarters. After he has done this, the mediator begins moving quietly back and forth, asking questions and listening very carefully to what everyone has to say. During this opening phase he does very little talking. His function is to evaluate the situation— to be an attentive listener, assessing and gauging the issues, the personality interplay, and the source and depth of the hostilities that have developed. He makes very little comment and, certainly, if he is skillful, no statements to either group about the validity of positions. There are several reasons for this. The mediator's role, as said before, is to be impartial. But, more than that, in the early stages of the mediation he may misread the causes before he thoroughly understands them. Or he may make a statement that is misinterpreted, increasing the hostility instead of reducing it, and turning the anger of both sides against him.

This is a critical time in the process. The mediator's objective at the beginning is to dissolve intransigence and reopen communications. His approach is to be calm and courteously impartial as he listens. While discussing the issues as each side sees them, he assesses the personalities of the individual negotiators to determine whether any of the problems lie in personality conflicts having little to do with the issues. Should he discover that such conflicts do exist, he has to set about ameliorating them by deftly explaining, first to one group, then to the other, the causes of misunderstanding.

A simple case will illustrate such a conflict that developed in a mediated negotiation. After a number of discussions, the mediator found that a member of one side was mad at one on the other. The former was a man of Southern background who resented a lot of swearing in meetings. The latter was an individual who used swear words in place of adjectives, and in one meeting, when the discussion became heated, he was coming out with every pithy four- to eleven-letter word. Somehow he cut loose with a blast of profanity just as he was looking at the man who objected to swearing. The Southerner took it personally, and as the negotiations reached the impasse state, his resentment grew. Having uncovered this, the mediator talked to one, then the other, finally relaying the message that the swearing was simply a habit and that nothing personal had been intended. His move salved a sore spot that was working against agreement.

By listening carefully and moving with deliberate sureness, the mediator builds confidence in his skills. As confidence rises, so does willingness to cooperate, and the way is opened for further progress. Making the right move is more important than the speed with which it is made. The illustration above is an example of a correct move, which caused a festering tension to dissipate.

While analyzing what the personal frictions blocking progress are, the mediator works to uncover the real issues and determines which can be easily resolved and which are more difficult. He places them in order of difficulty from the easiest to the hardest, then begins to mediate in that order.

This is not always simple to do. Often the true problems may be hidden in the past, deliberately screened, or so complex that they are not quickly recognizable. Sometimes a disagreement, in the form of active dissent, is more the result of a long-standing grievance than over any current question. Those who arouse the blacks know how to play on their long frustrations over housing and the opportunity to earn a decent living. These frustrations, more than any political conviction, have caused their active expression of dissent.

An individual may carry a smoldering grievance for years because he has been powerless to do anything about it, but will join in active dissent as soon as he has some protection from fear of reprisal. From the records, case after case can be cited to show that a man joined a union and a strike because, for a long time, he believed that his pay was not fair, that the man next to him earned more for the same job, or that his foreman had favorites.

Screening real intent behind moves is hard to detect when motives are deliberately obscured, as our diplomats well know from their experiences in international negotiations. Behind a claim of concern only for the group interest may lie a purely selfish motive, such as the craving for personal gain in power or money.

A move at the moment may be only a tactic that is part of a broader strategy. In one case, the mediator discovered that to understand the union leader's strike tactics and counteract them effectively required knowing that each of his moves was part of a long-range plan to organize the whole industry into a union shop under his personal leadership. His motives were mixed: in part they were for the best interests of the members, but to a measurable degree, they were the desire of a short man for personal power.

The point here is that a successful mediator will satisfy himself that he has probed deeply enough into the background, personalities, and issues to assure an accurate estimate of the situation before he makes any major moves. He does this by reflecting on all that he has learned about personalities and issues, and where there is still any question in his mind, he goes back to clear it up.

The mediator must be able to withstand pressures from all sides, including the public, and not give in to any demand for too rapid a settlement. The time he needs for opening communications and the way to agreement is directly related to how far apart the sides are on issues, and to what degree suspicion and bitterness may have grown up between them. The time can range from several days to months.

After opening communications between the parties by mollifying tension and appealing to fairness, the mediator brings the sides face-to-face in a meeting, deliberately short and introductory. Facts are reviewed and only one or two minor issues discussed. The purpose here is to get them used to being together again and to see how each reacts to the other, and the meeting is kept short to avoid the possibility that tensions will build and anger flare up. Is the air relatively calm, or is it tense? An assessment of this will give the mediator a gauge of how ready to discuss differences the parties are, so that he can set the direction and pace his actions accordingly.

Working back and forth, he calls meetings whenever certain issues seem to be ready to be resolved, disperses the parties to work on difficult problems, and recalls the meetings as issues near agreement. Near the point of accord, he withdraws to the sidelines to enable them to work together, with as little outside interruption as possible so that the relationship may be restored.

When mediating or using any of the other techniques for reconciling disputes, an important guideline should be observed. Past experience with strife and discord may be useful in seeking a solution to present and future problems, but to apply one or several past procedures by rote is a mistake. With contemporary disruptions, the proper action should be arrived at by weighing the effect of changing conditions on the situation at hand. In a complex situation, to attempt to follow a procedure that worked so nicely in a local area often results in failure—and wistful head-scratching over why it hasn't worked here. A common practice, for example, is to keep top decision makers apart from direct negotiations so that their decisions can be made calmly, away from the heat of the discord. But there are relationships in which, traditionally, the top has participated directly. To change this custom abruptly by removing the top from the meetings could be taken as an affront and in this case would be a mistake.

Arbitration

Arbitration, the fourth technique, is a court of last resort. It is defined as "the hearing and determination of a case in controversy by a person chosen by the parties or appointed by statutory authority." The person chosen is, of course, the arbitrator. The difference between arbitration and the other techniques lies in the words "hearing and determination." A mediator arranges the differences amicably. His authority lies in his insight into human action and his persuasive skills. The arbitrator, on the other hand, hears and determines. He holds a hearing during which each side presents the case for its position. Having heard both sides, he studies and weighs the facts, then determines and issues what he concludes to be a fair award to one side or the other, or both. Selected because of his professional competence in the field where the differences exist—wage determination, for example—he is considered qualified to make a decision, which may be final and binding on the parties by either mutual agreement or statute. His authority is limited to immediate issues and the facts surrounding them, but even with these limits, he has real authority to judge them.

The majority of union-management agreements contain a clause for the arbitration of individual or group grievances that cannot be settled otherwise. This practice has been in use for many years and, with a few exceptions, is by consent of the parties to the agreement. In the major industries, however, compulsory arbitration has been suggested as a solution for reconciling differences without strikes. This means that should the sides fail to reach agreement by the end of the contract, they are compelled to submit the dispute to an arbitrator and abide by his decision.

But no really serious attempt has been made to write this into the law. Although the question has been raised from time to time, particularly during nationwide strikes, nothing has actually been done to make arbitration compulsory, and it would seem that nothing will be done about it in the future. The unions do not want it; management does not like it; and administrations, Republican and Democrat, shy away from compelling it. Because of our characteristically independent nature, forcing settlement of such arguments by requiring the intervention of a third party goes against the grain. For us, it does not provide a satisfactory answer. We believe that having the public arbitrate what should be private concerns in the economic world is inconsistent with our concept of free enterprise. Moreover, it would strip the authority of those responsible for the operation of our economic system and subject them to too much public regulation.

No law sufficient to curb union power within reasonable limits has been passed, because of political expediency and the complexity of the problems involved. On the other hand, under the existing laws and practices, big unions are unable to control their muscle and management power has been reduced, so some kind of regulation has become inevitable. Certainly, the general lines set by presidential announcement and "jawboning" have failed, and firmer guidelines, backed by authority, have been the next logical step.

Public indignation over disruptive strikes and mounting wages, reflected in increases in cost of living, have strengthened the drive for wider wage and price controls. The Pay Board and the Construction Industry Board, with the authority to set and apply limits, are the result of this drive. Initially, government authorities indicated that controls would be temporary, but recently the head of the Cost of Living Council said that he did not know when controls would be lifted. Smaller business has been exempted.

The alternative is to reestablish wage and salary control boards, structured as they were during World War II and the Korean War, but there is great resistance against them. By setting limits within which unions and managements have to resolve differences, the supporters of the guideline approach believe that the number of crippling strikes and high wage settlements will be reduced substantially. That may be so, but unions are still free to strike within those limits, and they will probably do so when management stands on an offer that is less than the limit. What will happen is that most agreements will be at or near the maximum, and strikes will diminish, if the basic disagreement is over the amount of the wage increase and not work practices or a noneconomic segment of the total package.

This approach will provide the public with some protection against inflationary wage pressures on the cost of living, but it will not necessarily give relief from strikes. Only compulsory arbitration can solve that completely. One possible solution might be to allow a limited strike—setting a maximum time period—after which, if no agreement is reached, the dispute must be submitted to arbitration. The arbitrator would be selected with the consent of both parties. The strike itself and the threat of binding arbitration should induce the sides to work out an agreement.

Skills of the Arbitrator

How arbitration operates as a technique for settling disputes has been described. Successful arbitration depends upon several factors. First, the arbitrator selected must have a reputation for integrity and objectivity. Secondly, he has to be technically able in the field over which the points at issue arose. Thirdly, the limits of his authority have to be clearly defined, understood, and agreed to by the parties as well as the arbitrator. Fourthly, the preparation of the case to be presented to the arbitrator should be thorough and based on facts.

If the arbitrator is not objective or is without integrity, his decision may be swayed by personalities or persuasions, and he will lose the faith of the sides. If he is technically naive, his decisions will also reflect this weakness. Should his authority not be well defined, arguments and misunderstandings develop over his limits, particularly if he goes beyond what the parties understand the boundaries to be. And, a superficial presentation does not give the arbitrator a solid base for consideration, and can result in an unintentional error in his decision.

Effective Application

An understanding of the basic characteristics of these four techniques is essential for knowing when and how to apply them effectively. Skillful application brings success in resolving dissent. Misapplication in clumsy or inexperienced hands will only deepen the division between the parties involved.

One or all of these techniques may be brought to bear in the settlement of disputes of all kinds. Where attempts are being made to reach agreement, minor concessions are made first, with the major items at issue being held for the last. This is done with the hope that, by coming to accord on the smaller points, everyone will be in a more conciliatory mood when faced with the more difficult ones. There are times when this works, but often, in opening negotiations, it is simply a waltz and only delays facing up to the real problems.

When disagreements widen toward the impasse stage, conciliatory action should be introduced into the situation. Some form of compromise may be suggested. But the nearer the opponents are to an utter impasse, the more rigid the position taken by each of them becomes, and any try at compromise is unlikely to succeed. Settlement at this point may be impossible because of the emotionally charged atmosphere. The sides are still way apart, and the goal here is to bring them back to a willingness to concede anything at all. This gap has to be bridged before the tone can be set for mutual agreement to meet the major issues.

The purpose is not so much to settle as it is to set the stage for concessions later on, when a calmer mood prevails. Often a partial concession is offered by one side without either expecting it to be accepted. Occasionally, to everyone's surprise, it is, but more frequently it is intended as a basis for a final agreement in the future. This technique is common in labor-management negotiations: Management will make a money offer which is short of what it intends as a final amount by a percent or two, withholding the difference as a pot-sweetener for when the sides are close to agreement. Not only does this entice the union to accept, but, as a concession, it finishes the dispute on a conciliatory tone, offsetting any bitterness that may have developed and restoring relationships to a more workable condition.

Bringing conciliatory skills effectively to work is much more trying when positions have become rigid and unyielding. This is evident when one or both sides announces that theirs is "an absolutely final offer." No such position should ever be taken unless it can and will be held until the other side agrees. This may mean being able to undergo long and costly strife. When the steel industry tried the final take-it-or-leave-it-offer approach, the tactic failed because management was unable to back up its stand, politically and economically, long enough to win.

A pragmatic axiom in negotiating differences is: Never allow your position to become so rigid that no further room for maneuvering is left. Otherwise, as the saying has it, you wind up "on the hook," unable to get off without embarrassment—meaning you lose.

Compromise is not to be confused with capitulation, in which one side concedes on major issues without receiving any concession in return. In too many instances during campus scuffles between the university establishment, students, and professors, officials have conceded to the point of capitulation in an attempt to dispel unrest. Compromise, on the other hand, is the art of balancing concessions so that both sides are reasonably satisfied with the outcome. When a disproportionate share of concessions is made by one of the parties, it sows the seeds of expectation that this will become the pattern for future negotiations and weakens the position of the conceding party for the future. Should one side choose to stiffen and strike a firm stand, the other will discount it as a pose, not backed by firm intention.

When dissenters take extreme action—threatening or actually bringing about injury, causing the destruction of property, or engaging in any form of unlawful act—this is not the time for trying conciliatory techniques or attempting to reason. Such gestures will only be interpreted as weakness, and may encourage further disorder instead of quenching it. Firm action to quell the uproar is the right course. This includes moving in, isolating and dispelling groups, and arresting those responsible. If necessary, legal action ought to follow arrests. Failing to take strong action—not brutal action—causes loss of respect for authority, law, and order. This is what happened to certain youth groups, black and white, that flashed across the country. A degree of success in confronting authority in the university president's office led them to commit more extreme acts on the campus and in the cities, and they fell victims of their own rashness. As destruction, serious injury, and death followed their demonstrations, public indignation rose and demanded police action.

The authority of reason, however sound and persuasive, has no place here. This is not to imply that those in authority should be insensitive to the grievances of others. Far from it. A leader with a willing ear and an action-minded temperament, by resolving complaints when they are small, can prevent the need for active forms of dissent. But where dissent is already breaking out into violence, order must be restored before any attempt to use conciliatory methods can be of value.

Although, as mentioned earlier, it is essential to set the stage for final settlement by making initial concessions on minor issues, concessions made for immediate advantage or out of fear are likely to be bad compromises. Overanxiousness leads to compromising beyond the balance of fairness. Timidity in the face of the tough realities in meeting dissent may grasp compromise as an excuse for the easy way out, and short-range peace may be gained at the expense of long-term harmony. For example, corporations have bought transitory peace by conceding costly wage increases or seniority practices that eventually have priced them out of competition. The erosion of management authority over the past 35 years has given us a legacy of economic problems of serious magnitude. Some of these are the result of political expediency—the immediate advantage—with too little regard for the eventual consequences. What these are has already been discussed.

In any institution, irrespective of size or type, leadership must exercise its responsibility to act in the best long-term interest of its charge, often at the expense of instant popularity and personal comfort. Our wage-price dilemma is not President Nixon's creation. He inherited the accumulation of many years of too much expediency and too little statesmanship. To restore balance in the union-management power structure will not be easy to do. While not insurmountable, it is a problem of extraordinary proportions for which there is no overnight solution. What will happen remains to be seen, but the situation will require diplomatic and statesmanlike qualities of the highest order.

9

The Management of Violence

DISSENTING groups cannot always be negotiated into accord. Worn and pushed by grieving frustrations, they sometimes explode into striking or rioting. The chances are that this will occur when the discontent mounts, unrecognized by leadership, for a long time. While every effort is made to avoid strikes and riots—and the destruction, injury, and death that may follow—it is humanly impossible always to do so.

Destruction and violence will happen. When faced with the threat of violence, or with violence itself, there are a number of guidelines to follow which experience has shown to be effective in helping to bring the situation back to normal.

Control

Before or during a strike or riot, strong self-discipline and control are paramount. At such times leaders need to be bold, confident, and sure in action. A gathering of protesters may form simply to hear speakers voice their complaints or to picket peacefully, but inherent in such forms of dissent are mob tendencies.

And if a leader who appears before a group to appeal for dispersal is visibly timid, unsure, and unconvincing, his insecurity may be the very thing that detonates violence. The crowd senses a lack of control and becomes more aggressive; threats are hurled; small destructive acts, such as breaking a window, trigger larger ones. Smoldering frustrations push what was a crowd of individual dissenters into an uncontrollable mob. Exactly why this transformation happens is not always clear. Perhaps the reason is that the crowd's frustrations are heightened by the feeling that leaders are providing neither direction nor assurance of satisfaction, and they react by following the threats and acts of others within the group. Many threatening crowds have dispersed after listening to the confident reassurance of a magnetic leader.

One morning an aimless crowd, loosely organized, gathered before the executive offices of their organization to protest against what they considered to be a number of unfair actions taken to discipline older members of the group. The protest was tripped by a single such action that had taken place early that morning—a decision had been made to discipline a woman with long service by giving her a substantial layoff without pay. The word flashed around, and indignation at this, as well as other decisions, swelled. Urged by informal leaders, a loose crowd of dissenters had formed and marched to picket before headquarters. Shortly after the crowd appeared, an executive came out and stood facing them squarely from the top of the steps. Raising open-palmed hands, he called for quiet, then asked what the problem was. Several of the informal leaders spoke their complaints in direct language. For a while the executive said little except to ask questions. But because he listened attentively to what they had to say, so did others in the group. When the leaders had finished, he spoke calmly and clearly, making two points. With a disarming manner, he admitted that very possibly errors had been made, and he assured them persuasively that he would meet with the informal leaders, if they wished, to investigate and correct any mistakes that might have been made. More than that, he said, if there had been any errors, steps would be taken to assure that further inequities would not be committed in the future. Before he left the crowd, he arranged for a meeting to show that he meant what he said. Here was a leader who exercised control and moved with a sure hand. The pickets dispersed.

Decisiveness

Not only does a display of nervousness and fear cause loss of control, so does indecisive vacillation. Rattled by the threat of violence, a leader who is unsure of himself may become so distressed by the hard and critical demand for an immediate decision that he cannot decide what to do. While he hesitates in a quandary, the moment of truth passes and control is lost. Ironically, the cause of the dissent's heating to the flash point could be the executive's vacillatory temperament. Or it could be his lack of experience— nothing he has undergone in the past has prepared him for controlling active forms of dissent.

A university president vacillated over a decision about what to do when a small group of pseudomalcontents invaded his office and took over. What he should have done was invite them to leave in no uncertain terms, and, if they refused, to have them thrown out. But while he pondered what to do, the group enlarged, became arrogant and destructive, and ranged to other offices. What should have been confined to a local incident came to national attention and encouraged others to create similar incidents.

Vacillation in decision making is bad at any time, but it becomes a glaring weakness during crises. Conversely, quick decisiveness is a preventive act, far more likely to dissipate than to inflame violence.

Self-Restraint

Quick action differs from rash impulse. Intemperate outbursts, angry accusations, only add to the ferment by salting sore wounds. Even the coolest of our leaders occasionally lose control under severe strain and lash out acidly against critics. Invariably, they regret their public display of bad temper and have to set about repairing the damage done to important relationships.

President Truman, furious because the steel companies balked at meeting steelworker demands despite his intercession, ordered the industry to be seized by the government. This only stiffened the backs of the industry's "free enterprise" leaders and raised a public outcry. Mr. Truman had to withdraw his order.

Lyndon Johnson struck out at the critics of his Vietnam policies and had to salve the wounds he opened. Mr. Nixon leveled his fury at draft dodgers and demonstrators. His staff worked hard to explain this away.

For men bearing such awesome responsibilities, these occasional tirades are to be expected. That they do not occur more often is a measure of the high degree of their self-control. But should a leader allow himself the indulgence of impulsive outrage against a group of orderly dissenters, he risks igniting the coals of discontent into a flaming rampage. When this happens at a critical moment, the impetuous leader must be instantly replaced with one more characteristically calm and even-tempered.

One of our top industrial leaders, a man of bold competence in his field, admired by his brethren in the industry fraternity, could not contain himself when confronted with union pushes for more rights for members. For a number of years his organization was in constant upheaval. Only after he was forced to step down was it possible to begin calming the disruption, assuaging the bitterness, and repairing the divisive suspicion that had developed.

Instant Action

Impetuous and vacillating leadership is most costly when confronted by skilled professionals whose sole aim is to disrupt and divide. It plays directly into their hands, and they have a field day with it. While deliberately camouflaging themselves, professionals work to incite violence, and, when leadership lacks calm and force, they win the day.

Quick action as a preventive measure has already been mentioned. If there is ever a need for decisiveness, it is when a discontented gathering hangs in balance between reason and rage. Here is the time for the action-minded leader, whose experience and temperament enable him to make rapid calculations and incisive decisions. Realizing the force of the discontent is reaching the point of no return, he knows he must, and does, move quickly to dispel the emotional surge before it breaks.

One quick-thinking university president, new to his position but experienced in resolving dissent, heard that students were gathering to stage a demonstration. Instead of waiting, he went straight to the spot where the group was assembling. He moved among them and, in an open and friendly way, asked what their specific complaints were. By questioning, he brought home to them that he would be more than willing to discuss any grievances they wished to present. But the group discovered for themselves that they had difficulty trying to express anything more than vague dissatisfactions. At his suggestion they dispersed to form a more specific list of demands, which, when presented to him, he agreed to discuss and resolve with them. By moving at once, he prevented what could have swelled into a seething demonstration. He understood what to do, and did it. His actions were neither impulsive nor wavering, but rapid and positive.

When a sizable picket line forms, or any dissenting crowd grows, police or others trained in riot control should be sent quietly to the scene and tactically spaced around the perimeter. The leaders of the assembly should be watched closely to determine whether any attempt is being made to cause rioting or to fire up emotions into uncontrollable rage, whether that be the intent or not. Instantly, when the danger point is near, riot control should move to single out the leaders and remove them, if possible; or, if not, to isolate them in pockets and reduce their effectiveness. At the same time, moves should be made to prevent the crowd from poling toward the center and increasing its power to riot. During the late sixties the intensity of city rioting was increased when the rioters were in a concentrated position. By dispersing a crowd into localized segments, they can be made more controllable. Local incidents may—probably will—break out, but the massing and central leadership necessary to set off an uncontrollable riot are neutralized. Leaders are in no position to mass and goad a peaceable gathering into a mob, and a mob is brutal. Within the mass the individual becomes clothed in anonymity, loses his identity and his fear, and is caught up in mob action.

Once violence has begun, there is little, if any, chance to reason with it. Force has to be quickly brought to bear to keep the mob from running rampant. If rioting becomes uncontrollably vicious, the best that can be done is to curb it until the mob spends its emotions. The time for reason is *after* order has been restored —then is the time to seek for the grievances and to settle the issues.

Weather Effect

Weather conditions obviously affect crowd action. Hot weather, bringing discomfort and sleeplessness, raises irritability and lowers the flash point of tempers. Strikes and riots are more apt to explode during hot days. Those who incite them know this and use the weather to advantage. This is one of the reasons leaders of dissenting or radical groups have promised "hot summers." And, until recently, we have had them.

Little wonder that riots can be ignited in the teeming and oppressively hot ghettos. Heat irritates frustrations.

When thunder warns and rain begins to fall, man instinctively hurries to shelter. Whether he is plowing or dissenting, getting uncomfortably soaked has no appeal, and off he goes, leaving the tilling and demonstrating for later.

Rain helps to disperse restless crowds, and if a storm is coming, those responsible for control may have only to contain the situation until the rain falls and the crowd scatters. A review of the riots of recent times shows that when rain came the intensity of the clash dissipated—and sometimes burned out. This happened one evening during the Chicago riots of 1968, but, unfortunately, not until after the rioting had peaked.

Cold has the same effect on crowds as rain unless the striking and rioting is a protest against hunger, as it was in Russia. Snowfall, too, takes its toll, causing crowds to scatter from the scene of the action, whether it be a riot or a game. A shivering protester finds standing on the picket line hard when he is thinking of hot food and a warm bed; leaders find it difficult, if not impossible, to keep the fires of militancy hot. A cold man is more concerned with physical discomfort than with ideas.

For years unions and managements fought over the date on which an agreement ended and employees could go out on strike. Management wanted to make the termination date in the middle of winter, and the union obviously wanted the agreement to end in the middle of summer. Whenever management won that issue, a change of date became a perennial union demand. This skirmish has been fought, and is over, but it certainly illustrates what part discomfort can play in striking and rioting.

Avoidance of Extremes

In the face of a milling crowd of dissenters, two extreme positions have to be avoided: the yielding and the inflexible. Total acquiescence may dissolve this afternoon's crisis while creating a more troublesome one for tomorrow morning. Inflexibility solidifies and closes the ranks of resistance.

The mistake of buying short-term peace at long-range cost has been reviewed in the discussion of conciliatory techniques. Just as it is a mistake during conciliation, so is it an error at the threshold of violence, and for the same reasons. When, by threatening violence, dissenters succeed in intimidating leaders to capitulate, they are led to believe that menace will win their demands at any time.

One executive, inexperienced in union relations, gave in to all the initial demands of the union after he was advised not to. No one was more surprised than the union representative. This led the union to expect that the executive would be an easy mark in the future and set up problems for him the next time negotiations were due to come up. Not only did he jeopardize his own company's relationship, but he set a pattern that employees of other organizations having the same union would expect to be met. As well as causing problems for himself, he did so for other executives and the union leadership. To break the pattern in the future would require a strike, and the longer he took to do so, the more prolonged the strike would be.

At the other end, the rigid position, which sternly says no to every request, reasonable or not, spurs frustration into rage. Among dissenters, even the levelheaded let their disappointment overcome common sense, and they finally go along with their more militant cohorts. There is an observation in the field of negotiations that, while not expecting a complete victory, everyone has to bring back a trophy. Denied that, people are provoked into long and clamorous discord.

This is at the base of the black problem. And only now are we coming to realize how much it has been so. The longer we deny the blacks and other minority groups economic and social opportunity, the more lasting will be the uproar.

Long-overdue realization of this problem has goaded us into pell-mell action, such as trying to overcome the black educational lag overnight. The complex social difficulties created by two centuries of barring them from just opportunity do not lend themselves to superficial solutions. More deliberate long-range plans, as well as present action, will provide a base for opening the way out of the ghettos and for educational and social adjustment to positions of responsibility in the community.

Patience

As Americans, when we have made up our minds to do something, characteristically we want to solve it all today. But there
is no easy solution to our social difficulties. Patience and understanding of the intricacies of the problem must leaven our desire
to solve them now. Our error has been to allow our eagerness to
"set it right this morning" to deafen our ears to more common-
sense recommendations in matters of social concern. We must,
for example, be more patient with prejudice. A very human characteristic, it runs deep and cannot be yanked out by laws alone.
Steady and patient integration of minorities by gradual introduc-
tion and adjustment will succeed where bromide solutions fail.
As prejudice dissolves, as minorities are prepared educationally,
acceptance will come, and along with it dignity and respect.

No one is to be blamed for these social conditions. They have
evolved subtly over many decades. We can decry our lack of foresight, but as humans we are neither all-wise nor all-seeing. What
we need to do is to turn our innovative energies fully to the problems. Grand plans we need, but only those based on common
sense. We must not allow the guilt of neglect to rush us into ill-
conceived action.

Human relations, where differences are involved, requires a
spirit of give-and-take. No one is completely right, and an inflexible stand is almost invariably the wrong one. The skill is in
knowing when to stand and when to give.

Resistance to Insult

A leader must not stand by and permit an unruly group to
flout his position, nor should he give in to deliberate taunting.
Tolerating flouting and being drawn into a taunting bout are
taken to be signs of weakness and only increase the boldness of the
dissenters. To allow a student to deliberately mock authority in
the presence of the administrator himself demeans the authority
of both the position and the man. This is the time for firmness.
Authority has to be exercised promptly, for where taunting goes
unchallenged by a leader, he plays into the hands of the taunter.
Should the demonstrators find themselves in control, the possibility
of violence is increased. At this critical turning point, the exercise

of authority will curb the action, perhaps dissolve the group. Laxity only encourages a further display of arrogance, and can easily lead to rioting.

One night, in a military barracks housing soldiers all of whom had been reduced in rank from noncommissioned officers to privates, one of the soldiers, returning from a beery social hour, flouted the authority of the sergeant. He dared him to take off his stripes and have it out. Others quickly pressed around the two. The soldier shouted insults. The sergeant, after waiting for the man to run out his rant, firmly said that the stripes represented the authority of his position, that he would not take them off. Further, he said that if the man didn't quiet down and go to bed, he would call the sergeant of the guard and have him taken to the guardhouse. The soldier said he was afraid. The sergeant said no, that he was only doing what his duties said he should do under the circumstances. Again he repeated his warning, more loudly and, as he said, for the last time. One of the soldier's sober friends reminded him that he had already been disciplined, that the sergeant was right, and that he could only lose. The soldier quieted down. This could have turned into a bruising barracks brawl, but it was curbed in time.

This is a homely illustration, but should make the point.

Taunting is an old schoolyard tradition and has probably accounted for more preadolescent black eyes than any other youthful prank. The schoolboy takes it with him into adult life, where he may use it when disagreement is involved. For a leader to let taunts raise his blood pressure and tease him into bitter retaliation is to put a chip on everyone's shoulder, and reduces the conflict to back-alley bickering. Again the leader has played into the dissenters' hands, and his stature and authority are lessened in the minds of those around him.

Obscene taunts were common during the Chicago riots and contributed to the fury of the clashes that took place in the streets and in the parks. Even the mayor was visibly ruffled by them, and the news media did little to help. There appears to be some evidence that the taunting became so vicious that it measurably increased cuts, bruises, and bloodshed. This was a dramatic case, sweeping in scope, but in less massive confrontations the same holds true. In fact, clashing outbreaks are almost always preceded by taunts, which lead to the chip-on-the-shoulder and threatening jeer stages just before the action breaks.

Obviously, whenever a leader seeks to control a crowd from

turning to riotous acts, he should, as best he can, ignore the taunts aimed at him. Their purpose is to mock, embroil, and cause loss of control, and if they are ignored, the barb falls to the ground—useless and ineffective.

Sympathetic Projection

Even though firmness and decisiveness are necessary to ward off or control violence, care has to be taken not to project hostility. When faced by a leader, a crowd that is stirred up and unruly may already have feelings of hostility toward him and the institution, and any action, word, or gesture by him that can be interpreted as unfriendly will only intensify their animosity.

Because such an impression is so frequently an unconscious one, a leader must consciously alert himself to this possibility and observe with sensitivity the group reaction to what he does or says.

One executive flew quickly to a location on the West Coast to quiet a clamor among a group of employees who were threatening to join a union and go on strike. He was advised not to attempt this himself, but to leave the problem to others more skilled in employee relations. Within a day he sent a long wire to headquarters saying that he had met with the group and had tried to sell them on staying unorganized and giving up the idea of a strike; but, far from buying his plea, they had been hostile.

The facts were that promises had been made to these employees for a number of years by a manager who never came through with them. Wages were not competitive, and working conditions left a great deal to be desired. No one from headquarters had been to the West Coast location for some time and the employees apparently thought they didn't know about the complaints, or didn't care. Suddenly, as they turned to the union for help, an executive from headquarters appeared to sell them on the idea that all was going to be sweetness and light, and that they must not turn to the union for what management would give them. The executive was new to the group, and they had never seen him before. His hard-selling manner came through to them more as an order than a plea, and, as far as they were concerned, with the same old story. No wonder their hostility rose. In fact, all of them were simply damned mad. The union won the election handily.

In fairness to the executive, relations and conditions had deteriorated to such an extent that it was questionable whether any move could have saved the day. Nevertheless, his approach was all wrong. He took no time to investigate, to question quietly and candidly, to find out how the group actually felt about the situation. Nor did he spend any time with them hoping to win at least a degree of acceptance. Had he done this, some of the hostility could have been dispelled. But his brusque, almost dictatorial manner, although completely unintentional, and his promise to keep promises made and not kept in the past convinced them that a union was needed.

The Importance of Interpretation

When a crowd or group is already showing hostility, anyone who appears before them in an attempt to quiet the restlessness and resentment has to be exceedingly careful that the words, gestures, facial expressions, and general movements he uses will not be interpreted as hostile to the group and its grievances.

As we all know, the clenched fist at the top of a raised arm may express strength, defiance, or hostility. How it will be interpreted by a crowd depends upon who makes the gesture and for what purpose. If the leader of dissenters raises his fist before the crowd, it is taken as a sign of strength or defiance. If the leader against whom the dispute is directed raises his fist to emphasize a point, it may well be seen as a threatening gesture, particularly when emotions are running high. In contrast to the fist is the open-handed gesture. Arms stretched out with palms turned up implies an open, friendly attitude, or even a plea to be heard. Arms extended with raised wrists and palms faced toward others is read as a defensive, stay-away signal or a rejection. Arms at the sides may imply a neutral position, and extended behind the back, a defenseless one.

As emotions become more tense, the eyes of the crowd magnify and, in varying degrees, distort actions. At a critical point, a fist raised for whatever purpose will be read by a crowd as a threat, and they may turn in defiance to resist it. Hands outstretched may be accepted as a conciliatory gesture.

Facial expressions are also watched. A serious face or one void of expression may be interpreted as signifying extreme disapproval.

One executive turned a picket line away from imminent hostility to guarded acceptance by the simple act of appearing friendly and saying hello as he passed the line. The pickets believed he would be angry at them, but the executive was careful not to appear either angry or as having any desire for reprisal. By acting this way, he neither raised additional fears nor provoked heated resistance that might have caused serious picket-line incidents.

How actions can be distorted occurred in one plant where an executive carried a pistol inside during a strike. He was a pistol buff and, having time on his hands, decided to work on and test the weapon. Pickets saw him with the pistol and concluded that he was practicing to use it on them if necessary. His actions stiffened their resentment and resulted in restlessness and angry incidents on the picket line.

The use of arms as part of an attempt to control impending or actual rioting is dangerous. The dissenters may look on them as an indication that they are lawbreakers and culprits instead of peaceful men demonstrating their dissatisfactions. Hostility may rise as a result, as the presence of arms undoubtedly keys up the emotional pitch. And, when loaded, there is always the possibility of accidental firing, injury, or even death. If they must be used, arms should be kept unloaded and out of the way, or at least not held ready until absolutely necessary. Only as a last resort, when rampaging leaves no other course, should they be brought to the ready and fired.

The selection of words is also to be watched. Those that may normally inflame emotions will strike even more discord when the group is already incensed. Using words which are degrading to the listener, such as "fool," "dumb," "old," "worthless," and so on, are alone enough to cause smoldering restlessness to blaze. Careful selection of words—those highly imperfect transmitters of meaning—is critical during confrontation with dissent.

No vindictive act or threat of anyone should be used in front of dissenters. Singling out one or several from the group, castigating them, threatening them, or carrying out penalties such as discharge or arrest can develop a bitterness that will linger long after the strife is settled, as well as add to the difficulty of bringing it to an end.

A Lesson from Attica

The violent action during the 1970 prison revolt at Attica is now history, but what happened may serve as a lesson for the future. Although some of the causes and what actually happened will never become clear—it never does in the aftermath of violence

—some points emerged from the controversy that I believe are significant.

The seizure of hostages was not spontaneous, but planned to appear so by professional activists in the group, and possibly on advice from the outside.

Russell Oswald, New York commissioner of corrections, made a mistake in granting 28 demands immediately, leaving only two, amnesty and the firing of Attica prison superintendent Vincent Mancusi, for further negotiation. Because the remaining two were denied categorically, no room was left for maneuver, and an impasse was immediately set up. The concessions made too quickly may have raised hopes too high, and deepened the disappointment when nothing else was granted.

The committee that entered the prison for negotiations was a sort of ragtag bunch, composed of too many with too little experience and too much emotion. They were high on idealism and short on practice. Bobby Seale and William Kunstler began to argue for the prisoners, when their assignment was to help persuade them to dispel. This was ridiculous in the middle of this explosive climate, because, instead of helping, the turnaround tactic of these two became a disruptive force.

By the time the assault was ordered, it was unlikely that further negotiations would have produced anything constructive. What was there left to negotiate over? The prisoner demands left little flexibility. In my opinion, Governor Rockefeller's presence would have been an error. Unquestionably, the prisoners would have wanted to see him; he would have dominated the situation and undercut the authority of those immediately in charge, reducing their stature for the future.

Amnesty should not have been granted, aside from the fact that legally it was impossible. That would have amounted to capitulation. Whether or not the demand to fire Mancusi was a legitimate grievance, Oswald could hardly have granted it under the circumstances because it was presented as an ultimatum. A fact to be kept in mind is that Attica is a high-security prison, containing criminals with serious crimes on their records. Certainly they are human beings, but they have forgone certain privileges by committing crimes against society.

The throat-cutting report, later disproved, was the result of distortion through emotionally charged eyes and ears. Hostages were in prison dress; rain, smoke, and confusion made identity impossible.

While the riot was an unfortunate tragedy, Rockefeller believed there was no other course. Delay might have led to more death and injury, as the prisoners had entrenched themselves and were making weapons, including bombs.

The basic problem is the penal system. Although modernization is making progress, it lags too far behind the needs of the times. Some penologists say that the old system, which is still applied with a heavy hand and in the same rigid way that has been practiced for years, is unable to respond to the rapid changes taking place in society. Prison administrators and their staff are still entirely white while the prison population is predominantly black and Spanish-speaking. This racial dichotomy deepens the hostility between prisoners and the system. It is also said that dissenters, both on the inside and the outside, deliberately arouse prisoners. They do not accept what they consider to be unfair restrictions and punishment with the same stoicism characteristic of the "hard liner" of the past. The uprisings, in the opinion of these authorities, are only reflections of the social unease and restiveness in the world outside. At fault is institutional lag.

10

Institutional Causes
of Accord

THE characteristics of an institution that will cause dissent to rise
—the marks of an institution in decline—have already been discussed. Now it would seem appropriate to examine what the characteristics are of an institution that fosters reasonable accord and
agreement among its members. These are the ones found in progressive organizations—progressive in the sense that members are
generally in assent with the way their executives run institutional
affairs; they believe that their leaders have the best interests of
members as well as the general objectives of the organization in
mind. To a degree these characteristics are the opposite of those
fostering discord; but they are also more than that.

Searching Attitude

A progressive organization is never satisfied with the status quo,
never content with things as they are. The outlook is that, in a
dynamic world, to follow the mission of guarding the traditions
and old practices of the organization is not only to stand still but
to fall behind.

138

Ever present in such an organization is the expression of dis-satisfaction with ideas, approaches, techniques, programs and practices, systems, products, and services as they are. Seeking im-provements or new ideas is a daily, not an occasional or casual, activity. Dissatisfaction of this kind is not critical or negative, nor does it condemn the past for lack of foresight. In fact, respect for tradition is there, though not blind adherence to it. The attitude is a positive one, not of what is wrong, but of how we can improve to meet tomorrow's as well as today's challenge. Yesterday is a word of little use among those with this view.

A searching attitude is a quality of the young-minded, but it is not entirely due to youth. Truly inventive individuals seem to retain an eagerness for the new until they themselves are old, and a number of them appear to live longer than the rest of us. As we advance in age, most of us become more critical of the present, tending to measure its ethics and activities with standards of the past. What we forget is that the world is changing while we are not. The more one harps on the present, the further he is living in the past.

Within such an environment there is a strong bent for improve-ment, of never being satisfied with how affairs are being run now. Explanations marshaling a long list of reasons that attempt to prove why a suggested change will not succeed raise a restless push for seeing how it can be done. Even though the negative position may turn out to be the correct one when judged later from hind-sight, the "no" position is met with something less than enthusiasm, and sometimes the change is willfully forced against considered advice which time later proves to be right. But in a surprising percentage of decisions, the "yes" position proves to have been in the best interests of the organization.

Ebullience, the lively expression of ideas, is encouraged. En-thusiasm for new ideas is stimulated, not doused, and the air is full of zest, not pessimism. Generally speaking, this is a function of organization age. The longer an institution has been in operation, the chances are that it may have less of the searching attitude and be more comfortable with the time-tested patterns of the past. What is forgotten is that the patterns were fitted to conditions not in existence now. A belief that time-tested methods are practically infallible obscures the need for modified or new approaches. When, as pointed out before, tradition takes over, the institution loses its forward drive and slips into a decline. But, in a progressive organization, the questioning view and a willingness to try new concepts become the tradition, and smug satisfaction is not tolerated. Its actions are constantly being injected with new ideas that keep propelling it forward.

One organization increased its size by 300 percent within a period of seven years. Such success did not come about by accident. A number of reasons account for it, not the least of which was the top executive's insistence on and personal attention to searching for, analyzing, and testing new techniques. Some of them failed, but results have proved that many were valuable contributions.

Other organizations have enjoyed a surge of growth, not necessarily spectacular, but continuing. Much of it is due to the fruitful mind of an innovative leader, forever searching, testing, trying.

Flexibility

This is the ability of an organization to bend without breaking. Rigid resistance to the internal and external dynamics of change is absent. Some of our institutions, centuries old, are here today because their founders and successors have followed the philosophy that bending with the times is necessary to keep them alive, and have guided the affairs of their institutions with this supple principle in mind. But many others, failing to recognize this principle, have presided over the demise of crumbling structures.

Strict adherence to time-proven policies may be successful only so long as the conditions these were designed to meet remain essentially unchanged. But to stand adamant before the forces of societal upheaval that confront us today—the demand for more individual responsibility and freedom, for example—is to become organizationally brittle. Older organizations, because they are more susceptible to diseases of old age, atrophy, or wasting away, have to be more sensitive to proneness of falling victim to organizational senility.

Flexibility appears as willingness to accept the need for change. Those executives who cannot adjust to or accept suggestions for change have dissatisfied members in their units. To them altering the status quo is a threat, and their reaction is to treat a new idea as such, either fighting the proposal or ignoring it, hoping the danger will go away. These are unfortunate individuals. Fear drives them to build a protective fortification around their activities, which, battered by the insistence for advance, fall. So does the executive.

The satisfactions of those who belong to an institution relate directly to the degree that executives are flexible. The flexible leader manages not only the present, but the future as well. While considering what to do, he ponders the impact of today's decision and projects whether it will stand the test of time or cause problems as his organization moves ahead.

If, for example, his immediate problem involves member relations, such as his subordinates' insistence on deciding matters of concern to them, he does not overlook their demand simply because past and present practice has been to keep such decisions in top hands only. He decides to alter the system to include lower levels more directly in the decision process, believing it to be a fair and correct move. He knows too, that if the system isn't flexed to meet changing attitudes, dissatisfactions will mount into an active form of dissent, perhaps not now, but eventually.

One top executive and his group have done exactly that. The system has been changed from a paternalistic to a more democratic one. When a suggestion is made for a new approach to solving problems, the thoughts of those affected are sought. This is not confined to the top, but, depending upon its scope, the problem may be discussed at several or at all levels. Morale is excellent, and accord exists between the top and the lower levels. It can be seen in the attitude of mutual respect present when they face each other.

In contrast to this is another organization, whose leadership believes it knows more about the conduct of affairs than anyone else and excludes others as being unable to contribute except to a very minor degree. Advice about what can be expected in the future is politely ignored. There is a discouraged and negative atmosphere and the turnover rate is high. Dissatisfactions are reaching the critical stage.

Demand for Action

In an institution where accord and consent exists between the leaders and other members, the top command is action-oriented. Thoughtful consideration is given to decision making, but action is demanded and undue delay simply not allowed. The energy level of the leadership group is high; so is the accomplishment rate. To those used to a slack environment, the speed with which decisions are made is breathtaking.

When any executive exhibits an inclination to overdeliberation and inaction, his seniors and equals, as well as his subordinates, become very restive. Flimsy excuses for failure to act are unacceptable. And, if he cannot mend his ways, he either leaves or is invited to go.

Basic to a demand for action is that any appeal, request, or recommendation by a member be answered as rapidly as possible. Satisfaction is evidenced by such comments as "Things get done here," and "We may not always agree with it, but we get the answer."

Reasonably rapid action on requests from members is a right they have to expect from those in charge. This is particularly true today, in a society where there is a strong drive for more independence; more than ever no man is another man's master. Fast action does much to develop accord and consent among members: tension and concern over a problem that is bothering an individual or group is relieved, and the feeling develops that the top really cares about the well-being of those whom it is their responsibility to lead. Although a particular concern may seem to be minor in relation to all the problems with which leadership has to contend, to those who are bothered the problem is a real one. Otherwise, the appeal would not have been raised in the first place. So, to develop accord, it is important for leadership to be concerned with and act on all requests, not just those it believes to be important.

In one institution a number of groups waited for several years for adoption of their recommendations. After hopefully expecting action and seeing none, a high percentage left in discouragement. Had action taken place at a reasonable rate, a number of talented members would have stayed. The problem here lay in procrastination at the top.

In another organization, where time-limit guidelines have been set to measure the effectiveness of actions taken in answer to requests, the number who leave is small. Satisfaction with conditions, while not complete, is exceptionally high. Setting time-limit guidelines is an excellent technique for ensuring that requests are being satisfied.

It is well known among those familiar with the military services that the officers that men want to serve under are those who are competent in taking care of their needs and gripes; the officers labeled with derisive nicknames are those who do nothing.

Sensitivity

Sensitivity means an awareness of new conditions affecting the course of the institution. Leadership looks outward, beyond the immediate confines of the organization, into the world at large. The outlook is not parochial, not local.

Sensitivity combines with a searching attitude in recognizing the need for adjusting the structure and practices of an institution to align with different conditions as the world moves into another era. Sensitive leadership is aware of the ground swell of antipollution sentiment and has anticipated how widespread and real it would become. Instead of hoping that the public demand for eliminating pollution will go away, it makes plans and takes steps to cooperate in getting rid of the causes. There are those who have done exactly this.

Sensitivity is insight into the objectives of the organization in terms of its responsibilities to the public as well as its members, stockholders, alumni, and others. One of these is to cooperate with the various government agencies, political parties, welfare organizations, and other civic activities. This can take the form of lending capable administrators to assist them in operating their functions where competent managers are in short supply. This sort of contribution—of donating time and effort—strikes a note of approval both within and outside the institution.

Top commands that are sensitive in the sense intended here do not live, either mentally or physically, in a sterile atmosphere within the executive suite. They study economic, social, and other, more specific, conditions having an impact on the course of their affairs, and they attend and participate in meetings, programs, and seminars to keep themselves sensitively alert to what the trends are. Today many of these gatherings are international in scope as the need for a wider exchange of ideas and information is recognized.

Traveling to and from meetings is not simply an excuse to go to interesting places as an additional reward—a perquisite—although that can sometimes be combined with the more serious purpose. The intent is to select sessions and plan schedules for various executives, the purpose of which is to prevent them from falling into provincial, narrow habits and to aid them in developing and maintaining a more metropolitan concept and attitude.

Considerable contrast exists between the top echelons of an institution that is provincial and one that has a metropolitan point of view. When considering a new idea or technique, the provincial institution is characterized by the comment, "Well, that may be all right for somebody else, but we're different with our own problems, which only we know how to solve." The metropolitan one, when listening to new suggestions, observes, "The suggestion may have some merit. How can we apply it here?" In any institution these two types of statement will disclose how sensitive leadership is to the dynamics of change.

Effective Communications

All of the sophisticated communications techniques and systems we have available today are of no use when no one is listening. Effective communication *begins* with listening, and, until it, as well as telling, has begun, no actual communication is taking place. Listening is a skill requiring every bit as much sensitivity, insight, and experience as speaking. The primary emphasis in our training as leaders has been on speaking and writing, and too little time is devoted to the fine art of listening—we need to develop those skills.

In an institution where there is reasonable accord, leadership listens and acts upon what is heard. Otherwise, the temper of attitudes would be dissatisfaction. Sensitive listening—giving hard concentration to what someone is trying to get across—helps a leader detect dissatisfactions long before they can build enough pressure to force an active form of dissent.

Explaining actions before initiating them is basic to good communications; it encourages consent instead of allowing rumor to take over and distort the intent of the action. Silence may be golden, but not when actions are involved that affect others. In organizations where members express approval of leadership's conduct, communications are free-flowing, and everyone feels at liberty to say what he thinks without fear. "Furthermore," say subordinates, "they listen to what we offer."

Sound communications are not determined by volume, but by the accuracy, clarity, and timeliness of what is said. In fact, the greater the volume indiscriminately issued, the less effective the communications. This is a mistake made too often. Internally, we kill communications with overbulletinizing, with squandering needless instructions and information that confuse the eyes of the receivers; we lose their attention and with it the intended effect. Random, unrestricted communications bury the important beneath trivia, and increase discontent.

In an organization where members are satisfied with the information forwarded to them to explain what is going on, leadership is careful about what should be said, when, why, and by whom. Also considered is the audience to which the information is to be directed, and, above all, why it has to be sent in the first place.

In addition, an audit—a survey—to measure how well communications are working is taken systematically from time to time. In institutions enjoying good relationships such audits are scheduled for every two to three years, and comparisons are made between them to determine what improvements have been made and whether any new problems have developed of which the top group is unaware.

Where communications are excellent, experience has shown that the top does not assume that it knows how everyone feels about the conduct of institutional activities. Those who make that assumption for too long suddenly find themselves facing an array of active discontent, and are at a loss to explain the causes.

Inventiveness

Inventiveness is related to a searching attitude but goes beyond the point of simple inquiry. New techniques for accomplishing the aims of the institution are created. The unimaginative habit of clinging to the past for answers to the problems facing leadership today and tomorrow is not found in an inventive environment. Creative accomplishment is strongly encouraged, not hobbled by the traditional outlook.

The attitude is optimistic, and discussions center around the opportunities of the future. Pessimism is not to be seen. There is respect, but little nostalgia, for the past; what happened yesterday is of small concern compared to what is planned for tomorrow. Problems are met with the freshness and vigor of youth.

Consideration of new advances is not prejudiced by conventional thinking, nor is leadership reluctant to modify or replace policies or systems that have been adhered to for a relatively long period of time. And credit for new adaptations is carefully assigned.

Opportunities and support are provided for testing and developing ideas into useful devices. One of our successful and long-enduring corporations has a tradition of nurturing inventiveness. The organizational environment for its engineers and scientists is deliberately structured to stimulate research for the new, and every effort is made to allow as much freedom as possible. That the results be of immediate practical use is not always imposed as a standard. Freedom to develop new techniques is not confined to technology alone, but appears in other areas as well throughout the organization. As a result of its healthy outlook, this corporation has been able to remain supple and adaptive while many others have aged and passed into history. And because self-expression is encouraged in an inventive atmosphere, the satisfaction of those involved is high.

Much of the discontent in institutions today is caused by the structure's inability to provide opportunity for self-expression. Work has become so divided, routinized, and monotonic that the basic need for self-expression is thwarted and has to seek an outlet beyond the work location. For years some organizations and research groups, fully aware of the problem, have been experimenting with techniques to enlarge or enrich work by putting more variety and meaning into it. This approach has much to offer as a constructive innovation and will probably become widespread in the future, as more experience and more highly developed methods become available.

Inclusiveness

Institutions in which the climate is one of accord take a more open view of activities than others. The degree of participation by members is high. The decision makers have wider latitude than their counterparts in similar organizations. And participation in decision making at all levels will be more inclusive.

Independence of action is deliberately fostered. Defensive holding on to details is discouraged. Withholding information and secretiveness aren't allowed. Free exchange of information is not only permitted but encouraged.

Because of the inclusive attitude, more youthful participation will be found. Younger members are a part of higher-level activities to a larger extent than are their equals elsewhere where little latitude or delegation exists.

Inclusiveness enhances accord for a very basic reason. If an individual or group participates, really and not superficially, in deciding actions affecting them, it follows that they will favor the results. To put it another way, they have "a piece of the action." How can any rational person dissent against his own decision?

An inclusive environment contains room for disagreement. Disagreement is worked out during participation in decision making, so that much of what could create discord later is nipped before it has a chance to grow into a large problem.

Participation is not simply telling others what is going on. To call a number of people into a meeting for the purpose of informing them is not participation. That is good communication, but it is not, as sometimes happens, to be confused with inclusiveness. Participation in its true sense means actual inclusion in the decision-making process.

In one organization, the top. believes that it operates in a participatory style, and, in this case, the top is actually one man. Meetings are called at least once a week for the purpose of discussing problems and to bring others in to assist in solving them. But the fact is that the meetings quickly settle into a series of monologues by the top man. His subordinates hear him, but he never hears what their ideas or thoughts are. As a matter of fact, there is not only no participation but no communication. Much goes on of which he is completely unaware.

The opposite is the case in another organization. Major decisions at the top are group decisions. Important questions are placed on an agenda, and studies are prepared by those most directly concerned and forwarded before the meeting for review by those who are to participate. During the meeting, each question is taken up in turn and subjected to rigorous discussion. Following that, a vote is taken, and the majority generally rules. The top executive seldom exercises his prerogative to overrule the group decision.

This system is applied not only at the top level, but also down the line. Each of the executives participating in the top group has his own section, and he operates with it just as the top group does. The level of accord in this organization is high.

Boldness

A leadership position is no place for the timid or unforceful man. Timidity and lack of force lead to overdeliberation and vacillation, which, in turn, lead to delay and sidestepping in making decisions. The result is a loss of confidence in leadership and the rise of considerable unrest.

Boldness, on the other hand, does not mean rashness—committing the institution to actions on the basis of impulsive and ill-considered judgment. What it does mean is the willingness to take a risk after having carefully studied the alternatives.

Although this applies particularly to new courses of action, it relates also to a searching attitude. But a searching attitude alone, or the demand for action alone, is not enough. It is easy to decide on an action when a tradition of past practice has already established what to do under the circumstances. Far more difficult is the decision where there is no traditional pattern to use as a guideline.

Here is a key point that separates the successful institution from the ordinary one. Without boldness there can be no progress; and without real progress, no satisfaction with the institution's direction.

Bold men are the risk takers. The risk may involve money, reputation, career, or life itself. Hard is the decision to lay any one of these on the line in an attempt to progress. But, risk is the lifeblood of progress, and institutional leadership must be willing to dare if the organization is to move ahead into the future. When leadership loses the will to risk, the organization will decline as it falls behind the movements of the times. And as it declines, dissatisfaction with leadership direction and action mounts.

Winston Churchill was a risk taker. So was Douglas MacArthur. Churchill's boldness in the face of Nazi might and MacArthur's Inchon landing are forever written into history as great acts. The rubber industry owes its founding to Charles Goodyear's faith in an idea and his willingness to go ahead at personal loss. Whether one agrees with it or not, Nixon's decision to let the dollar float and to declare a moratorium on wage and price increases took considerable courage.

All of our great institutions were founded by men and women willing to risk and sacrifice. Christianity is one. Our country is another. Our great banking and industrial organizations are also examples. Whatever the organization, from the huge corporation to the small store manned by husband and wife—the "mom and pop shop"—risk had to be undertaken by the founders. One of our larger merchandising organizations was begun by a husband and wife.

Desire to Serve

Another quality found in a progressive institution is the desire to serve, not only those for which leadership is directly responsible, but also the community at large. This desire is neither superficial nor selfish, but an earnest belief that service to others is a responsibility of leadership as well as a personal obligation. No attempt is made to evade the responsibility; every effort is made to meet it. That an individual may make a legitimate profit at the same time makes service no less valid. The sense of service may be seen in the results—good products, efficient transportation, effective political action, healing, teaching, farming.

Today it is fashionable to criticize profit-making corporations—industrial, merchandising, insurance—as being interested in money and not service. In a number of cases this may be true, but the majority are sincerely trying to provide the best products or services at as reasonable a price as possible. Some of our great economic organizations were founded on this principle, but labor shortages and other difficulties have made flawless products or services more difficult to achieve than ever.

Hucksters, peddling cheap goods, are always with us, but a number of top executives can be justly proud and jealous of their organization's reputation for integrity. Hucksters are not only a blight in the world of trade, but are to be found in any type of institution, often disguised under a title of high status. A political idea of questionable morality, designed to capture a following of the more gullible, is more fraudulent than selling cheap goods—as it may be more damaging. A cry of antipollution to further one's own ends is a case in point.

11

How to Maintain Accord in a Climate of Dissent

TWO approaches should be considered for maintaining accord in a climate of dissent: the short-range and the long-range. The former includes planning for gathering crises, for meeting active dissent that may soon be or has already been set in motion. The latter involves anticipating causes of dissent and acting to remove them before discontent can solidify into the more stormy forms of disapproval. The short-range approach is defensive; the long-range is preventive.

Short-Range Planning

To prepare for such possible crises as picketing, a strike, or a riot, a number of factors should be evaluated: relative strength of position, limits of concession, firmness of stand, control of outbreaks, approach to settlement, and communications.

Relative Strength of Position

When dissent reaches the threatening point, the side threatened, before deciding to stand fast on its position, has to weigh its bargaining strength against that of the other side. The blunt question is: To what extent can the organization afford to take a strike? In a profit-making corporation this is, of course, determined by a look into the bank account, the cash register, and the business coming through the door. If the bank account is low but the register is beginning to ring, the top has no option and can only accede to the demands that have to be met to avoid a strike.

In battles between the industrial giants and the huge unions, such as those that occur in the automotive, steel, and electrical industries, relative strength is constantly on the minds of the top commands and staffs of both sides. Each side has a formidable amount of economic and political muscle available. For years the corporate sinews were stronger than those of the union. But beginning in the 1920s, and following 1935 after the passage of the Wagner Act, the balance turned definitely in favor of the unions.

Strength of position is a basic factor in negotiations. On the union side we see union leaders quoted in the media about the size of their strike funds and how long they can afford to stay out on strike, forcing corporations to suffer a burdensome loss of incoming cash. This is a demonstration of muscle flexing, aimed at scaring the manufacturers, the government, and the public. Industry leadership counters with warnings about the widespread loss of income that will result from a prolonged strike, the adverse effect it will have on the economy, and the severe pressure an out-of-proportion wage increase will put on prices. This is counter-flexing.

In the industrial world the nature of the production process affects the strength of position. The steelmaking process favors the union, whereas in the electrical industry the balance leans toward the manufacturer. Steelmaking, because of its size and the need for water, is highly concentrated in a few areas with large plants. A strike literally shuts down all but a small portion of the industry. The size, the heat—as much as 3000°F—and the process complexities make the shutdown of a basic steel mill a slow, complicated, and costly procedure.

In the electrical industry, on the other hand, many of the facilities are geographically widely dispersed, and the union organization is more varied so that the cohesiveness and militancy necessary for a total strike is practically impossible. The close-down process is less complicated. The strategic position places the balance of power more in the hands of management than in the union.

Few, if any, are the institutions where the cash cost of open dissent—strike or demonstration—is not necessary to assess. Even a university has to consider the effect of a strike on its tuition and contributions. There are also other factors to be considered in determining one's strength of position. If, for example, the dissent is not over wages, but politics, the politician or political group attacked has to think about public reaction to proposed action. When a group of veterans announces its intention to demonstrate peaceably on the Mall to voice anti-Vietnam sentiments, what alternatives does the president have? For one, he can threaten and carry out the arrest of anyone appearing on the Mall and break up the demonstration forcibly, whether the veterans are quiet or not. Suppose the decision were to follow this procedure—when demonstrators appeared in groups, the police would move in, shove, and club the resisters. Public reaction? Anti-Vietnam doves rumble. Those with sons, brothers, and other relatives in Vietnam are offended. And what about servicemen and women from other wars? Although, as citizens, they may not agree with the reasons for the demonstration, as veterans their sympathies go out to the veterans being beaten. Included in this group would be policemen who are also veterans. Obviously, a decision to adopt this tactic would be unwise, as the demonstrators' plight would raise public indignation and bring the public to their side.

On the other hand, if the demonstrators were allowed peaceably to assemble on the Mall or picket the White House, and if police or military force were used only to break up any attempts to disturb the peace, damage property, or cause injury, the public would largely approve, and sympathies would remain with the president.

This is the kind of reasoning it takes to determine accurately what the relative strength of positions between dissenting parties is. An impulsively or carelessly judged strength of position may weaken the bargaining power of either side. The steel industry's sudden attempt to adopt Boulware's strategy, successful within the conditions of the electrical industry, to the different characteristics of the steel world, is a case in point.

Experience has taught that it is unwise to exploit a weak position. If the calculation is that an institution cannot afford a demonstration or a strike because of the relative weakness of its position, which would make it impossible to win, only a foolish leader would decide to resist. Should he do so anyway, he can only lose, and, as pointed out earlier, others will expect that the same course will be followed in the future. And each successive time he holds to this pattern, his power and believability will be reduced.

Strength-of-position estimates should weigh the future, as well as present resources, as having an impact on the correct course of action.

Limits of Concession

Limits of concession means determining how far one side in disagreement with another is willing to go to meet the demands of the other and settle without open dispute. This is the "final position."

To a degree, these limits are determined by the relative strength of positions, which determine one's power to resist the demands of the other side. They are also set on the basis of what the institution can afford to give, unless its position is so weak that there is no alternative to acceding to the demands of the opposition.

If the argument is over a wage demand, the limits are set by the economics of the cost-price relationship and the effect the concession will have on profitability. For example, top corporate executives may decide that an 8 percent increase in wages for each of two years and a 6 percent increase in the third year of an agreement with a union is the most that can be paid without endangering the corporation's competitive position. After consideration of all the pertinent competitive factors, including foreign competition, the decsion is made to set this amount as the outer limit and to make no further concession without a strike. During the actual negotiations, part of this amount is withheld as the two sides trade back and forth, and the full amount may not be offered until immediately before the strike deadline. In fact, if a strike seems to be unavoidable, some percentage of the amount may still be withheld, to be used later in helping to settle the strike.

This is where relative strength enters into the consideration. The limits of concession move directly in proportion to position strength. Limits have to be realistically set equal to the institution's ability to withstand the various pressures brought to bear by all those who have a stake in a peaceful or quick settlement of the dispute. In addition to the union, these include those served by or serving the institution, such as customers, suppliers, the government at all levels, the community, and the public at large. These are the facts of life in all types of disputes, ranging from local squabbles to international crises.

In the community harangue beween the management and the

employees of the Barnard Corporation, described in the next chapter, each side was able to stand against pressures until a settlement within reasonable limits for both was reached; their relative positions of strength were balanced.

In the larger industrial disputes, the position strength and concession limits are complicated by the shadow of the president looming behind the bargaining table; and at critical stages, negotiations sometimes proceed under the watchful eye of the head of the Federal Mediation and Conciliation Service or some other intermediary from the White House. Because large industries and unions can seriously disrupt the economy and cause public discomfort, politics enters the scene. Although some may say that the government policy is one of "hands off" to allow free collective bargaining, this has been more fancy than fact since before the Wagner Act was passed. Curiously, politicians as a group have been led to believe that unions have more political power over member votes than some case studies would conclude, so union leaders have been able to maneuver disputes into Washington where they have won concessions and an enormous increase in position strength.

The political situation, as it is today between unions, government, and management, is in a very unhealthy state. Union leadership has failed to grow from life as it was in the thirties into the realities of the seventies—it is suffering from nearsightedness and orthodoxy from the past. Union leaders are failing to exercise restraint in the use of their powers, and their demands continue to be high and often unreasonable. They seem to be more interested in topping each other's costly increase wins than in whether the increases may be damaging to the economy.

When the 1971 wage-price freeze was announced, union leadership stamped, hollered, and defied the president. These rash acts caused public as well as official indignation to rise. As a result, several top union leaders had to issue statements saying that their remarks had been misinterpreted—a public relations technique, and a thin one, to avoid the embarrassment of making an outright retraction. But their willfulness in demanding and getting much of what they ask demonstrates that the relative strengths of position are so far out of balance that the union position is oligarchic, virtually establishing the concession limits.

Management reached such an arrogant position in the past, but its freedom to decide has been substantially curbed. Now union leadership is following the same course; it too will be curbed. The unions seem to be seriously overestimating the public sympathy for their position, forgetting that Americans are essentially fair-minded and that the force of public indignation can and will exert itself through political action. In fact, union power may be at its apogee and subtly moving into decline, as causes of organizational deterioration have set to work in their institutions.

The federal government has nurtured the power of the unions to such an extent that they are dominating the economy; the government is being forced into the corner and controls have to be exerted to contain the lack of self-discipline in the interunion rivalry. Unions have pyramided their power structure into one controlled by the few. Caught in this web, some of the present leaders lack the desire, maturity, and innovative ability to adjust the direction of unions to new conditions. These well-meaning, unquestionably patriotic men simply lack the capability to see beyond besting each other at the bargaining table; or, if the capability is there, it has yet to be demonstrated. Some years ago certain union executives, echoing that the time had come for "labor statesmanship," claimed with pompous rectitude that this was the direction they intended to follow. Today the statesmanship has yet to come and is never discussed.

Ironically, as leaders seek more power, their actions threaten to weaken their long-term position strength.

As mentioned before, the principles of relative position strength and concession limits are not confined to the labor-management arena; they apply to almost any kind of dispute, whether national or back alley, and should be weighed carefully by any leadership faced with a disagreement, either internal or between organizations. Unfortunately, during the campus rioting the top administrators of some universities were innocent about these principles and did not seem to grasp that the strength lay in their own hands; or, if they were aware of their strength, what to do about it. This is not intended as a snide criticism of the administrators, as their background would not include managing dissent, which demands tough-mindedness as well as experience.

Firmness of Stand

When leaders faced with open dissent have deliberated over the problem and weighed their position strength and concession limits, the decisions they reach should be solid—not to be changed easily, not based on either fear or short-term convenience, and not hastily conceived.

Firmness of stand is not rigidity. Within this context it means "not easily moved," and implies elasticity to resist pulling and pushing. Elasticity is the ability to bend without breaking. Decisions include alternatives that can be substituted for parts or even all of the main position so that maneuverability—elasticity—is provided without going beyond the concession limits. The Barnard Corporation case will illustrate this principle.

In negotiations over wages, alternatives are sometimes offered or demanded in what is known as "end loading." If, for example, the bargaining is for a three-year contract, not only is the total dollar amount in question, but also how it is to be distributed over the three years. Suppose the total package—the concession limits—is set at \$1.20 initially, and the outside limit at \$1.30. Evenly spread, the increase for each year of the contract would be \$.40. One alternative might be to agree to \$.60 the first year, \$.30 the second year, and \$.30 the third year. This is front-end loading. Another might be to agree to \$.30 the first year, \$.30 the second year, and \$.60 the third year. This would be rear-end loading. Obviously, the union or other negotiating agency would want the money loaded on the front because it tallies up to more money over the three years, and management would want the opposite because it costs less. Different scales can be calculated as trading goes back and forth until a settlement is reached, with or without a strike.

This is a simplified version and does not cover the complexities involved in negotiating for pensions, insurance, medical benefits, holidays, vacations, and a variety of other items; but it does show essentially how elasticity is brought to bear—how to be maneuverable but firm. The giving is kept within, not outside, the concession limits.

Firmness of stand is possible only if it is solidly constructed for the realities of the situation, and must be reasonably held to if present and future believability is to be established. Government intervention in negotiations weakens the capability of the parties to hold to a position, and is one reason for Washington's reluctance to intervene. But, as discussed, the imbalance of position strength between big unions and business has made it practically impossible for the government not to become involved.

Control of Outbreaks

When dissent is tending toward an active form and may, within a short time, break out into a demonstration, strike, or riot, plans should be laid and procedures set up and thoroughly practiced to prevent mistakes and develop coordination. Instructions have to be clear and concise; steps should be taken to assure that everyone involved understands what he is supposed to do to avoid confusion when the breakout occurs. Faulty plans and sloppy procedures for control of active dissent have frequently caused more violence and destruction than they have prevented.

First, plans and procedures should outline *where* the breakout will probably happen—in front of a plant, a government building, or a number of different plants, government buildings, parks, or other locations.

Secondly, the estimate should predict *when* the crisis is most likely to occur—on a weekday, weekend, holiday—and at what time. Frequently this is set by agreement, as in labor-management contracts. Or it may be announced publicly, as in marches in Washington, in other cities, or on campuses. Otherwise, informal lines of communication have to be set up to signal the warning.

Thirdly, *how* it may begin has to be outlined. Is the protest to be in the form of a demonstration? A strike? What are the chances that a demonstration may suddenly turn into a riot? Plans and procedures should be designed to cover each of these possibilities. As experience has shown, a dissenting demonstration may inadvertently turn from a peaceful one into a riot; and without coordinated procedures for quelling a breakout, the rioting and destruction will spread and run rampant, stopping only from exhaustion or a lucky piece of bad weather.

The proper authorities, concerned with keeping the peace, need to be advised as far in advance of the incident as possible, and any plans and procedures should be reviewed with them to get their advice and enlist their aid. One of the reasons for the success of the Chicago Labor Detail was the spirit of cooperation between its officers and those anticipating picketing when a strike was imminent.

For years large corporations with complex operations have had manuals covering strike procedures in which every necessary move is carefully detailed. Shutdowns, for example, are carried out quietly and efficiently.

Along with what might take place, the size of the dissenting group has to be considered. This would seem to be obvious, but at times too little attention, or none at all, has been given to this question, and an underestimation of the size finds well-trained but undermanned forces helpless in the face of a threatening riot.

It is absolutely essential that the procedures firmly and clearly fix who is in charge of what, where, and when. Authority should be delegated as much as possible to those at the scene of the crisis so that quick decisions can be made and actions taken to quell the outbreak before it runs rampant. Delegation also provides the flexibility to meet unexpected turns of events, which surely will occur.

Very important in such plans and procedures is the selection of personnel to carry them out. Selection is a question not only of numbers, but of personalities and temperaments as well. The situation calls for coolness and the ability to think rapidly under pressure. High-strung, impulsive individuals will act rashly; timid ones may not act at all at a time when action is paramount. This is no place for Nervous Nellies. Nor is meanness of temperament desirable—these are the ones who will overreact with a vengeance.

The right temperament for the job isn't enough by itself. Training in what he is to do, how he is to do it, and how he can meet the unexpected has to be added, and it must be drilled into him so that he can become self-disciplined under pressure.

As within any group of human beings, the perfect man for the job does not exist, but by eliminating those who score low on the scale of selection standards, a capable group can be assembled.

If the criteria spelled out here are followed, an organization should be well equipped to meet dispute emergencies—able to control outbreaks when they form or to keep them from happening in the first place.

Approach to Settlement

How to reach agreement following a dispute is covered in other chapters, so that little need be added here except to stress again the point that, if at all possible, nothing should be said, written, or done that will spread bitterness during the dispute. Words and acts that create bitterness in others are not easily forgotten, a bitterness that stubbornly refuses to go away, and may linger long after the argument is settled. Certainly it makes reaching agreement much more difficult.

Personal insults, which strike a particularly sensitive chord in others, are to be avoided. Following the announcement of the 90-day wage-price freeze, a government official verbally assailed a labor leader for balking against compliance. While doing so, he inferred that the man was behind the times and old. Although the leader was vigorous he was clearly sensitive about his age, as his blast back at the official revealed. The insult only made him balk even more against cooperating to help the administration hold the wage-price freeze.

Unnecessary mistreatment of a protester should never occur. The history of dissent is full of incidents where needless or vicious physical attacks have only created bitterness and immeasurably increased the difficulty of settlement.

In one corporation a request was made by a group of employees to work an overtime day on their own. The reason for this was to give a day's earnings to the family of an employee permanently disabled in an accident. Compensation was already being provided for him by the company, and legal counsel advised that, technically, permitting this could set a costly precedent. Relationships with the group were good, having been carefully restored after a period of considerable discord.

The decision was to allow the men to work. Objectively, the decision would have had to be no. But other reasons overrode the purely legal ones—humaneness was the foremost. Another important consideration was that the group understandably would have reacted bitterly and set relationships back into the discord of before.

Communications

Here, too, much has already been discussed in other chapters, and little can be added. However, sensitivity to what will inflame and what will mollify angry dissenters is so important that it should be stressed again.

Care must be taken that communications are accurately sent and accurately received. During an uproar of active dissent, communications have a way of being distorted, at times deliberately by those whose purpose is to increase the fury of the discord, and at other times unconsciously by those whose eyes and ears see and hear through emotional distortion. By repeating the same communication several times in several different ways the sender can improve the chances that the message will be received accurately.

A line of communication should be kept open between the dissenting groups so that no void is created between the two which will require mediation to repair. While this is not always possible, mediation can often be avoided by pointedly directing attention to maintaining an open line. For example, communications should be routed through individuals who are calm and conciliatory as well as experienced in working in an atmosphere of discord.

Important also is to keep in mind that, during periods of disputes, emotions rise, and when people are inflamed, appeals to reason may fall dead while those to the emotions are heard. Appealing to another's sense of fairness may be more successful than outlining the facts coldly and explaining why an offer to negotiate a difference is logically just. The explanation of the logic should come after the other party has heard and responded to a sense of fair play, not before. Reversal of this order has caused many unsuccessful attempts to win over another.

Long-Range Planning

Long-range planning anticipates the causes of dissent. Institutions live in a dynamic environment, and only by remaining current with the changing world and adjusting to different conditions can an organization avoid disruptive disagreement.

A number of techniques are available to an organization for use in preventing the more active forms of dissent from happening. Primary among them are listening devices for gauging the changing attitudes and wants of its members.

Listening Devices

Reliance cannot be placed on the normal channels of communication to provide a complete profile of the attitudes of members and others affected by top decisions. The more authoritarian the command style of an organization is, the less accurately will attitudes be gauged through regular communications systems. The reason for this is simply that the authoritarian structure is habitually tuned to telling instead of listening. Present also is a fear of reprisal for speaking up. A democratic style will encourage more openness and produce a better grasp of attitudes; but to get a truly accurate measure of the degree of accord and discontent, definite techniques for sensing attitudes ought to be used.

A system for processing grievances needs to be an integral part of an organization structure. To be effective, such a system has to protect members from reprisal; resolve complaints rapidly; and have representation for members less able to speak for themselves. Final appeal must be beyond the unit of the organization within which the grievance arises. In union-management relations, the grievance and arbitration system is a common one, spelled out in hundreds of agreements. It begins with an employee's appeal to an elected representative from his own group. Next, a discussion is held with the supervisor. If the grievance cannot be solved there, the question is taken to the next level of supervision and employee representation. Failing at that step, the grievance is taken to the third level of supervision and the professional union representative. If the two still disagree, they may submit the problem to an independent arbitrator, or take it one step higher and then place it in arbitration.

The system can and does work well, depending upon the intelligence, fairness, and trust that exist between the employee, the union, and management.

Adaptations of this are used in other organizations, allowing members to form and present their suggestions or complaints through the group rather than forcing the individual to speak for himself—which for many of us is very hard to do because of shyness, fear, or inability to talk to those in a senior position. For these reasons, no matter how much we may encourage others to speak out individually, the majority will not do so, preferring to stay silent before their seniors. Within their own group and to their own representatives, however, they will express grievances and ideas.

Where a system of this type runs parallel to and supports the regular organization lines, grievances that may grow into active dissent have a much better chance of being brought into the open and solved before the situation becomes serious. The reverse is true where no parallel system is integrated into the structure.

In this sense the "open-door policy" may be a myth, and those who believe that by keeping the door open all problems will come through may be ignorant of sore grievances beyond the door. What does come through may be largely what others believe those on the inside want to hear.

An excellent listening device is the attitude, or opinion, survey. This is an anonymous appraisal of individual and group attitudes on certain questions by means of interviews or questionnaires. Public opinion polls are common, and reports from them are published almost daily by the press. Some are excellent, carefully constructed and taken; others are less reliable. On the whole, survey techniques, because of continuing refinements introduced into the methods, are reliable and useful.

The survey is used to sound out attitudes of members of institutions of any type, from employee groups to members of parishes. Many organizations have used this technique for years, but it is not yet so widely applied as it will be. As accountants review the financial position of an organization on a systematic basis to discover the state of its health, so should an audit be taken to reveal what attitudes toward the organization are and to spot conditions where dissent may rise out of dissatisfactions. Almost invariably, attitude surveys reveal discontent of which the top has been unaware, and the revelation always comes as a surprise. But they also bring the positive attitudes into clear relief. Taken together the positive and negative results provide a base for systematic correction.

The attitude survey is a positive technique. It enables the top to seek out what the members feel should be done to improve the organization, without waiting for trouble to bring complaints to the surface. The survey is also positive in the sense that, when it is completed and the top acts on the results, members of the institution believe that their leaders truly are interested in their well-being.

One of the most important aspects of an attitude survey is that the anonymity of the individual is carefully safeguarded and he can speak up without fear. Surveys in written form are coded and processed in such a way that no one inside an organization sees them, or could identify one if he tried. Interviews, if this approach is followed, are conducted by professionals, skilled at interviewing and known for their personal integrity.

The survey may be extended into the community where the organization is located if a broader profile of attitudes seems desirable. Actually, these surveys are quite important, since they reveal any changing conditions in the community that may be affecting the direction of the institution. "Community survey" here is used in the broad sense, to include the total area in which the organization operates.

Through these listening devices the leaders of an institution, of whatever kind and size, are able to keep a sensitive ear to shifts or changes in attitudes and wants of members, and can respond accurately and rapidly to them. The structural insulation that superior-subordinate relationships create between leaders and members is reduced, and the top level remains acutely aware of new conditions, not innocently immune to them.

Being aware of attitude changes is not the whole answer. Action in response is essential to satisfy members and to maintain faith in the sincerity of leadership's interest in their welfare. Responsiveness increases believability and approval. Failure to respond, as always in human affairs, fans disapproval and finally produces active dissent as the only way to get action. This is even more true if members and others know that the top is aware but does nothing. Ignorance of the problems may be excusable, but failure to act in the face of the obvious is not.

Listening for the need for change and responding adaptively to current needs keeps an organization healthy and prevents structural obsolescence from developing. Listening should not be concentrated only in the present, but turned toward the future, so that the institution can anticipate and prepare for its impact and be ready to adapt to its needs with minimal disruption.

12

Case Study:
A Fall from Accord

THIS chapter and the next present a case study in dialogue to illustrate how a calm situation can suddenly fall into a welter of discord. The case follows the development from passive to active dissent—a strike—and continues until a peaceful conclusion is reached. Chapter 14 gives an analysis of the on-stage personalities and the forces at work.

The case study is a composite of real events. The Barnard Corporation is, of course, fictitious. For illustration purposes, an industrial setting has been chosen because of the long experience unions and management have had with problems of dissent. The language has been cleaned up, as it would serve no useful purpose here to include profanities.

While the scene is industrial, the basic elements of dissent in this situation are universal to all types of institutions. By changing the name of the organization, the terminology, and the location, and by modifying the characterizations and scenes of action, the illustration can apply to a university, a public institution, a religious group, or any other organization.

The Barnard Corporation has been in existence for 60 years. It is headed by its third chief executive officer, who has been in that position for the past 20 years. He manages in the traditional patriarchal style. Although the corporation has not been particularly noted for progressive management, neither has it had a reputation for being backward. It has simply run the middle ground. Management is gray-haired, hard-working, and pragmatic.

The organization has grown from the founder and one employee to 10,000 employees. Still occupied are some of the original facilities, along with newer ones added over the years. The corporate offices are not plush, as though in deference to the founder, who scowls shrewdly on the doings of his successors from a portrait in the board room. Among the employees, some are second-, and, in some cases, third-generation.

Management has tried to encourage good relations with its employees by supporting athletic teams, outings, picnics, and awarding long-service pins. Retirement dinners are also held. It participates in community activities, such as charity drives, when asked to do so by the community leadership.

Communications with employees are maintained largely through a publication that includes thoughts from the president on free enterprise and government control, reports of employee activities, and accounts of events in the lives of individual employees. It is a modest but well-presented publication.

Although the corporation is not so profitable as it once was, earnings are still respectable. Between management and employees, a state of accord appears to exist, and there has been no apparent dissension. Viewed from the top, employees seem to be reasonably satisfied and loyal. In the past, the employees have not asked to be represented by a union.

Then it happened and management was dumbfounded.

A group of five employees asked to see one of the younger officers, Charles Rogers, to discuss a matter privately with him. Suspecting that they wished to talk about employee activities, Rogers readily agreed, even though he was not directly in charge of them. He asked them to come to his office at the end of the day. Rogers, in his late forties, was a heavyset, gregarious man.

At four o'clock the five employees walked into his office. As they stood uneasily before him, he asked what it was they wanted to discuss. He observed that they were an unusual group, ranging from young employees to one lean and grizzled old-timer. Four of them looked at the fifth, Bob Murray, a young redhead with a boyish face known as an informal leader.

Murray began, "We have been asked to represent all the employees, and I have been asked to speak for us. Before I talk about why we are here, let me say that we believe this is a fine place to work. We like the company, and we like to work for you.

"We have no union. Don't really want one. But, over the past few years, things have changed, and we have put up with things around here that stick in our craw. We hoped that changes for the better would be made. We have tried to suggest. We go to the boss and say, 'We would like this or we would like that.' He listens and says, 'I'll see what I can do.' 'O.K.,' we say. What happens? Nothing! They're good guys, but seems as how they have no say-so. For some time now, we've been talkin' it over with groups among ourselves, and we have been asked to come and tell you how we feel."

"Why me?" asked Rogers.

"Because we think you'll listen, and maybe do something."

"Oh."

"We think some things need to be changed around here. We've waited for them to happen, but they don't. So we came here to talk to you. We're not rabble-rousers, but we want to tell you what we're not happy about, and ask you to meet with us about these things after you've had a chance to consider them. We have a list here. Thanks."

With that they put on their hats and shuffled out of the office.

After they left, Rogers began to read the list. As he read further and further down the list, his eyebrows went up and he whistled in astonishment. Here is the list:

> We the employees of this company have for some time tried to seek what we believe to be fair improvements for us through proper channels, but there has been no action. Therefore, we have formed a committee of five to represent us in asking you to discuss the following items with us.
>
> 1. Representation of some sort for us to submit grievances and suggestions outside the normal channels.
>
> 2. A means for appealing discharges and other disciplinary punishment.
>
> 3. A joint means for reviewing safety and working conditions.
>
> 4. Employee representation for reviewing wage rates and changes in wage rates, particularly where we believe they are unfair, and to ask for increases, which we believe we are entitled to.
>
> 5. The right to strike over disagreements on 30 days' notice.
>
> 6. More holidays and longer vacations.

7. Transfers, promotions, and layoffs to be based on seniority only.

8. Ten minutes at the end of each day to clean up.

9. No overtime work without 48 hours' notice.

10. Vacations to be allowed to be taken throughout the year instead of only between June 1 and September 1.

11. No layoffs without two weeks' notice.

12. No new hires while any full-time employee is on layoff.

13. May leave two hours early on any day when the temperature exceeds 95° for the third day in a row.

14. Ten-day allowance for being off sick with pay, and pay for days not taken.

15. A guarantee of 45 weeks' work a year.

16. All safety, protective clothing, and other devices paid for by the company.

17. Employees be advised 60 days in advance of any planned, substantial changes that affect their jobs, and that they may appeal those they believe to be against their best interests.

18. Employees may appeal a change of job made without their knowledge and consent.

19. The workweek be reduced from 40 to 32 hours for the same pay.

20. Everyone receives the same pay for the same work regardless of sex.

And so on went the list, containing many specific department demands, until it reached a total of 56. Included was a 50-cent-an-hour wage increase, a pension plan, insurance, and hospitalization improvements and additions such as dental care.

Rogers went on studying the demands and wondered what he should do. Obviously the group meant business and could not simply be ignored. According to them, being ignored is what caused this bomb to fall. The president, he knew, hated the thought of unions, and if he handed over this list to him as it was proposed, the boss would be stunned for a moment, then explode into anger. After all, he was proud of the many long-service employees and of their loyalty to the company.

After sitting at his desk long into the evening, Rogers decided to have another meeting with the group first, even at the risk of having the old man find it out. He wanted to see whether there might be some other way around the problem.

In the morning he got hold of Murray and arranged for a

meeting at four o'clock that afternoon. The group entered his office on time, and he waved at them to sit down.

Rogers began. "I have read your list, and it's quite a list, believe me. What I'm wondering is whether we can't find another way to do this through channels and with some modifications."

Murray looked at the others, hesitated, and said, "We see no other way. As we said at the last meeting, we hoped over the years that management would act on our suggestions—but, nothing."

"While I know it isn't intended that way, this smacks of unionism, and you know how the boss feels about that," said Rogers.

"We know that, although we've never talked to him. But, as we keep saying, we tried the other way and it don't work. What we would like is to sit down with you and talk over these as reasonable things we are asking for, and to talk about them in a reasonable way."

"Well. Let me consider the next step, and I'll let you know as soon as I can."

They agreed and left his office.

Rogers finally decided no course was open to him but to place the list before the president, Mr. Athey. He planned to present the list orally at first, hoping to ease the shock as he handed over the written version. He met with Martin Athey, tall, patrician, and distant in bearing.

"Mr. Athey," he began, "I have been approached by a committee of five employees. The committee claims to represent all of our employees, and is asking for a meeting to discuss some employee matters with us."

"What is it they want—more money for their activities? We'll certainly consider that, if it seems to make sense."

"No, it isn't for that. There are some other things they want."

"Suppose you give me a for instance."

"Well, they would like to meet and talk about some time being allowed at the end of the day for clean-up—and some other items."

"Why should we discuss that with them? That kind of practice is for us to decide, not the employees. Why should they want clean-up time? In all the years we've been in business, this kind of approach has never been taken. Why now?"

Rogers decided that little would be gained from trying to make this easier. He put the list on the desk in front of Mr. Athey.

"Here is a list of what they want to talk over with us."

Athey began reading the list. As he read further, his eyes fixed on the paper in utter disbelief; his face reddened. Suddenly, he jumped up, tore the list into shreds, and threw it into the waste-basket.

Pointing his finger at Rogers, he roared, "Who in the hell do they think they are? What do they want to do? Tell us how to run the company? Who is this Murray? And what in the hell is an old-timer like Sam Brown doing with a group like this? What are they—a bunch of Commies? Is this the thanks we get for providing all these good steady jobs with good pay for all these years? Obviously, some damned union is behind this. We ought to fire that committee. Maybe we will. That ought to stop this kind of nonsense. When do they get the time to cook up this silly business? On company time when they're supposed to be working for the company doing what they're paid to do?

"You go back and tell them we have nothing to talk about, that I'm still running this company and don't need unsolicited help. If anyone doesn't like it, he is free to quit. In fact, tell the committee that if there's any more of this time-wasting, I'll fire the whole lot of them."

Rogers knew it would be impossible to try and reason with him now, so he left Athey's office as fast as he could.

Back in his own office he puzzled about what his next move should be. He could not, he thought, repeat Mr. Athey's blunt statement to the committee. On the other hand, he couldn't disobey him. Suddenly an idea struck him. Mr. Athey was leaving town on a two-week trip—this would allow him to play for time. Stretching the truth slightly, he could tell the committee that he had not had time to discuss the requests in detail with Mr. Athey before he left for a two-week trip, but would do so as soon as he got back. He asked for a meeting, met with the committee, and told them about the delay. Murray expressed their disappointment, but agreed little could be done until Mr. Athey got back, and asked for an answer then. Rogers said he would get one.

Rogers was in a real quandary. He had won two weeks of time. For what he wasn't sure. All he could hope for was that the boss, with time to recover from the initial shock, might be in a more tractable mood when he approached him again. Why, he wondered, had they come to him and not the personnel manager? The reason probably was that the position, in the minds of the employees, did not have the stature nor the manager the experience to cope with a problem of this size. In his own mind, he agreed with that outlook. He was flattered that they felt enough confidence in him to seek him out first, but he was deeply concerned by being placed in the middle of what could develop into a very explosive situation in this outwardly calm and placid organization.

Rogers decided to meet again with the committee toward the end of the two-week period to discuss demands, and to see whether he could persuade them to modify the list. He asked for a meeting two weeks later on Friday afternoon. The committee agreed to come.

At the meeting Rogers explained that more progress could be made if the list weren't so long, and he asked them to consider withdrawing some of the demands. Murray hesitated and asked Rogers to let the committee meet alone for a few minutes. He agreed. They met, then returned. Murray said they would like to study the matter and meet again after the weekend.

At a four o'clock meeting on Monday, Murray told Rogers that the committee had agreed to withdraw ten demands, including the 45-workweek guarantee. Murray said that nothing more could be given up because the list had been made up of the wants of the groups they were selected to represent. He added that these were long-standing grievances. Rogers expressed disappointment, but realized that the committee was in no position to go back for more concessions.

Mr. Athey returned, but Rogers still had no answers to the problem. He decided again that his only choice was to go to him and admit that he had met with the committee and got them to reduce the number of requests, but that the committee still wanted to talk.

He went and explained the situation to Athey, who exploded, "Why in hell don't they do this through the normal channels instead of acting like union men! I see no reason why I should meet with them. Maybe I ought to fire Murray as an object lesson."

Rogers said, "May I suggest that such a move would worsen the situation. These men are in a very serious mood, and if you fire Murray, it will be difficult to account for what they might do next. Perhaps it would be better if we were to agree to meet, listen to what they have to say, and give them a direct answer. Having done this, no one could say that we refused to talk and forced them to turn to the union for help."

For over an hour Rogers tried to persuade Athey, until he reluctantly agreed to "make our position clear to them, but not give in to any of their demands."

Rogers called Murray to his office to tell him that Mr. Athey had granted a meeting, and that they should arrange a time. He said, "Mr. Athey would not want to do it during the working day, so I suggest Thursday at four o'clock."

"It's O.K. with us."

On Thursday at four, the committee filed slowly into Mr. Athey's office where he and Rogers were waiting. As they were introduced to Mr. Athey, he waved them into chairs. He chatted with Sam Brown, a saturnine old-timer with wrinkled features, next to whom Athey had worked years before when he first started with the company.

Then, clearing his throat, Athey began. "I understand you have some complaints to make which you believe can't be handled through regular channels. What I can't understand is why, after all these years, it suddenly becomes necessary to jump outside normal channels to bring up a long list of outrageous requests. For 60 years this sort of thing has been handled to the satisfaction of everyone through the regular way. Anyhow, I'm prepared to listen to what you have to say."

Murray, very nervous, spoke next. "Mr. Athey, we have a number of grievances and requests that aren't being answered through our bosses. Many of us have had long hours of talk about what to do, and we finally decided to come to Mr. Rogers. Those of us here have been selected to represent the group and bring a list of requests. We went to Mr. Rogers first because we believed he would listen to us.

"We like the company, and we like working for you, but over the past few years we have had trouble getting action on our requests, so we decided on this way of trying to be heard. We believe what we are asking is reasonable and fair. We could have gone to a union, but we aren't interested in a union, so we are doing it this way. Here is a copy of the list we gave Mr. Rogers, showing what it is we would like to talk about." He handed the list to Athey, who glanced at it and pushed it aside.

"This is a most unusual move," he stated. "As I said before, and I say again, for 60 years we have been handling employee matters through your bosses, and I fail to see why, after all these years of settling such problems this way, it now becomes necessary to come up with this approach, which I frankly view as being subordinate."

Murray reddened. The others shuffled uneasily.

"Mr. Athey, the reason for coming here is that, as we said, the old way isn't working today. If we believed it did, we wouldn't be here with this list."

Athey's voice rose: "I want to repeat. Why should our system that has worked so well for 60 years suddenly break down, and how could a new employee like you become an expert on running a company that has been going for as long as we have?"

Rogers, seeing the tension rising, asked; "Murray, isn't it true that the items on the list are not outright demands but points you want to talk over with us to see what, if anything, can be done to clear them up?"

"That's right, Mr. Rogers. And these aren't just the thinking of us here, but requests of most of the employees."

Athey broke in, "However you put it, these are demands. I still see no reason why, if you want to present them, you shouldn't put them through regular channels. This is what you are to do. This is your answer." With that he got up, indicating that the meeting was over. A grim-faced committee left his office.

The committee met that evening and argued late into the night about what they should do. The conclusion was to report back to the others that the president had refused to discuss the list and had told them, in no uncertain terms, to go back to the old system. This solved nothing, and left them with no alternative. They would recommend going to the union for help. This they did.

Meanwhile, Athey told Rogers, "I want our supervisors to watch each of the members of this so-called committee to follow what they're up to. They could be real troublemakers. What I can't understand is why an old hand like Sam Brown can be taken in by these young punks."

Rogers said nothing and left to do as he was told.

The supervisors reported to Rogers that a lot of talk seemed to be going on between the members of the committee and the other employees. Rogers informed Athey of the reported activity. Athey scowled. "That so! Well, I guess I'll have to make an example. I'll fire Murray."

Rogers blanched and said, "Mr. Athey, if you do that, in my opinion, it could backfire on us. They could resent it to the point where they will go to the union for help."

"Look, Rogers, I don't believe that. Eight years ago we beat a union attempt to get in here. So I don't see why our employees should want to join now. They know when they're well off. No, we'll fire Murray and make an example of him. That ought to shut that committee up."

Murray was fired on the basis of below-average performance.

His employee activity had affected his immediate performance, but his long-term record was very good.

A majority of the employees polled by the committee favored turning to the union for help. A collection was taken to help support Murray for his committee work, and he was asked to meet with local officials of an international union, which he did. The union assigned an organizer to conduct a campaign. He was Bill Clayton, tall, broad, long-nosed, an ex-steelworker.

Clayton and Murray began making visits to employees at home to explain the need for and the advantages of a union and to enlist support. Rallies with free beer were held at the union hall. Employees were asked to sign cards for an election. More help was enlisted, including Sam Brown.

One day Rogers got an urgent call to come and see Athey. As he walked into his office, Athey demanded, "What in the hell is this?"

He handed over a letter. As he read, Rogers noticed that the letter was addressed to Athey and signed by William Clayton, an international union representative. In it Clayton said that the majority of the employees had designated his union as their representative for purposes of collective bargaining. He asked that management recognize them as the exclusive bargaining agent and that a meeting be called as soon as possible to bargain concerning wages, hours, and working conditions.

When he had finished reading, Rogers explained, "As I understand it, this is a routine approach that a union follows preliminary to petitioning for an election. Clayton probably doesn't expect that you will accept."

"You're damn right we won't! This is preposterous. Can't we simply ignore it?"

"We could, but I think we should get the advice of a good employee relations consultant. You know George Smith—he's reputed to be the best."

"I don't want to, but you're right. Call Smith and ask him to come over."

Rogers left, went to his office, and called George Smith. After carefully explaining the problem, he asked Smith to come to Athey's office. Smith offered to come immediately. A balding, round-faced and mentally nimble consultant, he had a wide reputation for his success in union-management relations. He came to Rogers's office and together they went to see Athey. The three met, and it was decided that Rogers, Smith, and Phil Hanson, the quiet, sincere young personnel manager, should work as a committee to recommend company strategy and tactics.

Smith drafted a letter from Athey to Clayton, refusing his request, and it was sent immediately. Within a few days, Athey received a letter from the National Labor Relations Board informing him that the union had filed a Petition for Certification of Representatives, and that the case had been assigned to a staff member for investigation. This was followed by a Notice of Representation Hearing several days later.

The hearing was held. Several weeks later, Athey received a Decision and Direction of Election, ordering an election to be held within 30 days; this was later amended, upon request by the company, to 60 days.

During the 60 days before the election, a tough campaign was waged by both sides. The union handed out a barrage of handbills taunting the management for its lack of concern for its employees and promising better pay and working conditions. Cartoons caricatured Athey and Rogers, making acid cracks about their refusal to hear the grievances of employees. The union also played hard on the firing of Murray, using the theme "it could happen to you."

Management, through letters to employees and their supervisors, made hard thrusts at the union, pointing out the advantages of present wages, benefits, and working conditions—all given without having to pay large dues to a fat union to win them.

As election day approached, the campaigns became increasingly bitter. Smith advised, however, that it would be unwise for management to fall into personal mudslinging, as that would make bargaining very difficult should the company lose the election.

Election day arrived. Employees filed to the voting booths. Athey, Rogers, Smith, and Hanson were confident that their loyal employees would elect not to have a union. But as the counting of votes moved along, management confidence began to ebb. The vote for a union led down to the final count, and a clear majority was tallied for the union.

This was a hard day in Athey's career. His first reaction was to refuse to meet with the union. But, as he said in a meeting with Rogers, Smith, and Hanson, "Like it or not, it's the law, so we have to do it."

A meeting was arranged and bargaining began with Athey, Rogers, Smith, Hanson, and Mitchell, the block-featured, impassive plant manager, who was added to the group. Clayton, Murray, Brown, Clark, and Zowalski represented the union.

The meeting was stiff and formal. Smith and Clayton discussed preliminaries and agreed that the union should present its demands. Clayton handed over a list, essentially the same as the one the committee gave to Rogers. Added was one demand calling for the reinstatement of Murray.

Smith asked questions about the meaning of certain items. Clayton explained them. At Smith's suggestion, the meeting was adjourned on the condition that management would take the demands under consideration and call a meeting for further discussion.

A management meeting was held in Athey's office. He began, "Murray has been fired. He is no longer an employee. He has nothing to do with this. Why should he be in the meeting and sit there smirking as they insist upon his reinstatement? I consider that way out of order. We should refuse to meet as long as Murray is present. Tell Clayton that."

Smith explained that Murray was temporarily assigned to the union and was in the meeting not as an employee but as a union representative. "Technically, it would be difficult to keep him out." Wisely, he did not bring up the fact that it was the firing of Murray that had triggered the organization drive, or that further harassment of him could only lead to a hardening of employee feelings and their bargaining position.

"Well," said Athey, "it's a hell of a situation when you can't fire someone. This union wants to run the company. I still think we should tell Clayton we won't meet unless he removes Murray from the committee."

"But Mr. Athey, as I said, whether we like it or not, technically he has every right to be there."

"What kind of law is it that protects an employee who deserved his discharge?"

"That's what the law is."

"All right! I don't like it, but if it's the law, we have to obey it, I suppose."

Rogers suggested, "We ought to review these demands and decide what to do."

Athey sputtered, his somewhat impetuous nature inflamed by the election defeat, and galled by having to deal with a third party over matters he considered strictly management's concern.

"Why should we agree to give them anything? Just because they elected to have a union doesn't mean we have to start a giveaway campaign this afternoon."

Again Smith and Rogers quietly argued that this would result in a violation, reminding him that the law required them to bargain in good faith.

"What a law! But if that's the case, then we'll go ahead, but only to the extent necessary to meet the law." They began to study the list. Rogers suggested that they agree to a joint review of safety and working conditions. Athey wanted to know why they should do that. "We have a safety department to supervise that responsibility. They're experienced technicians. Why do we need a union to tell us how to run safety activities?"

Rogers answered, "Maybe there's a real advantage in a joint effort—it could make everyone more safety conscious. On the other hand, if we refuse, couldn't it be interpreted by employees as a lack of concern for their health and well-being?"

"But we have been stressing safety for years."

Rogers quietly persisted, with Smith's assistance, until Athey finally agreed.

Other demands were brought up. Athey flatly refused to consider bargaining the right to set wage rates. That, he said, belonged to management, as management alone was responsible for costs and profits. Rogers and Smith began to point out that the law required bargaining wage rates, but quickly dropped the argument for the moment when both sensed the strength of Athey's resentment.

They moved on to review further demands on the list. Rogers and Smith were looking for one that, if not palatable, would at least be digestible to Athey. These were hard to find. Athey's view was that the demands infringed on management's—his— authority, and were being made by those who had enjoyed good jobs and pay for years, such as Sam Brown and one man he had fired.

With difficulty they got him to agree to a compromise offer of 24 hours' notice for overtime work, even though, as he said, "Scheduling is a part of management's job."

Rogers insisted, "It still is. All we're doing is agreeing to let them know ahead of time, and it seems to me that there's no real reason why we can't set scheduling 24 hours in advance."

"But deciding that remains a management responsibility!"

Rogers and Smith felt this was as far as they dared go, and with

Athey's approval, they decided to call a meeting with the union. Later, at an informal meeting among themselves, the four others agreed that Athey, because of his traditional background, could not be pushed too hard on some of these demands, some of which were, in their opinion, not too unreasonable. Rogers called Clayton and arranged a meeting.

The two committees met in the plant conference room to continue bargaining. The atmosphere was stiff and at arm's length. Athey said little. Most of the talking was between Smith and Clayton, with occasional remarks by Rogers and Murray. Brown said nothing. Nor did Hanson and Mitchell.

The union committee wanted to start out discussing Murray's reinstatement. But Clayton, as well as Rogers and Smith, sensed Athey's silent hostility toward Murray, dropped the discussion quickly, and went on to other items.

Smith suggested talking about the demand for joint effort on safety and working conditions. Clayton readily agreed to consider the question. Various procedures were discussed, such as a combined investigating committee for reviewing safety and working conditions monthly. Agreement was reached on the procedure, and Smith was asked to draft language for both sides to discuss later.

The overtime question was raised. Rogers offered the 24-hour notice to Clayton, and asked, in return, for a management rights clause. Clayton answered, "Twenty-four hours is hardly enough, but we'll consider that along with the management rights clause. What else, if anything, do you have to offer?"

Murray blurted, "Let's talk about how much money you're goin' to give us."

Clayton flashed back, "Unless management wants to discuss this demand, I believe we've had enough for today. It's been a long meeting."

"We agree with you. We have nothing to say on wages today," added Smith hurriedly.

After setting a date for the next meeting, the sides adjourned.

Rogers, Smith, Hanson, and Mitchell held a meeting to determine what the next step should be. First, it was decided that four were too many to tie up in long meetings and to excuse Mitchell from all meetings, as he had a plant to run. He agreed quickly, saying that he not only had a plant to run, but believed he could contribute little to negotiations. Later, Rogers told Smith confidentially that Mitchell didn't have the best temperament for employee relations. After he left, the three others examined many points in the demands, as well as possible approaches that might be taken. They concluded that some of the demands, such as the employees' right to question discharges and other acts of management, would be rigidly rebuffed by Athey.

"He would take these as threats to the very core of management authority," Rogers observed.

They studied the list further, looking for something that would be acceptable to Athey, and agreed to see whether he could be convinced to accept some type of advance layoff notice and to agree to stop hiring new employees while any full-time employees were on layoff. The three believed this was as much as could be put to Athey at this point with any chance of persuading him to concede.

Meanwhile, Clayton met with the union committee. He advised:

"Murray, the reason I called for ending that meeting is that it's too early to ask management to talk about wages. You got to realize that this is new to them—and to you—and hard on Athey with his habit of sole authority. Smith knows that too. Right now the word is 'Take it easy.' I suggest that from now on you don't raise any demands that we haven't agreed among ourselves to talk about before we meet with management."

On the other side, a meeting was held with Athey, who prompted his group with a tirade: "We should give nothing more. The union wants to manage the company. But they do not own it, and they are not responsible for profits. Nor do they have to answer to the shareholders."

"Granting that to be the case, we still have to work within the law, don't we, Mr. Athey?" Smith asked. "If we take an unyielding position with them, they can file an unfair labor practice charge for refusal to bargain within the meaning of the law."

"It's some law that makes me bargain away our right to run the business while leaving me with the responsibility for it. The union has the right to question how we run the business for profit —but is absolved from any responsibility. What's the logic of that kind of thinking? Obviously, the union is favored and the reasoning specious."

"But it is the law, at least until we can influence changes."

For three hours the discussion ranged back and forth on questions of law, management rights, profit responsibility, and the right for management to manage as it sees fit. The three worked hard to convince Athey to allow a layoff notice. Smith pointed out that this was hardly touching on the fringes of real management authority.

Reluctantly, in a touchy mood, he agreed, but only to a highly modified version of the original demand. Along with this, he was persuaded also to consent to a watered-down statement agreeing not to hire new employees while old ones were still on layoff.

The two sides met again. Clayton asked, "What answers have you got for us today? Would you care to talk about a grievance system?"

"No, we would not like to discuss that today," Rogers answered.

"Well, what do you want to bring up—if anything?"

Sparring over demands began, and continued until Clayton asked about the layoff notice. Rogers and Smith agreed to discuss it. In a dragging tone, Rogers offered, "We'll agree to give a 72-hour notice for layoffs that will last longer than one week."

"Hardly enough, but at least something," said Clayton in mock exaggeration.

An impasse on this point was reached, and the bargaining moved on to other items. Further down the list, the hiring of new employees during layoff periods came up.

Again Rogers, reluctantly, offered, "We'll agree not to hire anyone for a job for which any laid-off employee has the skill and ability to perform."

"That doesn't mean much to us. What is skill and ability? Something defined by management to suit its convenience?" questioned Clayton.

"Yeah! What does it mean?" added Murray.

In a sharp tone, Brown asked, "Just how will seniority be handled under this? Or don't that count around here any more?"

"You know damn well that long service and loyalty count a lot in this company, and have ever since its early days," Athey countered.

Brown frowned, but said nothing. He, Athey, and Murray sat glaring at each other. Smith and Clayton deftly turned the meeting to adjournment until a date set for the following week.

Both sides got up and silently left the room.

As they had before, Rogers, Smith, and Hanson met to decide what further steps could be recommended. Smith observed that Athey was stiffening rapidly.

"One of our problems, or, I should say, two problems, are

Brown and Murray. Mr. Athey sees one as a disloyal old-timer and the other as a troublemaking newcomer. From where he sits, I can understand his reaction to their attitudes in the meetings," reflected Rogers.

Smith, nodding, said, "I couldn't agree more. For him, he is showing remarkable restraint. But we've got to move ahead. I can see that Clayton is beginning to show signs of irritation, and for a union leader, he's a pretty patient guy."

"If Clayton could shut them up, it would help," observed Rogers.

"I believe he's trying," Smith countered. "He recognizes the animosity, but probably is having trouble controlling Brown and Murray. Those two are feeling their oats in their new position of authority."

Suddenly Hanson spoke up. "Why don't we offer to pay a limited amount of the cost of protective clothing and safety glasses? A number of companies do this, considering it to be good employee relations—and it *is* visible proof of our interest in the safety of our employees."

"That's a damn good idea! Don't you think so?" Rogers turned enthusiastically to Smith.

"It is. Safety will be promoted at a cost that won't be too substantial. We need this kind of offer at this point."

"And Mr. Athey may accept that," added Hanson.

Again they went through the process of a long meeting with Athey, but had even more difficulty than before persuading him to agree. He believed too much had been conceded already.

While Athey and his committee were meeting, Clayton met with the union group to review progress.

"I must admit that we're not getting them to move very fast," he observed. "We may have to start being tougher in our approach. We've got one real problem, and that's Athey himself. He is tightening more with each meeting. Probably part of the cause is you two," he said, looking at Brown and Murray, "Brown, he looks on you as a disloyal old-timer, and you, Murray, as a rambunctious upstart."

"Can't they do something with him?" asked Murray.

"He's the boss," Clayton replied.

"By the way, can't we start asking for Murray's reinstatement?" asked Brown.

"We won't get very far now, but we might as well get them used to the idea, so go ahead," said Clayton, adding, "Soon we should begin asking about money, but we'll hold for the moment."

On the following Tuesday afternoon, the two sides filed into the room to resume bargaining. They looked at each other coldly, and the air was cautious. Smith and Clayton opened the meeting by reviewing what had been conceded to date. Various items were gone over again, but little progress was made. Small arguments began to flare up as tension developed between the groups and individuals.

At one point Brown insisted, "When are you going to hire Murray back and give him back his seniority?"

"We don't care to talk about that now," Rogers announced.

"Seniority don't mean anythin' around here any more," Brown criticized.

"You're still here, aren't you, Brown?" Athey flashed.

Silence.

"Suppose we look at other demands—such as safety equipment," suggested Smith.

"That's important. What have you got to say about it?" Clayton asked.

"We would agree to pay for safety glasses when needed," Rogers offered.

"That's helpful, but what about paying for other safety equipment for employees who need it for their jobs. Why should *they* have to pay because the job is dangerous?"

Athey fumed. "Never before in the history of the company have we been asked to buy safety equipment, and buying glasses is giving quite a bit. In fact, if you don't appreciate the offer, maybe we should withdraw it. Perhaps we have given too much already."

Smith suggested that they adjourn until Friday. Clayton agreed, and the meeting broke up with each side ignoring the other as they filed out of the room.

For the third time the management three met to review tactics. They decided the point was being reached where Athey would balk at anything.

"Perhaps this would work," ventured Smith. "Since the union has the right to strike at any time, why not agree to a clause in the contract saying that a strike can be called only at the end of an agreement period, and only on 30 days' notice."

"Dammit! That *could* work. Let's try it anyhow and see whether Mr. Athey will buy," said Rogers.

Other moves were discussed, and the three decided that further delay over moving into the more knotty problems of wages, grievances, and discharges was no longer possible.

"These are real demands and probably strike issues. On the other hand, the 32-hour-workweek demand is something the union doesn't expect to win now. That's a 'trading' item," Smith observed.

"The union is becoming plenty restless because we aren't moving fast enough, but they don't understand how strongly Mr. Athey feels about some of their demands. In fact, his feelings toward having to deal with them at all are still deep," a solemn Rogers said.

"Clayton may understand that, but he has to show progress to the members," Smith explained.

The conclusion was reached that these problems had to be faced, and that the recommendations to Athey should be: allow the right to strike at the end of the contract; allow the right to appeal a discharge except for stealing, drinking, or fighting or for acts of outright insubordination; grant a 20-cent-an-hour wage increase.

Meanwhile, the union committee were meeting with Clayton to plan what their future tactics should be. Brown, even more than Murray, was becoming increasingly angry and restless over the lack of progress. Clayton argued for patience, pointing out that seeking agreement between two parties when the conditions are new and strange for the people involved is difficult, requiring time and patience. Even so, he said, he was beginning to wonder whether Athey's resentment and suspicion of the union could be overcome. If at all, it could probably be reduced only slightly at this time.

Clayton explained, "Athey seems to be more than ordinarily resistant. But resistance of this type is not unusual, where the top man takes the demands as a personal affront instead of the result of grievances that were years in the making."

He persuaded Brown and Murray to hold their horses for at least one more meeting, and not to let anger trip them into saying things that would only build more resentment in the management group. He cautioned Brown against raising the issue of Murray's reinstatement for the moment. "It will gain nothing except to make Athey madder."

He continued: "They have been making offers on the fringe issues. This is the usual move. I'll bet a dollar to a doughnut that's all Rogers, Smith, and company can get Athey to agree to. Anyhow, let's have another try and see what they come up with before we hit the bigger demands."

"Not much, I'll bet," growled Brown.

Once again the management committee met with Athey. They explained what they proposed should be offered to the union at the Friday meeting: the limited right to strike, the limited discharge appeal, and a 20-cent-an-hour wage increase.

Athey stared at the three and sarcastically said, "Whose side are you on—the union's? Why don't you suggest that I resign, and that we turn the company over to that committee to run! Seems to me that I'm paying a lot of money for advice on how to give the company away."

He went on berating them and the union for five minutes. Finally, he stopped. Carefully, Smith, helped by Rogers, explained that the union could strike, with membership agreement, any time they so elected, and that the management offer would restrict that right to the end of the contract term. Admittedly, they said, their discharge offer would place some limitation on management's disciplinary authority, but not on its right to fire for the most important discharge causes without question.

"As for the wage increase," Rogers said, "we have studied this carefully—or, I should say, Hanson has—and we find that other companies have been settling for a 35-cent increase. Last year we granted 15 cents on our own."

Smith added, "Mr. Athey, if we don't come up with a reasonable wage offer, my best advice is that you'll have a strike, and possibly a long one."

After three hours of discussion, argument, and repeated explanation, the three finally got Athey to agree to the strike clause and to a 15-cent-an-hour increase. He would not give on the discharge question. He allowed the 15-cent increase because, as he said, he had planned to give that anyhow had the union not interfered.

On Friday the two groups met for the fifth time. Clayton opened the meeting by saying, "This is our fifth meeting. While we have certainly made some progress, we need to move faster on some of these demands, or we'll be here forever. Besides, the people here in the unit have been asking when they're going to get a raise like they've been readin' about in the paper. But before we get to that, is there anything else you want to discuss? What about the request for a grievance system?"

Smith quickly said, "We aren't ready to discuss that yet."

"Are you ready to discuss anything at all with us?" asked Brown.

Rogers watched Athey bristle at this.

"Certainly we are," Smith replied. "Suppose we talk about the right to strike. Do you think it's fair to ask for the right to strike during the term of a binding agreement—simply by giving 30 days' notice—because you may be unhappy about something which you've agreed to in the agreement?"

Clayton argued, not very convincingly, that the union could call a strike any time by taking a vote of the membership, but was willing to give the company 30 days' notice and time to work the problem out.

Smith and Rogers argued with Clayton. Smith knew that Clayton wanted a strike clause, but that he didn't want an unrestricted right to strike any more than he did, since an unrestricted strike clause could be just as much of a headache for him as for the company. But Smith also knew that Clayton would use granting a restricted strike clause as a trade-off for something he wanted.

As agreed before the meeting, Rogers said, "What if we offered to accept this, but only on notice toward the end of the agreement?"

"At the end of the contract we have that right anyhow. As it stands now, you have offered nothing in the way of an appeal system so that we can raise grievances for settlement during the life of the contract. Without that, how can we agree not to strike during the contract period?"

"We don't care to discuss that point," said Rogers flatly.

Clayton's ears and face turned red. In an annoyed voice, he quipped, "And I suppose you don't care to talk about the question of a wage increase or anything else today!"

"We do," said Rogers. "But we think 50 cents in unrealistic. Do you realize what this would do to our costs and competitive position?"

"What you've been giving our people here leaves them far behind in the competitive parade. Maybe with the size salaries you executives draw, you don't feel the grocery pinch, which is putting *us* more and more behind. Other companies with better rates than yours are giving good increases, so we don't think 50 cents is out of line."

"There's a lot of complaint about our rates compared with

what people in other plants in this town are gettin'," Murray added.

"For 60 years we've always paid what we believe are fair rates, and besides, where do you get the idea they're your people? We're the ones who've been responsible for providing jobs for all this time, not you," pronounced Athey.

"They used to be," complained Brown.

Clayton asked, "What are you prepared to offer?"

"We'll offer 15 cents an hour," Athey announced.

"That's what you doled out last year, and it was too damned little," shouted Clayton. "We can't recommend that to our people —they'd laugh at us!"

"And *we* have a profit to make, or there won't be any jobs for *your* people," Athey roared back.

"And our people have to eat and pay bills! Is there anything else you wish to hand out to us?" leveled Clayton with cold sarcasm.

"That's all," yelled Athey.

Smith intervened. "Suppose we adjourn until next Thursday. Meanwhile, we can both review where we stand." Clayton tersely agreed.

The air was tense and silent, except for the scraping of chairs and the shuffling of papers as everyone got up and quickly left.

Between the meetings, Rogers, Smith, and Hanson, after many hours of discussion and argument, persuaded Athey to agree to the discharge appeal, as they had suggested earlier; to discuss departmental problems on working conditions; and to offer to meet monthly on grievances. He would not give in to offering any more money—he bluntly refused to talk about it at all.

Clayton met with his committee.

"Bill, speaking for the committee, we think we ought to strike. We aren't getting anywhere, especially with Athey," said Brown solemnly.

"I admit that progress is far from satisfactory, and we may have to do just that. But let's give them another chance, and hold off the strike talk for just one more meeting. Athey has stiffened plenty as it is, and that kind of talk may make him even more so at this point."

"So what! He's givin' damn little. He'll have to learn the hard way," Murray yelled.

"Calm down, Murray. You're new and too eager. Besides, we have to worry about eventually winning a reinstatement for you."

"O.K. for one more meeting," Brown offered hesitantly.

On Thursday another meeting was called. Both sides were tense and bristling. Discussion was curt.

"Well, Mr. Rogers, have you anything more to dole out to our people?" Clayton asked in a scoffing tone.

"We offered plenty. Where do you get this 'dole' business?" Rogers shot back derisively.

"Big deal!" Brown laughed.

"But we do have something to talk about, Clayton," Rogers said evenly.

"What?"

"We'll raise the layoff notice from 72 to 96 hours. We'll also offer to meet monthly to discuss grievances and discharges for causes other than stealing, fighting, drunkenness, or insubordination. We'll also talk about working conditions in various departments."

"From you that's quite a bit."

The meeting moved on to consideration of working conditions. They discussed locker rooms, lighting, ventilation, and other specific points. The tension dropped slightly. The layoff notice improvement was argued. Clayton and the committee still wanted more time. No conclusion was reached.

"Let's talk over the question of meeting monthly on grievances and discharges, and see if we can work something out," Smith offered in a conciliatory voice.

"Well, Smith, that sounds nice, but it seems to be only an offer to talk about them without any guarantee that anything will be settled. Talking around the subject and not doin' anything seems to be one of the problems our people have around here," answered Clayton sarcastically.

Brown added, "And we'd be back to where we are now. It's all talk and no action!"

"And you're all talk and no work," parried Hanson.

"Maybe we should withdraw the offer entirely," threatened Athey.

"What good is it anyhow!" Brown snorted.

Clayton broke in. "Perhaps we ought to reconsider that offer. And I see no more on the question of a wage increase, or anything on vacations, holidays, or fringe benefits. We've got a long way to go."

"We've made three offers today. You haven't said anything constructive. All you do is drone 'it's not enough.' Are those the only words you've got? If so, don't waste our time in meetings. Put it on a record and send it to me," Rogers said scathingly.

"We stand on the wage offer," said Athey. "I agree with Rogers. For 60 years we've been providing jobs and a living for many people in this town. Suddenly you show up, telling us that nothing's right, and that you want to take, take, take." He lashed out at Clayton.

"It's been a long day. Let's call it quits until, say, next Tuesday, if that's agreeable," offered Smith soothingly, hoping to divert any further chafing of personalities and nerves.

"O.K., but I hope something better is coming, or we may have to do something more drastic," warned Clayton.

"There'd better be," Brown echoed.

The meeting ended in strained silence.

Clayton and the committee met. "Their position is hardening," he said, "and Athey seems to like us less than ever. So, I think we ought to take a strike vote tomorrow night. A strike is a real possibility now."

The meeting was held on Friday evening, and the vote was overwhelmingly in favor of a strike.

In a meeting of the management three, Smith advised, "Frankly, we've got to come up with something on wages, fringes, holidays, and vacations. The union's stiffening. Clayton is finding it hard to control the committee—not to mention his own patience. At this rate we're headed for a strike. Could we convince Mr. Athey to increase the wage offer to 20 cents, 5 cents for fringe benefits, one more holiday, and three weeks' vacation after seven years of service? This will not bring a settlement, but it would move the negotiations well along."

"That's a lot to ask from Mr. Athey at this time, but we'll have to try," Rogers agreed.

Several long, hard sessions were required to get Athey to allow the offer to be made, and then only on the basis that a strike was probably the only other alternative. During these meetings the other three had to sit silently, listening to a number of furious tirades about giving the company and management's authority away to the union.

On Tuesday the two groups met. The meeting was a somber one.

Clayton began. "Well, what have you got to offer? I hope more than before. Our people are impatient—in fact, they took a strike vote and overwhelmingly gave us approval to call a strike. And I got to say this is moving too slowly," he growled.

"We don't see you giving much," Athey retorted.

"We don't give. We're asking for what is due us," yelled Brown.

"Yeah, we're behind everyone in this town," Murray shouted.

Smith said, "This isn't getting us anywhere."

"Have you got anything to offer?" Clayton asked.

"Maybe yes, maybe no. How about stopping long enough to listen," countered Rogers evenly.

"What in the hell have you got to give?"

"We've already given more than we should," Athey shot back.

"Suppose we talk about holidays and vacations," Rogers proposed.

Clayton argued vehemently that the present schedule for holidays was two days less than the average, and that the vacation schedule was also far behind.

Rogers and Smith forcefully presented their case that the schedule was only slightly off recent settlements, *not* way behind.

"Rogers, you're a company 'yes' man, and you don't know what's going on," Brown taunted.

"That so! I've helped make and keep jobs for guys like you," fumed Rogers in return.

"Brown, quiet down! What have you got to give us?" Clayton wanted to know.

Athey broke in, bellowing. "Before he says anything more, let me tell you, Clayton, that we don't intend to sit here listening to goddamn snide cracks that are aimed personally at one of us by someone who has made a good living here for 30 years—and now smears those who made it possible. That's real loyalty for you."

"Suppose we move on," Smith said quickly.

"We offer one additional holiday, and three weeks' vacation after seven years," proposed Rogers.

"Big deal!" Brown derided.

"Quiet!" Clayton ordered. "That's not exactly what we were expecting, but at least it's an offer—not much, but an offer."

"Why don't you just ask if you can run the company," Athey raved.

Clayton, ignoring him, went on. "Is there anything else you have in the way of money? Our people won't hold still for 15 cents. They'll strike first," he warned.

"Yes. We'll go to 20 cents an hour and add 5 cents for fringe benefit improvements," Rogers countered.

"Well! Some move after all! I doubt if we can sell it, but it is a move."

"I move we adjourn to give you time to consider these offers, and that we meet again on Friday," Smith intercepted.

"Agreed," Clayton said curtly.

The meeting broke up in a glaring mood. Later, Rogers, Smith, and Hanson met with Athey about what should be done next. Athey was adamant. Flatly, he said, "Not one damn thing more! Too much money and management authority has already been given, and all Brown does is yell for more."

Clayton and his committee met. Brown, still smarting from Athey's remarks about his loyalty, complained and demanded that they strike.

"Sam," said Clayton, "I've told you to watch your temper. After all, you asked for it by your crack at Rogers. My idea is that we should meet with them once more to see if they'll make any moves, and I think it's time to ask for Murray's reinstatement. If we get nothing, then we walk out. Nobody can say that we haven't tried. Frankly, though, I'm not too hopeful at this point."

On Friday they met. The meeting was abrupt and cold.

"What's your reply to our offers?" Rogers demanded.

"Before we get into that, we'd like to discuss Murray's reinstatement," said Clayton.

Athey broke in. "There's nothing to discuss, dammit! He's fired!"

"Isn't there any room for discussion?"

"None," said Athey.

"Because he's loyal enough to fight for his rights!" Brown added bitterly.

"What about our last offer?" interrupted Smith.

"We find it unacceptable," said Clayton. "What else do you have?"

"Nothing! That, Mr. Clayton, *was* our last offer," Athey said in a final tone of voice.

"Cheap! That's what it is—cheap! Let's go!" Clayton glared at Athey as he rose, motioning the committee to follow, and walked quickly out of the room.

"Gentlemen, we now have a strike on our hands," Smith said as they left.

13

Case Study:
Return to Accord

NO attempt was made over the weekend to prevent the strike. On Monday, Rogers arrived early to find that a picket line had been set up at the gates and no employees were crossing the line. The strike was on. As they had planned, Clayton and his committee met with groups of employees in a rented space near the plant, and organized the strike. Picket schedules were set up and food supplies arranged.

Neither side moved for a week. On the following Monday, Clayton called the committee together to size up the situation.

"It's unlikely that the company is ready to change its position, but we should make an attempt to meet with them, if only for public relations reasons, to show that we are trying to get this settled," he advised.

At a meeting of the management group, Smith also suggested meeting for the same reasons.

"If we refuse, or make no move, we can lose any sympathy we might have in the community. By remaining silent and withdrawn, it may appear that we don't give a damn what happens to our employees."

"I don't like it, but I can see your point," agreed Athey reluctantly..

During this discussion a call came in for Rogers from Clayton, who asked him for a Wednesday meeting to see whether anything could be done to bring the two sides together. After checking with Athey, Rogers agreed to a meeting. Then he, Smith, and Hanson asked Athey whether they should consider making any additional offer to the union.

"Absolutely not!" Athey answered flatly.

On Wednesday the sides filed into the meeting room. No one spoke; they only nodded curtly as they sat down.

"Clayton, you asked for this meeting. What have you got to propose?" demanded Rogers.

"This strike has been on for ten days now, and we asked for the meeting to see what can be done to bring it to an end. What we'd like to know is this: Have you reconsidered your last offer, and are you ready to make any other proposals? As I told you before, I can't sell your money offer to our people." Clayton spoke in a conciliatory tone.

"And we, too, are here to see if anything can be done to end this strike. What we want to know is whether you are ready to withdraw your demands and accept our last offer. We aren't here to give," Rogers announced.

"You heard our last offer! That's it!" Athey rasped as he leaned forward, glaring at Clayton.

"We heard, and it's not enough," Brown yelled at Athey.

"Are you sure there's nothing else?" asked Clayton in an even tone.

"You heard me. That is *all*," Athey bellowed.

"O.K.," said Clayton. "I can see there's no point in trying to get anywhere with you. You've taken a rigid position—think you've given a lot, which you haven't. I warn you, we are set for a long strike. We mean business. Come on! Let's get the hell out of here," he stormed as he jumped up and rushed from the room, followed by the committee.

The management group left quickly.

On the following Monday, Clayton called Rogers to set up another meeting. Athey agreed, and it was set for Wednesday. Because of Athey's unwillingness to concede anything more, the meeting was short. They would make no move. Again the agreement to meet on Wednesday was for public relations purposes, to keep the channels open for what little it was worth at the time.

The strike had been going on for two weeks, and reporters and community leaders were asking questions about the possibility of settlement. The answer given was that the sides were continuing to try and reach agreement, but that progress was slow.

Clayton and his committee met and decided to make no move in the Wednesday meeting. Their readiness to meet was for the same reason as management's. The meeting of the two groups on Wednesday was short.

"Have you anything to give?" demanded Clayton.

"You have our final offer," Rogers said tersely.

"What have *you* to give?" asked Smith.

"Nothing."

"Well, nothing's just what we'll gain by sitting here," Athey scoffed. "Let's get out of here." He stood up and strode through the door, followed by the others.

Rogers, Smith, and Hanson met. They agreed that Athey would not move, nor would Clayton and his committee, so trying to call another meeting immediately would be pointless.

Pressure for settlement was building up from the outside. Radio and television commentators were asking why, in this day and age, the two sides couldn't settle their differences and get back to work. Directors of the company were calling Athey to ask about progress. Customers and community leaders wanted to know when a settlement would be likely.

Nothing happened until Friday, when Athey and Clayton both received a call from the Federal Mediation and Conciliation Service. The call came from John Hunt, regional director of the service. He asked if he could be of any help. Athey said that he didn't think so, but that he would discuss it with his staff and the company counsel.

Athey called the three to a meeting in his office, and told them about the call. He wondered, "Why should we have the government interfering? Hell, this is a private matter between us and the union."

"I agree," said Smith. "Maybe they can help later, if we can't come to terms. But as far as interfering is concerned, they have no authority to force a settlement—it's only a service for mediation."

"It seems to me that we have to do something. We're getting plenty of pressure from radio and TV, not to mention the mayor's office, and customers are asking when we believe it will be over.

Maybe we ought to try another meeting," said Rogers in a worried voice.

"What good will that do!" Athey asked in exasperation.

"Well," counseled Smith, "at least we can find out whether the union is getting pressure from the employees, and whether it's ready to give up some of the demands. We've been on strike for almost a month now, and their savings must be running low. If we don't try to meet, the public, customers, and everybody else will blame us, not the union. Sympathy runs with the man out of work, with a family to support. If we do call another meeting, we can tell Hunt that we appreciate the offer, but that we are still trying to settle."

"And I must admit, the directors are showing a great deal of concern," Athey remarked quietly.

"It makes sense to me," said Rogers hopefully.

Athey agreed. The decision was that Athey should call Hunt and tell him the sides were meeting and would not need his services. Rogers was to call the union and ask for a meeting on the following Wednesday.

Meanwhile, Clayton was meeting with his own committee to discuss his conversation with Hunt. "We may have to call for his help," he told them, "but it would be better if we could do without it. Athey is so fixed in his position that mediation is probably the only way we can get him to move, but we ought to try one more meeting to see whether they are softening. We've been out four weeks now, and they must be feeling the pinch and getting pressure from customers—and others as well."

"We're gettin' lots of calls from members. Their wives are on their backs askin' when they expect to go back to work," said Brown solemnly.

"Well, we've got to make some kind of a move. I'll call Hunt to thank him, and tell him we're still meeting."

When Clayton got back to his desk, he found a call from Rogers. Maybe they're weakening, he mused hopefully. He called Rogers and a meeting was set for Wednesday.

On Wednesday the sides gathered silently around the table. The meeting was short. Each side asked briefly if there was any change of position. Both answered with a sharp no, and the meeting was over, ending in cold silence.

Clayton said quietly to the committee, "Now we have to go to mediation. There is no other way. If Athey would move, so would we, but he isn't about to."

"We got to do somethin'," said Murray, troubled.

It was agreed that Clayton should ask Hunt for help.

The management team met in Athey's office. He remarked sarcastically, "Well, that went nowhere. They just don't want to move. They're being pigheaded, and misguided by that Clayton and Murray."

"I must admit I had hopes that they would soften, but there was no sign of any weakening, although the employees, pushed by their wives, should be putting pressure on them to do something," observed Smith wearily.

"What's the next step? Do we sit tight until they move?" Rogers asked.

"For a number of reasons I wouldn't advise so at this time," answered Smith. "We can't meet because of the rigidity of each side's position. Little love is lost between us at the table. We are in the fifth week of this strike and pressure on us from the outside is building up fast. While I'd prefer not to, I suggest that we call in Hunt."

"Isn't there some other way?" asked a haggard Rogers.

"Not that I know of."

"I never thought I'd see the day when I'd have to go to the government for help with our own employees, but I suppose we have to try," admitted Athey in a strained tone.

Rogers agreed to call Hunt to discuss a meeting. He did, and Hunt said that Clayton had also called wanting to talk about a meeting, so it would seem timely to set one up in the service's offices. Through Hunt, it was arranged for the following Wednesday—not earlier, because Labor Day weekend intervened.

On Wednesday, Athey and the others went to Hunt's offices, where they were met by a tall, graying, straight-featured man, dressed conservatively.

"Hello, George." Hunt greeted Smith, whom he knew. As Smith introduced him around, his affable smile and cordially offered handshake extended a friendliness that was easy to accept. Later, Athey was to admit that Hunt was not what he'd expected to find in a government official, and that he found himself liking him in spite of himself.

"If you don't mind, I'd like to ask you to come to Room 705, where you will be for this meeting. Clayton and his committee will be at the opposite end of the hall. He called to say that they would be a few minutes late," explained Hunt. "By the way, would you like some coffee?" They accepted.

Someone knocked on the door, and Hunt opened it. Before him stood a secretary who told him that the union had arrived. "Please take them to Room 775, tell them I'll be there shortly, and offer them some coffee." She left to do as he asked.

Turning to the group, Hunt said, "Let me explain our suggested procedure. For the moment, each side will be in separate rooms—usually no attempt is made to bring the two of you together at the beginning. My job is to listen carefully to each of you to find out what the basic issues are and where the real differences lie, then to suggest to each of you possible approaches for reaching a settlement. This morning I plan to listen so that I can learn more about the problems. I suggest that this is all we try to accomplish today. Also, I would like to stress that my role is to serve as mediator. This means I act as an intermediary between the two of you, without prejudice for either side, to help reestablish communications between you and to assist, hopefully, in bringing you back together. I am not a negotiator, nor am I here to tell you what to do. I can only suggest. Now, if you'll excuse me, I'll go see the union, introduce myself, then come back to discuss the situation with you. I'll send Miss Jarrett in to see how you want your coffee."

Hunt left, went to Room 775, and introduced himself to the committee and to Clayton, who knew him. He repeated to them what he had told the management committee about his position as a mediator; then he excused himself and said that he would be back later.

Meanwhile, over coffee in the yellow-walled room where they sat around a table on hard, wooden chairs, Athey wondered what would happen next. Smith explained the procedure that was usually followed.

Twenty minutes later Hunt returned. He sat down at the table and began in a conversational tone: "Let me explain the procedure. As I understand the situation to be, no progress has been made in your negotiations for the past several meetings, and an impasse has been reached. Obviously, the first step is for me to become thoroughly briefed by both sides to help me develop an understanding of the differences and to see where I might assist. A joint meeting between you today would probably serve little purpose—I wouldn't know enough to be helpful, and you would be back where you left off at your last meeting. Is this agreeable?"

They agreed.

"All right. If you will be kind enough to brief me thoroughly from the beginning and bring me up to this point, I'd appreciate it. First, let me call Miss Jarrett." He buzzed, and she came into the room.

"Would you please tell Mr. Clayton that I'll be here for several hours, and that they can do what they want until one o'clock. Mr. Clayton will understand. I've explained this, and they're agreeable." She left.

"I'm happy to hear that committee is agreeable about something," Athey laughed.

"O.K. Let's begin. Who will describe the situation for your group?" asked Hunt, politely ignoring Athey's remark.

"I want Smith, our counsel, assisted by Rogers, one of our vice-presidents, and Hanson to do the talking. I'll add to it when I think it's necessary," instructed Athey.

Turning to Smith, Hunt asked courteously, "George, would you explain the situation as you see it, beginning with the employees' first move?"

"I will, with Mr. Athey and the others adding to or correcting my comments as they believe necessary."

Smith began to describe the events, starting with the employee committee's first request for a meeting with Rogers. Hunt made no attempt to express an analysis of what had happened as told by Smith and the others. He only asked questions to clear up what he didn't understand. Most of the time he listened carefully. Several hours passed. While he was listening, he tried to sense the personalities and temperaments of the individuals, from how each one spoke as much as from what he said.

As he outlined the moves and countermoves of each side, Smith handed Hunt copies of the original demands and those formally presented by the union as the committee's representative. Hunt sensed that the two sides were still far apart, not only in money offered, but in attitude, when he heard Athey observe defensively that too much management authority had been given away already.

At noon Hunt suggested, "Well, now. That briefs me pretty completely for the moment. Suppose we break up. I have to meet with the union in an hour, and you've given me all I need for now. The next step will be for me to study carefully what both of you have told me today, then I'll ask for another meeting. Would next Tuesday morning be all right?"

"I guess it'll have to be," said Athey tonelessly.

"Thank you—I'll see you then."

They got up, shook hands with Hunt, and went to lunch.

At one o'clock Hunt met with the union. He greeted Clayton with the same cordiality he had shown Smith. After they sat down, Hunt asked them to agree to the same procedure the management committee had followed. Clayton approved, then outlined for Hunt what had taken place from their point of view. As he had with the management group, Hunt listened to sense the personalities of the various members of the committee, guessing correctly that Clark and Zowalski were not the talkative type in meetings, that Brown and Murray were. As Clayton continued to explain what had happened, again he felt that the sides were far apart, in attitude as well as money. Brown's caustic remarks about management bothered him, as did Murray's tendency to blurt out and then think.

At four o'clock he said that he had been well briefed, would study the situation, and would like to call another meeting the following Tuesday.

"Management's agreeable, if you are," he said.

"That's the first thing that group has agreed to in a long time!" said Brown acidly.

"We'll be here, John," said Clayton quietly, ignoring Brown's crack. They got up to leave.

Hunt studied the demands and the notes he had taken during his discussions with both sides. Although they were apart in demands and offers—and so much so that it would take time and patience to bring them together—he knew that they could be reconciled, as he had seen happen so many times in the past. But he felt sure that the problems here involved personal differences, possibly deep animosities. If this were the case, the situation would be much more complicated than it appeared, and much more difficult to handle. What these differences were he wasn't sure, but he knew he would have to isolate them before he could get the two sides to move toward agreement.

Hunt decided that at the next meeting he would probe to see where they might be willing to give on the demands; at the same time, he would try to deduce where the animosities lay. In his own mind that was more important than trying to get the two sides to move on money differences—he believed they could not reach accord until the hostilities were understood and resolved.

On Tuesday the meeting was held. Again Hunt made no attempt to bring the groups together. Each committee stayed in its own room, and he moved back and forth between them, as he had at the first meeting. As he discussed the demands, he found that prestrike positions were still held, but he could sense that both sides were beginning to have second thoughts, now that the strike had been going on for six weeks.

Hunt continued to talk over the demands with them, knowing that it was too early to expect much movement, but it gave him time to study the individuals on each side as they argued their points. He made only one attempt at asking them to move on what he gauged to be minor issues, the 45-week-a-year guarantee and jury pay, but neither side was willing to give first, so he dropped the suggestion.

As he observed each committee, he tentatively concluded that Murray was the disruptive element on the union side, with Brown playing a lesser role. Clark and Zowalski were quiet; they spoke rarely, so they could hardly be causing tension between the groups. On the other side, Hanson could be no cause—he was not in a lead position, only a participant. Smith and Clayton had been opposing each other for years; they fought but respected each other. Rogers, he learned, was well regarded throughout the company, but Athey's attitude he guessed to be a gall to the union committee. Hunt could see that his patriarchal manner would hardly be acceptable in this new relationship. On the other hand, he could sympathize with Athey, who, after all these years of giving unquestioned orders, was suddenly faced with employees questioning him on how he ran the company. From past experience he knew that this sort of relationship was always hardest on the top man.

Hunt made these deductions tentatively; he tried to guard against jumping to answers too fast, not wanting to make a mistake on this fundamental issue.

The meeting ended with no noticeable progress. Before it broke up, Hunt thanked each side and asked them to meet on the following Wednesday. He also asked that during the intervening time they carefully reassess their positions.

The strike entered its seventh week. The company was under more and more pressure from customers, who were showing anxiety over the length and possible settlement date of the strike. Employees were really feeling the pinch of no pay coming in, and their committee was under increasing pressure from them as they anxiously asked what progress was being made.

Athey met with his committee. He was still opposed to any offer, but the pressures on him for settlement were heavy, and his drawn look showed the strain. He asked, "What is it we can do? What can the union do? George, what's your opinion?"

"John Hunt has given us an idea. If you remember, he suggested that we might want to give jury pay to employees called to serve on juries as a public duty. In return, he proposed that the union withdraw its demand for a 45-workweek guarantee. In any employee group, jury duty is an infrequent occurrence, so the cost in money spread over the total wage cost is negligible. In my opinion, this would be a good thing to give on to help John move this off dead center. At very little cost, we give to support a public service."

"What do you think, Rogers?"

"I think George is right, Mr. Athey. We've got to do something on our side to help move this. We're getting plenty of kick from customers and people in the community. As one man in town said, 'It's beginning to look as though both of you are being downright pigheaded.' And, from what I hear, the union is feeling this pressure too—from the community as well as the employees."

"All right, George, we'll go ahead, but only on this demand."

Clayton and the employee committee met to review their position. Clayton listened to Brown and the others describe the constant questions coming from other strikers about when they were going to settle. They were becoming more restless because nothing seemed to be happening.

Clayton said, "We've got to make some move, if only for outward appearances. If *we* don't and the company does, that will put us in the position of being the block to progress."

"What do you suggest we do, Bill?" Brown asked in a quiet, strained voice.

"John Hunt suggested we give up the demand for a 45-workweek guarantee in return for jury duty pay. We can be sure that Athey will never buy the guarantee at this point, and, frankly, it may not even be practical. My suggestion is that we concede this."

The committee agreed. On Wednesday they met at Hunt's offices for the third time. Again he made no effort to bring the sides together. After moving back and forth between them, he noticed the signs of strain and fatigue. They were having second thoughts. All of them were beginning to look at themselves and wonder whether their positions weren't too rigid. How long could they expect others to stay away from work, lose pay, and go into debt? Athey and his group had additional worries—the health of

the company, the cost of lost sales, and the possible loss of customers, should this continue too long.

Hunt sensed that, although he could see the development of
these feelings, it would be a mistake to assume that they were
strong enough for him to press hard toward a settlement at such an
early date in the mediation.

During the afternoon, he again suggested the possibility that
a move to trade jury pay for the 45-workweek guarantee be considered. He saw signs of weakening, so pressed quietly but firmly,
as each side was reluctant to be the first to move. Working through
Smith and Clayton, he got both sides to agree to make these concessions. Knowing the depth of feeling involved, he made no
attempt to push further that day, but suggested time for reconsideration of positions and called a meeting the following Wednesday. Both approved.

After the meeting, Hunt also reconsidered the situation in
terms of his own position and of the relationship between individuals on both sides. As he reassessed it, he decided, on the basis
of Brown's occasional verbal flings at Athey, as well as his actions
as a whole, that it was he, not Murray, who was the disruptive influence on the union side. On the other side, when Brown's name
was mentioned before the management committee, Athey's comments were caustic.

This posed a serious problem for Hunt. Progress, he believed,
could be nullified if, when he brought the two groups together in
face-to-face meetings, Athey and Brown were present. He was in a
dilemma. Athey was president of the company, and Brown was a
long-service employee well regarded by his fellow workers. He
decided that it was too early, if not virtually impossible, for him to
suggest withdrawing the two men from the meetings.

Hunt visited each of the committees prior to the scheduled
Wednesday meeting. He reminded them that all this had begun
in March, that it was now October, and that the strike was entering
its eighth week. He pointed out that he, too, was under pressure
from his superiors, as well as from others on the outside, questioning why more progress hadn't been made. He pleaded with both
groups to do as much as possible to make some progress at the
next meeting. He had hopes, but privately didn't expect much so
long as the interpersonal bitterness was present.

Athey's group met. Again an attempt was made to figure out
where a move could be made without giving too much. Rogers
suggested they should consider raising the layoff notice to four

days, observing, "After all, if we're doing the right planning job, we need to plan much further ahead than that anyway, so what are we really giving away?"

Athey answered wearily, "Nothing, except that determining how and when to lay off has always been management's job, as part of its responsibility to control costs and make a profit. But, since we have already conceded three days, one more won't make too much difference, As you say, we need to plan further ahead than that."

"I think that idea is a good one," Smith offered.

"Let's go ahead," said Rogers.

Clayton and his committee also met.

"We've got to make a move," he said worriedly. "We're not only under pressure from the members, but I'm getting plenty of static from my bosses, asking why we aren't making more headway."

"Let Athey make a move," scoffed Brown.

"Brown, we trade hard, but bargaining is a two-way street. You can't expect to get everything the first time around," Clayton retorted coldly. "Here is what I suggest. We have asked for a 32-hour week. This is a long-term union objective. You can be sure Athey won't give in on that one now, and, frankly, even if the company did, it could cause all of us more problems than it would solve. Let's withdraw the demand."

"That makes sense," offered Murray anxiously.

"We got to do something. And I'll tell you—we're livin' on savings. Every day, when I walk down the street, I hear plenty from our neighbors when I tell 'em nothin's happened. They ain't in any mood to wait. I get plenty at home, too," muttered Zowalski.

"O.K.," said Clayton, "We settle on that."

On Tuesday morning Athey received a call from a man who introduced himself as Scanlon, a district vice-president of the union.

"Mr. Athey, I called because this negotiation between you and us isn't getting anywhere. Can't you and I get together and talk this out?" coaxed Scanlon in a voice that boomed over the wire.

"I can't answer that now, Mr. Scanlon. My staff and counsel are working on this with me, and I'll have to ask them," a wary Athey replied. "I'll call you back."

Athey hung up and dialed Rogers to describe his conversation with Scanlon.

"Call Smith and Hanson, and come to my office as soon as you can," he ordered.

They met in Athey's office.

"George, what do we do? Why is this guy calling me?"

"Mr. Athey, unions sometimes do this. It's one way of putting pressure on. Also, when a standoff occurs locally between the union and a company, the international level—such as Scanlon— may have to move in to help the Claytons bring a rambunctious local back into line. I've done this, but I wouldn't advise it here. For one thing, it would bypass Clayton, and, for another, Hunt's efforts would be upset. Such a move could create future problems in our relationship with the local. My suggestion is that you call him and give him a courteous no, with the explanation that we are working this out through Hunt."

"Anyone disagree with this?"

Rogers and Hanson shook their heads.

Athey called Scanlon and told him. Scanlon didn't sound surprised or distressed, said he was available if they wanted help, boomed a thank-you, and hung up.

On Wednesday another meeting was held in Hunt's office. Hunt decided that little purpose would be served by trying to bring them together, so he kept the committees separated. His move was simply to ask each side what it was prepared to do. Through Hunt, the union group agreed to a 4-day-layoff notice in exchange for dropping the 32-hour-week demand. But, having come to that agreement, Hunt discovered that neither side was prepared to do anything more. At his urging, however, both agreed to come back with something more substantial at the next meeting, scheduled for the following Wednesday.

The strike entered its ninth week.

At the next meeting of the management committee, Smith opened with a question. "Mr. Athey, is there any reason why an employee can't be given prior notice of any change affecting his job? Isn't it possible that communicating a change beforehand would be helpful in avoiding confusion in his mind, and in others around him?"

"That's always been our prerogative. Rogers, what do you think about this?"

"Mr. Athey, maybe George has a point. Our employees want to know more about what's going on, particularly when it affects their jobs. And I'll have to admit that their not being informed has caused us some confused tangles."

"Mr. Athey, we had a problem like that just before the strike," explained Hanson in his quiet voice. "A production-line improvement caused a change in the position Bob Jones had on the line in the assembly department, and he came to see me about it. He was plenty mad, and wanted to know why he had been changed. He was earning his rate, he said, and wanted to know what was wrong with him. Didn't we think he was good enough? I checked into it and found that the change would make it possible for him to earn more, and that his foreman rated him as one of the best workers on the line. I told this to Jones. He was satisfied, but as he left my office, he asked why no one had bothered to tell him before. After all, it was his job, and had we let him know, this and other problems could have been avoided."

"Well, if that's the way we do it, I can't say I blame him. Go ahead, on the basis that we will make every effort to explain beforehand, but that we are not bound to do so when circumstances make a quick change necessary."

The union met. Clayton started.

"Some demands we can give up or at least soften, but until we can see some more money, I would like to hold off. On the other hand, we have to make some sort of move to show progress. What I suggest is this: give up the year-round vacation schedule. Most of us take a vacation during the summer anyway, although I must admit there is a trend toward vacations at other times. But we can go after that later."

"Athey takes a winter vacation. Why can't I?" complained Brown.

"Well, for one thing, you're not the hard-working president. Murray? Clark? Zowalski? How do you feel about this?"

"I think you're right, Bill. Sometime we'd like to take a winter vacation, but right now most of us go in the summer, and I hear that some plants go only during a two-week shutdown period during July or August," Murray agreed.

Clark and Zowalski said they felt the same way as Murray.

"O.K. That's it."

"I don't like it," shouted an angry Brown.

"You're outvoted."

The Wednesday meeting was held. Beforehand, Hunt had decided to chance a combined meeting to see whether the hostile tension had softened.

Both sides filed into the room and sat down at the table across from each other, with Hunt in between at the head. As they had not faced each other for some weeks, there was an air of self-conscious stiffness in the room. Hunt noticed that Athey and Brown completely ignored each other.

Hunt reviewed the progress made. "Some encouraging give-and-take has happened since you asked me to assist, and I commend you for it. But you are still a long way from settlement, and this is our fifth meeting. I hope you will be able to move faster together—that is why we're here today. And before we go on, I'd like personally to thank you for the excellent cooperation you have given me. I hope I've been of service to you—after all, when you get down to it, you're really my boss.

"Who would like to open the meeting? I assume, as agreed before, that you, Bill, will speak for your committee, and that you, George, will speak for yours. Is that so?"

Clayton and Athey nodded approval.

"I'll start, if it's all right," said Clayton.

"Agreeable, George?"

"Right."

Clayton began, "We've looked at the demands and still think many of them are fair and reasonable. But we also know that others, frankly speaking, are negotiable. We're here to see how we can work this out and settle."

"What are you willing to discuss, Bill?" Hunt asked.

"Any of the outstanding issues," Clayton answered cordially.

"There are some demands we won't discuss," pronounced Athey irascibly.

"You won't, eh?" Brown erupted.

"But *we* will, and if we have something to offer, have you?" Clayton cut in swiftly, turning to Smith.

"We are prepared to make a counteroffer," Smith shot back before anyone could interrupt.

"O.K. Our people would like more freedom to plan vacations for times other than during the summer. More and more families are taking winter vacations, and we're no different from anyone else. After all, a vacation is only useful and restful if a family can plan one to suit its own interests and living pattern. But apparently you don't see it this way yet. So we're willing to concede on this point," Clayton said.

"That's something," Athey snorted sarcastically.

"You bet it is!" blazed Brown.

"We'll counteroffer. We have considered your request that,

before we make any unusual change in an employee's job, we notify him in advance. We have looked into this thoroughly and are willing to concede it as fair, provided management is not so completely restricted that emergency changes can't be made without notice beforehand." Smith offered this directly to Clayton.

"Is this acceptable to both of you?" Hunt queried calmly.

"It is to us," Clayton quickly agreed.

"We'll buy it," Smith concurred hurriedly.

"Let's record that as agreed," Hunt said. "Now, are there any other points to be resolved at this meeting?"

"Let's talk about money instead of all this garbage," Brown yelled.

"What you call garbage *is* money. What you want is the whole company without any responsibility for making money," roared a red-faced Athey.

Hunt intercepted, "It's nearing lunchtime, and I suggest we adjourn for the day. I'll call each of you tomorrow about the next meeting, if that's agreeable."

Smith and Clayton approved. Chairs scraped back on the wooden floor as they got up silently and filed out of the room.

As the strike entered its tenth week, Hunt sat down to plan his next move. He decided he had made a mistake by bringing both sides together too soon. On the other hand, the flare-up in the meeting proved conclusively that no real progress was possible so long as Athey and Brown were present in any joint meeting. His best approach, he thought, would be to meet separately with Smith and Clayton, explain the problem as he saw it, and ask them what could be done to solve it. He had worked with the two before and knew they were hard, but fair, bargainers. He had also observed that each had developed a quiet respect for the other.

Hunt called Clayton and told him that he wanted to discuss the situation, not over the telephone but in his office. He asked whether Clayton would be kind enough to come and see him the next afternoon. Clayton understood and said that he could meet with him after three o'clock, following a union meeting.

Then Hunt called Smith, repeating the request. Smith offered to come at four, pending Athey's approval, which he obviously had to get.

Smith went to Athey's office for a meeting of the management committee. He described his conversation with Hunt, and suggested that although he did not know what he wanted, as a courtesy he ought to go and see him. After talking it over, Athey and Rogers decided there was nothing to lose, and Athey gave his approval.

The next afternoon Clayton met with Hunt.

"Bill, as you well realize, we aren't making any real progress in this negotiation."

"How well I know, John, how well I know! This is one of the toughest I've been through in a long time. The situation is still very rigid, even though there has been some softening. Frankly, I know George has some problems in his group, but so have I. I'm sure you recognize that this guy Brown can be a real pain in the ass. He's hard to control."

"I'm glad you offered that thought, because that's what I wanted to speak to you about. I would like to pass along this observation between you and me. As long as Brown is in the meeting along with Athey, it seems to me that real, flexible bargaining can't take place."

"You're right."

"There is simply too much emotional conflict between the two, and nothing can be done to resolve it now. Something from the past seems to exist between them that isn't obvious to me. Would you, and could you, get Brown to stay away from the meetings?"

"He's a rambunctious cuss, and it will be hard to do—but I can't see any other way around the problem. Part of it hinges on whether George Smith and Rogers can persuade Athey to stay out. Their problem with him is even harder to handle than mine is with Brown."

"That will be a tough one, but I plan to talk to George later. I'll let you know. I assume I can tell him that you will persuade Brown to stay out if he, with Rogers, will ask Athey to do the same?"

"Yes."

"Thank you."

Clayton left, and Hunt waited to see Smith. At four George Smith walked into the office and sat down.

"George, as you know, the meetings are not producing much in the way of progress toward a settlement."

"John, you can say that again. We're still in a locked position, even though some evidence of concession has appeared. In the last meeting Bill Clayton signaled he was ready to begin negotiating a settlement, but Brown keeps getting in his way. He's got a problem there. But so have we. Mr. Athey is a fine man, and an excellent executive, but he sees all this as an intrusion on his real authority and a threat to the successful management of his company. He is deeply sincere about that. He was trained in the old school where management ran things with few questions asked. But negotiating isn't his 'bag,' as the kids say. He isn't temperamentally suited for it, and being taunted by an old-time employee from a group that always accepted his authority with respect is more than we can expect him to take gracefully."

"This is what I want to talk over with you. I've already talked to Bill. As you say, he's got a problem. I asked to see each of you separately from the others because you're old hands at this and understand what's going on. The others are all too new to grasp what's actually happening. Bill agrees that he's got a problem with Brown—that as long as he is in the meetings, movement can't be made. But, he says that he can't ask Brown to stay out of the meetings unless you and Rogers can persuade Athey to stay away. He will try it if you will."

"I was afraid you would ask that. I'm sure you realize that this puts Rogers and me in a touchy position. Athey is Charlie's boss and my client. It's a tough one, but we have to try. Otherwise, this could drag into a long and bitter strike that will leave scars for years."

"I'd appreciate it. Would you let me know? Bill is doing the same."

"Yes."

"Thank you. It seems pointless to ask for another meeting until we can work this out. If I may say so, everyone seems to be overtired from the strain, and a breather might help."

"You're right. It's already cost me my annual fishing trip."

Smith shook hands and left. When he got back to his office, he found a telephone call from Athey. He returned it immediately.

"George, I've had a call from one of our directors, Frank Marlin. It seems that one of the union officials with whom he used to bargain called him to see what he could do to help settle the strike. Isn't that getting way out of line? What business does he have calling one of our directors? I'm supposed to be running this company, and I don't like it!" stormed Athey.

"What did Mr. Marlin tell him, Mr. Athey?" asked Smith quietly.

"Fortunately, Frank said that he had been through all this, and

he told Scanlon—I think that was his name—that he was a director, that I was doing a competent job running the company, and
that he was in no position to interfere."

"It's unfortunate, but that happens occasionally." Sensing that
Athey was calming down somewhat, he suggested, "My advice, Mr.
Athey, is that you should simply ignore that move. It's simply an
attempt to put more pressure on you."

"That's what Frank said. O.K., let's forget it," said Athey in a
more conversational tone.

Luckily for Smith, Athey, in his excited concern over the phone
call from Marlin, forgot to ask him about his meeting with Hunt.
Smith didn't want to talk about it until he had a chance to explain
to Rogers. He called Rogers and asked if he and Hanson could
come to his office for a meeting to discuss his conversation with
Hunt. Rogers said that they would come right over.

The two men, looking strained and apprehensive, came into
Smith's office and sat down.

"Charlie, I've met with John Hunt, and he has a suggestion
for Bill Clayton and us. It's tough enough for Bill, but even
tougher for us. John believes, and Clayton and I agree, that as
long as Mr. Athey and Brown are in the meetings, no real progress
can be made. Bill Clayton has told John that if we can persuade
Mr. Athey to stay out of the meetings, he will keep Brown away."

"Whew! That's a beaut," whistled Rogers softly.

"How can we ask Mr. Athey to stay away!" asked an astonished
Hanson.

"Well, we've got to try. Scanlon put pressure on Mr. Athey
through a director he knows from his earlier negotiating days.
Scanlon called Mr. Marlin to ask him if he could do something to
help end the strike. Marlin told him that he did not interfere with
the running of the company, and that Mr. Athey was president and
a very competent one. Scanlon expected that. But he's pretty
certain that his move hasn't eased the strain on Mr. Athey. As you
can see, the pressures are really building up. I listened to the
radio driving into town this morning, and one commentator be-
rated us both for standing like stubborn schoolboys with chips on
our shoulders while families go hungry. And the editorials in the
evening and morning papers aren't exactly complimentary. There
are also letters to the editor asking the mayor to intercede."

"I can tell you, our customers are plenty unhappy," Rogers
added.

"And I hear that a back-to-work movement is under way among the employees," remarked Hanson.

"So, that brings us back to this very sticky problem. Charlie, I've been thinking about this for some time. I could see it coming, and believe me, I had hoped that somehow we could avoid this, but here it is in our laps. The best approach is to say to Mr. Athey that, at this stage in negotiations, the top man usually withdraws if he has been there; or if not, that he does not enter and run the risk of introducing new complications into an already intricate set of problems, technical and human. We could say, further, that as we reach the critical point where settlement may be near, he cannot be trapped into making a commitment he might not make in a less tense moment, and regret later on. Although he would be outside the meeting, we can't make a commitment without his approval. In that sense he controls the negotiations, and he could think about them in the calm of his office, not in the middle of an uproarious session. I also have another thought that might be helpful. This is the procedure we use at the Xylon Corporation. Tom Hendrix, the president, is a friend of Mr. Athey's. Tom has often said that the two of them exchange views on management problems. We could suggest that Mr. Athey call him."

"Say! That might work. It might just work!" said Rogers thoughtfully.

Rogers arranged a meeting with Athey to report on Smith's meeting with Hunt. At Smith's suggestion, Rogers and Hanson had agreed that Smith was in a better position to approach Mr. Athey than they, as subordinates, were.

In an apprehensive mood the three walked into Athey's office and sat down before him. Athey's face was drawn, and he slumped in his chair as he waited for them to begin.

"Mr. Athey," Smith hesitated, then went on, "I've met with John Hunt, and he has a proposal for both sides. He observes that your presence in meetings is upsetting to the committee. They are not used to meeting with the top man—as employees, they have only heard or seen you at a distance up to now. This is more evident in Brown than in the others."

"Am I something of an ogre to them?" Athey asked querulously.

"No. Far from it. It's just that these men stand in awe of you. This is more usual than not in similar situations. Hunt has suggested that we meet without you present. He also suggested to the union that Brown be taken from their meetings, too, as he upsets everyone, including Clayton."

"That's the understatement of the year," grumbled Athey sarcastically.

"True. There are more important reasons, in my opinion, for having you available, but outside the meeting. If you are present as top man, every statement you make is taken as a commitment. During heated sessions the committee might misconstrue or twist your words into a decision you had no idea of making. This is more likely to be true as we reach the critical point near settlement. On the other hand, if you are not present, they know that the rest of us can't make a commitment of consequence without your approval. This gives us leverage because, when we want to divert or stall while we consider the significance of a move, we can simply say that we want to check with you. We could only use prior or subsequent limits set by you. This leaves you in complete control of the situation, frees you from time-consuming meetings, and allows you to consider moves here in the quiet of your office."

The three waited for the storm, but Athey was thoughtful.

"There is one other thought. I believe Tom Hendrix is a friend of yours. This is the tactic he uses at Xylon. Perhaps you would like to review it with him?"

"He is, and I will." Athey picked up the phone and dialed Hendrix's number. He waited. Hendrix's secretary quickly put him on the line.

"Tom, this is Martin. As you damn well know, we've got a nasty strike going over here. We're meeting in my office to decide our next move. The suggestion has been made that, at this stage in the bargaining, I ought to stay away from the meetings but be around for decisions. George Smith is here. He has explained that you operate this way over there, so I'm calling to get your advice, as you have been at this for some years."

Athey listened as Hendrix spoke in a staccato voice that could be heard by everyone. Intermittently, Athey asked a question, or nodded with an "I see." For twenty minutes Hendrix talked. The others waited anxiously, but Athey gave no indication of his feelings.

"Tom, that's very helpful. Thank you," Athey said as he put down the phone.

He turned to face the committee.

"George, Tom gives exactly the same reasons you do—he says

he finds it works much better that way. So, consider me removed from the meetings, but be sure to check with me and keep me informed of all moves. Charles, that is basically your responsibility."

"Yes, Mr. Athey."

The three men left the office visibly relieved. In the hallway, Rogers looked at Hanson and Smith, and let go a long whistle.

Meanwhile, Clayton called Murray and asked him to come to his office. After Murray had sat down, Clayton began.

"Bob, we've got a tough one. I've talked with John Hunt, and he has a suggestion. His thought is that we can make little progress in meetings as long as Brown is there. He tends to blow his lid, particularly at Athey, and causes meetings to break up. I happen to agree with John. He also suggests that more progress could be made if Athey weren't present. We left it that I would get Brown out of the meetings if they can get Athey out."

"Wow! That is a sticker. Sam is very proud of his position on the committee, but for some reason he seems to like baiting Mr. Athey. That's no good. How do we do this?"

"I've been worried that this might happen, so I've given the matter a lot of thought. We may have to vote him out of the meetings, if you, Clark, and Zowalski will agree. But I'd sooner not do that except as a last resort. He's well thought of around the shop. What I suggest is this: We actually need someone familiar with the situation to oversee activities at strike headquarters and to answer questions about where we stand. He could also keep aware of the pulse of feelings toward the strike, and warn us if a serious back-to-work movement is developing. This isn't a put-up job. Sam has our people's confidence, and he could handle it well. Meanwhile, he would attend all of our own meetings."

"Say! That could work. That could do the trick."

"Just in case, you'd better cover the bases with the other two."

"I'll do it now."

Within an hour Murray was back in Clayton's office.

"Clark and Zowalski like the idea of putting him in charge of headquarters, and have voted him out of the meetings in any event."

Clayton called Brown in.

"Sam, we've got a real job around here that needs to be done, and I hope that you will volunteer."

He described the job, watching carefully for Brown's reaction. As he came to the part about not being able to attend meetings, disappointment spread over Brown's face, but, Clayton noticed hopefully, more mildly than he had expected.

"I don't like to miss the meetings. I've been around here a lot longer than the others, and know a lot more about what's going on," Brown complained.

"We make the important decisions about what we're going to do in our own meetings, and you'll be there to help make them," coaxed Clayton.

"O.K. I'll do it."

Clayton smothered a sigh of relief.

Outside criticism continued to mount. Newspaper reporters, radio and television commentators constantly called both sides. They reported to the public only that "some progress is being made, they tell us, but how much isn't clear. Something ought to be done. If the union, management, and Hunt can't do anything, maybe the mayor can. How about it?"

The management committee met. Smith suggested to the others offering three days' sick leave. "This," he said, "is something of real substance to them, and experience shows that if it is carefully administered, abuse can be minimized. Spread over all the hours worked by employees, the cost would be nominal. If we offer this, we could also tie it in to our demand for a management rights clause."

After considerable discussion, the others agreed that it was a good offer, and Athey approved it.

The union committee met to decide their next step.

"We have to move," said Clayton. "My idea would be to drop our demand for the right to appeal a change in an employee's job without his consent. In return, we could ask for the grievance system we want." They talked it over, and approved.

Hunt reviewed the situation. The strike was now entering its twelfth week, and he thought that the time had come to press for a settlement. He decided, however, that he would not bring the groups together until he could observe the tenor and progress of the next meeting, which he called for Tuesday morning.

As the committees arrived, Hunt again placed them in separate rooms. He conferred with Clayton and his committee first.

"John, we will drop our demand for an employee's right to appeal a job change without his consent. In return we want a strong grievance clause with an arbitration step," Clayton offered calmly.

"O.K., Bill. Now, without revealing your position, let me go and see what management's position is." He went to the management committee room.

"John, we are willing to grant three days' sick leave in return for a strong management rights clause," said Smith in a cordial tone.

"O.K., George. With your committee's consent, I'll take this to the union and come back with their counteroffer."

Rogers and Hanson nodded agreement.

Hunt worked back and forth, exchanging the positions of the two sides. Nothing was definitely settled, but movement was picking up momentum. He observed that the offers created a favorable reaction on both sides, and he noticed a diminishing of tension throughout the meeting. Since real progress was being generated, he concluded that he would not press too hard and risk throwing the negotiations back into bitterness. This was a delicate point in the procedures, and he believed he should not crowd progress, even though the public clamor would undoubtedly rise.

He called for a meeting the following Tuesday.

Between meetings Hunt studied the problems and finally isolated the real issues. On the union side, they were money, a grievance and arbitration system, and reinstatement of Murray; on the management side, money, the cost-of-living formula, and a strong management rights clause.

Management met, and Athey approved a recommendation that Hanson had made: By agreeing to supply all safety equipment, management would not only enhance its safety efforts, but it would bring about a favorable response from the employees and be able to do so at much less cost than originally estimated. In return, they could ask the union to drop the cost-of-living demand. Clayton and his committee decided to drop the demand for clean-up time in return for more money.

At Tuesday's meeting, Hunt still kept the two sides apart. He worked between them, exchanging the concessions made and the contingencies asked for in return. Still he did not press, but asked for a meeting on the following Monday.

In his office later, Hunt was planning. "Progress is moving solidly along. Now is the time to bring them together and suggest moving into the basic issues. But," he thought, "in the first meeting I had better confine them to a review of the issues—at least until they have time to get used to being together again."

The strike was now about to enter the fourteenth week. It was almost Thanksgiving. Public pressure was growing daily.

The media stepped up their demands for public intervention. Customers were less cordial about wanting to know when the strike would end and shipments begin. Members of the clergy appealed to both sides to put a stop to this unfortunate strike. Their parishioners were without money and running low on credit. Brown reported to the committee that he sensed a strong back-to-work movement was developing.

Hunt held to his position, although he too was feeling the press from the public and his superiors to "get this thing settled soon."

Monday arrived. Hunt guided the two committees into a bare meeting room with a long table in the center, and asked them to sit across from each other. Clayton and Smith greeted each other by their first names, and the others followed suit.

Hunt opened the meeting, saying, "It seems to me that now is an excellent time to review where we stand at this point. Both of you have made concessions in the spirit of give-and-take, and, in my opinion, that is what this system is all about. It can't be too much take, nor can it be all give. Otherwise no bargaining exists. Let's get to the issues."

He outlined, step by step, what had happened so far, then asked for a review of the unresolved demands.

"Who would like to discuss a particular point?" he asked, looking around the table.

"If it's all right with them, I'd like to talk about the grievance clause," Clayton replied.

"O.K.," Smith answered, after glancing at Rogers and Hanson.

The discussion flowed back and forth between the committees and Hunt. As the meeting went on, Hunt had less and less to say. He noticed that in the case of the grievance system, management balked at the request for arbitration, but he said nothing about it.

At Rogers's request, the grievance question was put aside and the cost-of-living demand discussed. Hunt saw that management was strong in its belief that granting this would be detrimental—because of the unpredictability of the trend, projecting costs would be difficult in their highly competitive industry. The union, in return, asked for more money and the reinstatement of Murray.

Although progress was made, nothing was firmly settled. Arguments between them were long and strong, but much of the bitterness and tension was gone.

Hunt recommended that since it was Thanksgiving week no further meetings be held until the next Monday. He appealed to both sides to review their positions carefully and come prepared to move into a settlement. He reminded them that he, too, was under considerable stress, from the outside as well as from his superiors. "I know that you are under much more pressure than I, and I can appreciate the burden placed on each of you. In my opinion you are making a great deal of progress, and I would suggest that a joint statement of progress be made and released to the press."

Hunt's delaying the next meeting until after Thanksgiving was deliberate. The weary negotiators needed rest. Between them a joint statement was prepared, which Hunt released to the press. They adjourned.

The management committee met. Mr. Athey opened the meeting; he was calm, but his voice had a tone of anxiety in it.

"Gentlemen, I must admit that I'm under very severe pressures from our customers, and even our directors and stockholders are asking why we can't seem to get this thing settled. As you know, we, as well as the union, are the objects of a severe lambasting from the press. What do you suggest?"

Rogers spoke next. "Mr. Athey, George, Phil, and I have carefully studied where we stand. Our conclusion is that more money will be needed to reach a settlement. We have made a more extensive study of the settlements in the area and believe it will take at least 30 cents in wages and 10 cents in benefits to settle. That is what the Xylon Corporation gave. But for the next meeting, we suggest that we offer 25 cents in wages and 7 cents in benefits in return for a strong management rights clause to keep control—and no cost-of-living adjustment. The rest of the money we recommend be held until we are near settlement to help to clinch it." Rogers reported in a strained voice, and Athey noticed that all three were tired and drawn.

"George, does that make sense to you?"

"Yes, it does, Mr. Athey."

"All right, Charles, go ahead."

At strike headquarters Clayton argued persuasively with the committee. "As you know, we are under heavy pressure to settle. Sam reports that a meeting was held at Ralph Hausner's house the other night to organize a back-to-work movement, and it was well attended. My superiors are pressing me to finish this. All of us, particularly Sam, have been getting a lot of blunt demands that we get busy and settle the strike before their credit runs out. And all of us are taking a lacing from the press. My idea is to lower the money demand shortly, but, before we do that, to put more emphasis on the question of ability to do the job than on seniority. After all, if a substantial difference in skill and ability exists, it's to no-body's advantage to put one of us into a job he can't do simply because of his seniority. We'll ask in return that an employee's inability to do a job must be definitely proven."

The committee discussed this and agreed. Sam Brown readily nodded after Clayton carefully explained it to him. During the meeting Clayton observed that Murray was beginning to grasp what this was all about and was finally developing a feel for nego-tiations. He also noted that everyone was tired and a little irritable.

Thanksgiving weekend passed.

On Monday the two sides again faced each other across the table. Hunt asked, "Who would like to open?"

"We'll be glad to begin," Rogers offered cooperatively.

"Please do."

"We have considered our position carefully since the last meet-ing," said Rogers. "We still want nothing to do with the cost-of-living adjustment. It would affect our cost projections in that we can't predict what the trend in living costs will be. As we see it, we'll take care of that by keeping our wages in line with trends. We want a clause that will clearly spell out management's rights in running the business. In return we are willing to move to 25 cents on wages and 7 cents on benefits."

"Bill, what have you to say?"

"We appreciate the offer. Obviously, I have to take it back to the membership—they're pretty strong on the cost-of-living adjust-ment. We want an arbitration step in the grievance system, but we'll offer to go along with a modification in the seniority section that will allow an employee with less seniority to be placed in a job where there is a measurable difference in skill and ability. That will have to be defined."

This led to a lengthy give-and-take over the seniority system. Considerable argument took place, but there were no angry flashes. At the end of the afternoon, they decided to adjourn and meet on Friday.

The strike was now in its fifteenth week.

Hunt believed progress was heading toward a settlement. Basic issues were being negotiated. He concluded that he could begin reducing the importance of his role. The union met.

"I have the feeling we're really moving now. What do you think, Bill?" asked Murray.

"You're right. I suggest that our next step is not to accept or reject the money offer outright, but to indicate that we are more pleased than we have been and that another move might get us to see things a little differently. As I said in our last meeting, the time has come to lower our money demands. My recommendation is to lower wages to 35 cents and the benefit demand to 15 cents. What do the rest of you think?"

"If you remember, you told us at the start of this that we should not expect to win everything we ask for the first time around. Now I can see how this works. I think you're right," answered Murray enthusiastically.

Zowalski and Clark nodded in agreement.

Management convened in Athey's office. "Where do we go from here, Charles?" asked Athey calmly.

"Mr. Athey, at this time we recommend that we stand for the moment on money and push for the other things we want, such as the management rights clause. We suggest we move on the vacation schedule, offering four weeks after 20 years of service. We figure it won't cost very much, and it's attractive to the union."

This was argued at length until Athey approved. Smith suggested that, before holding any meetings in the future, Rogers check to be sure that Mr. Athey would be available, as his approval of last-minute changes might be needed. Athey said he would make it a point to be available until the strike was settled.

On Friday they met in Hunt's offices. Clayton looked at Hunt and said the union would like to open the meeting. Hunt turned to Rogers, who nodded. "O.K. Bill, go ahead."

"Bob Murray would like to speak first, and I'd like to add to it. Bob?"

"We have reviewed the demands carefully, as Mr. Hunt has asked us to do. In reply to your offer to increase the money package, we will lower our demand to 35 cents on wages and 15 cents on benefits. Bill?"

"Yes, we are here to negotiate seriously, and we believe we're making progress. Some things you want, and there are those we would definitely like."

"May I suggest that you start working on these items, and keep working on them for the rest of the day?" Hunt asked. They agreed. After bargaining began, Hunt quietly left the room, returning occasionally to check progress. At the end of the day, he asked them to summarize what had been done. He found that considerable progress had been made on the grievance, seniority, and management rights sections. Both sides agreed to the suggestion that they meet again on Tuesday.

Meetings were held on Tuesday and again on Friday. Advances were made on everything but money, the cost-of-living adjustment, and the arbitration clause. The reinstatement of Murray was not discussed.

During these meetings Hunt participated very little in the actual discussions, but as they progressed, both Rogers and Murray played increasing roles.

Public pressure rose to a high. Radio and television reporters and commentators asked the mayor to intervene. Brown told Clayton that the back-to-work movement was gaining support daily and becoming serious. The mayor called Athey and Clayton, wanting to know whether his office could be of any help. Both told him politely that real progress was being made and that an early settlement seemed likely.

The next time management met, Rogers had a suggestion to make. "Mr. Athey, if we give on the arbitration demand and reinstate Murray, we are almost certain we can settle. An arbitration step in the grievance procedure is commonly found in contracts today. If you want to find out more about it, George thinks you should call Tom Hendrix. He's got such a clause in his contract."

"That's not a bad idea—calling Tom, I mean—although I still don't see why we have to have an outsider help us settle our differences."

Athey called Tom Hendrix, and the two discussed the question at some length. They could hear Hendrix's rapid words as Athey nodded into the telephone. He thanked Hendrix, said good-bye, and hung up.

"I'm not absolutely convinced, but Tom says it hasn't really been a problem over there. He says they manage to settle practically all of their grievances before the arbitration step is reached. If granting that will bring this to an end, I'll agree. But as for reinstating Murray, how can I do that? I fired him. Bringing him back would be bad for discipline—any employee who gets fired could expect to be reinstated."

The committee discussed the state of negotiations further, then planned the next meeting. The others did not press Athey on the Murray issue.

Clayton met with his committee.

"I believe we are coming to the point where we've got to accept the company's offer. As Sam says, the back-to-work movement is gaining ground. We can't afford to have that take over, or we'll lose control now and in the future. I suggest that if they make one more move on money, give us an arbitration step, and reinstate Murray, we should take it. This strike is about to enter the seventeenth week, and is no longer serving much purpose. It's bad for the company as well as for us."

The committee planned their moves for the next meeting, and all agreed with Clayton's tactics.

On Monday everyone met again. Hunt, believing a settlement was near, reduced his role to a minimum.

"Bill, do you or Bob want to go first?" Rogers asked.

"O.K., Bob, want to take over?"

"Thanks. If you'll agree to an arbitration step, we'll grant the seniority clause that you want, along with the management rights clause."

"That's our proposal. What have you got to offer?" Clayton asked, turning to Rogers.

"We'll agree to work out an arbitration clause, and we'll add a vacation improvement—four weeks after 20 years of service. We still won't agree to a cost-of-living formula."

For the rest of the day the committees worked on various parts of the agreement, arguing and adjusting language to meet each other's thoughts.

At the end of the afternoon the meeting was adjourned and another one set for Wednesday. In the Wednesday meeting, they continued drafting the agreement. Meetings followed on Thursday and Friday. By now Hunt was barely involved. A joint press release was issued saying that a settlement was pending.

On Saturday, Rogers made the final offer of 35 cents on wages and 10 cents on benefits. After they talked it over, the committees agreed to have benefits experts from both sides work out how to distribute the 10 cents.

At the end of the day Clayton said pointedly, as the meeting was breaking up, "You know, this isn't a bad package. I don't see any problem with the cost-of-living formula, but the reinstatement is a tough one."

Rogers and the others went to Athey. "Mr. Athey," he said, "we can understand your point on Murray. But if you approve his reinstatement, we are almost certain we can settle this tomorrow. We would like to say this in all fairness. Murray has not been arrogant in the meetings; he's been reasonably cooperative, and he has tried to learn. Also, he *is* popular with the others. We believe this is a case of a young man who made a mistake and got off to a bad start. If we agree to reinstate him, it will take away bitterness on the part of the others. The only suggestion in taking him back—and this is George's—is that the union must agree that the reinstatement will not set a precedent." They waited.

"Well, let's talk about this further," Athey said doubtfully, and for an anxious hour the three discussed the problem. Athey was reluctant, but he approved it.

The union committee was also meeting.

"I think we can settle this tomorrow," Clayton predicted. "They know that if Murray is reinstated, we'll give on the cost-of-living demand. My guess is that they'll come through, and we can go for the cost-of-living adjustment at another time. I doubt that Athey can prolong the strike on that alone. It would be an ill-advised and very unpopular position."

On Sunday the committees met. An air of excited and anxious expectancy spread among the weary bargainers. The meeting opened with a discussion and agreement on benefits. This was annoyingly slow, as the experts had to examine the many technicalities involved. By mid-afternoon, however, the basics were settled.

Rogers turned abruptly to Clayton.

"Bill, if you'll drop the cost-of-living demand, we'll agree to reinstate Murray as long as it isn't considered to be precedential."

"We'll buy that."

After the necessary wording had been worked out, Clayton turned to Rogers. "O.K.," he said in a friendly tone. "We'll take this to the membership and recommend acceptance. We'll do it tonight, and I'll call the results to you."

"Good."

The meeting adjourned with much cordial handshaking.

The union met that evening. Clayton had a little trouble with a few diehards, but the recommendation was overwhelmingly approved. He called Rogers right away, who put the back-to-work schedule into action. The strike ended as it entered its eighteenth week, five days before Christmas.

14

An Analysis of Causes

WHAT are the underlying causes that brought about this violent disagreement and strike, and what are the skills and forces that were brought to bear to resolve it?

Athey, Victim of Change

Athey, with the board of directors' approval, manages the affairs of the corporation in the traditional patriarchal style set by his predecessors. He has been raised within it, and to him it is the proper way of life. Within the framework of that style, his personality and bearing—tall, patrician, and distant—fit. That is one reason why he succeeded to the chief executive officer's position. He is never addressed by his first name except by his peers.

But, over the years, the aspirations and the attitudes of the employees of the corporation have changed. They are more informed, more independent in outlook, and more demanding in those matters that affect their well-being. While they are not conscious of it, the employees have become unwilling to submit to a somewhat dictatorial leadership, however benign the leader. The fact is that Athey, unwittingly, because his experience has been totally confined within a patriarchal framework, hasn't sensed the need for adjusting to a more democratic, inclusive style. Had he been able to recognize this need, he might have been able to make a successful adjustment. This realization, however, would probably have been more intellectual than actual, because his personality and temperament are more exclusive than gregarious.

The patriarchal style has outlived its usefulness and has become obsolete.

Athey's style may be obsolete, but one should not make the mistake of assuming that he has not been an excellent executive. He did not become chief executive officer—and continue to direct a profitable economic enterprise, providing a livelihood for 10,000 individuals and their families—by being stupid. He was elected to head the corporation because he was hard-working, intelligent, and suited to the traditional style of the organization. Had he not had these qualities, he could not have succeeded. Athey is less the victim of his own shortcomings than of the traditional management approach.

Inadequacies of the Communications Structure

Custom demanded that employee problems be processed through the management hierarchy. But as attitudes changed, employees became more vocal and daring in their demands. The traditional paternal outlook of supervision was not in tune with this approach, but was confused by it. The old system broke down, and inaction resulted.

Because these changing attitudes developed slowly and subtly, they passed unrecognized, and management was unprepared for them. It lacked the training to understand what was taking place, and it had no system for meeting these new attitudes effectively. Had the organization been sensitive to the problems, the unionization and the strike would not have occurred. Of all this, Athey was completely unaware.

The employees turned to the union and struck, because they found the system denied what they believed to be just demands in a changing world.

Not obvious at the time of the organization drive and the strike was the depth of the impact on employee relations of Mitchell's personality and performance as plant manager. We saw that he withdrew very willingly from the committee, and that Rogers didn't believe him to be strong in employee relations. During a review of the unionization and the strike, it became clear that he was a hard-working technician with little feel for employee relations. He was a poor communicator, uncomfortable with people. As a result he shied away from problems of employee relations and delayed resolving them until forced to do so.

Unwittingly, he was causing communication breakdowns and frustrating delays in answering employee suggestions and dealing with grievances. His failure in these areas had much to do with bringing the employees' grievances to a head and forcing them to go to Rogers. But until the causes were analyzed, no one, Rogers included, knew the extent to which his lack of action was damaging relationships.

The Firing of Murray

This was a bad mistake made by Athey. It triggered the events leading to the strike. This sort of thing had become unacceptable to employees whose attitudes toward the organization were no longer those of the past. During an earlier time, when the patriarchal style was still accepted, Athey's firing of Murray might have caused grumbling, but there it would have ended. But, it must be recalled, to Athey, Murray represented an insubordinate upstart who dared to defy the system and the chief executive officer in the presence of others. According to the old style, this sort of behavior warranted excommunication. Athey did not recognize that Murray was a part of a new generation. His was a very human error.

Rogers as a Symbol

The original committee went to see Rogers because they recognized that he seemed to be interested in them—that, although a member of the system, he would listen to their complaints. In this they were correct.

Rogers had succeeded within the company by complying with its customary behavior, but he was interested in learning new techniques, so he went to seminars, attended schools, and read as much as he could. Being gregarious by nature, he was also interested in improving employee relations. He tried to introduce new approaches within the company, but was only moderately successful, as neither his superiors nor his peers were as sensitive to the needs in this area as he was.

He was loyal to Athey and the organization, but he could see the need for change and did as much as the system would allow. He knew there were problems with employee complaints, but he could not overcome the deep inbreeding of the system; nor had he completely plumbed the depths of employee resentment or understood that it had reached the critical, eruption point—the flash point.

Rogers represents the coming generation of leadership that recognizes the need for change, but, in its present capacity, has limited power to bring it about. Only when and if he becomes the chief executive officer will he be able to order those changes in organization and communications necessary to develop the more inclusive style needed to meet the demands of the new attitudes.

Murray as a Symbol

Murray is of the young generation whose family structure is more open and permissive and less patriarchal in attitude. The patriarchal style is foreign to him. He has not been raised in such an environment, either at home, at school, or in the community. The opposite is the case with the older employees who have had a long period of service within the organization.

In this situation, Murray was inexperienced and brash. His actions were not insubordinate in terms of how he was used to acting with those in authority. But, as his later actions revealed, he is smart and quick to learn—he is the raw material from which leadership can be developed. Through necessity and a sensible acceptance of subordinate advice, Athey made a sound decision to reinstate him without fully understanding its long-range positive effects.

Murray was placed on the committee because his coworkers sensed his unpolished leadership qualities. His leadership potential was not lost to the company, and it is not beyond the realm of possibility that he will rise to the executive level in the future.

Brown, the Paradox

Sam Brown has many years of service with the company. He once worked with Athey, when he was a young man beginning his career with the organization. Normally, in this situation, Brown would have cast his lot with management, as Athey did. He symbolizes the core of long-service members that are the very fiber of strength in any institution that stands the test of time. When he appears as a member of the committee on the other side, Athey is, naturally, both astounded and disturbed. He simply does not—cannot—understand why he appears with the dissenting and not the supporting group.

What happened to Brown? While he is an older member, he is not immune to the changing attitudes in the community and the company. As do the others, he wants the right to be heard in matters that affect his well-being. He no longer accepts the injustices of the old approach.

Later, it was discovered that he had been passed over for promotion to a supervisory position ten years before, and the man who was promoted was found to be long on favor with his superiors and short on acceptance by his subordinates. Brown considered this to be unjust, and so did his coworkers, of whom he was the informal leader. Bitterness had remained within him for all those years and motivated him to act as he did.

Clayton, when he wanted to remove Brown from the bargaining table, was shrewd in his decision to place him in charge of strike headquarters, where he could exercise some of his latent leadership talent.

The Basic Problem

The employee demands met with stiff resistance because they implied an approach that was foreign to the organization's long-standing and cherished life pattern. This move was counter to any custom.

The overt divergence between the two groups began here, but it had been a long time in the making. The basic problem began some years before, when attitudes started to shift, but the system, whose leadership was only vaguely aware of and insulated from changes in employee and community attitudes, continued insensitive to these changes. The result was a gradual breakdown in communications that failed to answer the needs of employees.

Accumulated dissatisfactions and tension forced the grievances out into the open, where they appeared in the form of the employees' committee. The act that triggered the unionization and the strike was the firing of Murray.

At this point it was inevitable that an eruption would occur. The members of the organization found its action, of which the Murray incident was only symptomatic, unacceptable to the point where they had to confront its leadership and demand change. It was also inevitable that its leadership—Athey—could not suddenly adjust to this new situation.

The Role of the Professionals

Both Smith and Clayton are highly experienced in resolving problems of conflict. They represent a stabilizing influence. They are mature men who understand the process and maneuver it skillfully. For example, they move quickly to adjourn meetings when the tension reaches a high level—before it can become even more critical.

Both recognized the problem between Athey and Brown and, when the time was right, moved to resolve it. Smith understood very well that Athey would respond to his suggestion to call Hendrix, a friend and a peer. Athey belonged to an era where top leaders associated with each other and were on a friendly basis, socially as well as in the world of business. It was an astute move to suggest that Athey call Hendrix about staying out of the meeting. It solved a sticky problem.

Clayton was as astute, in his own way, as Smith had been, in his move to take Brown from the meetings and place him in charge of strike headquarters. There he could use his talents— and at the same time remain active on the committee outside the meetings.

This was a critical turning point in moving toward settlement, and until it was accomplished, no real action could take place.

Curiously enough, neither Athey nor Brown reacted as strongly against the suggestions to stay away from the meetings as might have been expected. Why? Because neither of them actually wanted to be there. Athey was uncomfortable in this new arrangement, and Brown, while wanting to be a part of the committee, was tense and nervous, particularly in front of Athey, who symbolized his older loyalty to the company. And he was divided between two loyalties—the old and the new.

Smith and Clayton had been opposing each other for a number of years and had learned long ago that the other's word was good. Even though they traded hard at the bargaining table, they had a healthy respect for each other. They knew beforehand where they would come out at the end of the strike. In the last meeting before they brought in the mediator, Clayton had signaled to Smith that he was ready to begin trading, but the Athey-Brown feud erupted before Smith was able to do anything about it.

During the tense periods each remained calm. They were used to being under fire. Clayton appeared to lose his temper in the next-to-last meeting before they moved into conciliation and mediation—he got up and left the room abruptly—but that was a put-on meant to jar Athey loose, if possible. It didn't bother Smith, because he knew exactly what Clayton was doing.

They had been working with Hunt for some time and respected his fairness and good judgment. Also, both men understood how strange each member of the two committees felt in this new relationship, and they did what they could to lead and guide them into an understanding of the process as the strike deepened. Toward the end, as the members developed a surer feel for what was happening, Smith and Clayton brought Rogers and Murray more actively into the bargaining, working toward the future when, with sound experience, the two sides would be able to negotiate and resolve problems by themselves with minimum outside help.

Hunt's Role

Hunt is also an old hand at assisting in the resolution of conflict. He is good at his job. Otherwise, he couldn't have won the respect of Smith and Clayton. He set the tone for his relationship with the two by making it immediately clear to them that he was there only to assist and suggest; he was not a negotiator, nor was he there to tell them what to do. He was equally cordial with both sides, knowing that for him, in his role as mediator, it was essential not to sympathize with either.

What Hunt did in the first meeting was to listen. This was intentional. He knew that before he could do anything constructive, he had to get to the core of the problem. To do this he had to avoid the temptation to jump to quick and possibly erroneous conclusions.

He moved deliberately, as the timing and pace of the meetings indicated. Even under pressure from his superiors and the community, even when subjected to public verbal whippings, he refused to rush, knowing that the relationships were at a delicate point. He did not try to hurry, because that could have caused further deterioration instead of improvement. He quietly held off on meetings until the Athey-Brown removal was a fact.

The one attempt Hunt made at an early stage to bring the two sides together was as much to observe and gauge the degree of the divergence as it was to hope that they might be ready to settle.

After he had carefully isolated the real issues as well as the interpersonal conflicts, the pace toward settlement quickened. This was deliberate, as Smith and Clayton understood. The smaller issues were taken first, so that the sides could get used to the idea of exchange. Then he moved on to the larger ones.

Another skillful move Hunt made was to call off the meetings over the Thanksgiving weekend. This was not simply out of respect for the holiday. He recognized that everyone was tense and overtired—and thus less reasonable.

The Importance of the Professionals

The value of the skill and integrity of Smith, Clayton, and Hunt is hard to estimate. If any one of the three had been of less than average competence, the strike could have dragged on to the point where public indignation would have forced the mayor to intervene, and the strike could have ended with an acrid bitterness between the sides that might take years to mend.

If Clayton had been rigid in his stand instead of flexible and patient in the knowledge that he would continue on another day, the strike certainly would have been prolonged. If Smith had insisted that his side stand fast, that would have brought the same result. If Hunt had not been astute in his analysis, patient and able to stand the pressures, that too would have lengthened the period of conflict.

These were mature men who knew their jobs. But as we know, human beings come in all shapes, sizes, temperaments, and outlooks. They differ, too, in experience and ability, so that the ending of conflict of this kind is not always so skillfully brought about. And where skill is lacking, the conflict can be prolonged and eruptive, as was often the case when the collective bargaining process as we know it today was new.

This stresses the vital importance of using deliberate care in selecting those who are to operate the negotiating process. Too often, it is decided precipitately.

Internal and External Pressures

At the beginning of the strike, little pressure was brought to bear for a settlement. Beyond the employees, there was little effect on customers, owners, and the economy of the community. "Wait and see" was the attitude of all.

As the strike continued, the employees were the first to become concerned. They began to dig into savings, and the more they did so, the deeper their anxiety became, particularly at the end when they were asking for an extension of credit. As always, it was their economic well-being that was most seriously damaged.

This insecurity was the cause of several abortive back-to-work movements, and a serious one was building up toward the end of the strike. The real pressure here came from the wives, who were practical economists of no small order. No one understood the cost of living better than they, and, as they saw the bills mounting and the savings dwindling, they viewed standing on principle as something less than practical.

Customers tolerated the early period of the strike. Some had been through this kind of strife before, and they understood the company's difficulties. But when it seemed to go on and on, their concern increased sharply. Their own economic well-being was at stake. They informed Athey and his chief marketing executive that, while they were loyal, there was a limit to how long, practically speaking, they could wait.

The stress and tension of these anxieties became visible in the number of calls and visits from customers and in employee calls and visits to strike headquarters.

As they saw members of their parishes suffering more and more from the effects of the strike, the clergy began to approach management and the union to see whether and how they could help. With all due respect to them, there was little the clergy could do. They were not trained to think, feel, or respond to the rigors of this sort of process.

The damaging effect of the strike widened. The local economy was hit—an estimated $3½ million a month in wages was lost to the community. Local suppliers of goods and services to the company were the ones to suffer. As time passed and there was no visible evidence of an imminent settlement, the pressures from the community mounted and appeals were made to the mayor to intervene. He was reluctant to do so because he did not want it to become a practice to go to the mayor with every labor problem that could not be quickly settled. But by the end of the strike he was about to step in.

The press, radio, and television reported the progress or lack of progress, and as the strike lengthened, commentators asked why it was that the two sides could not exercise common sense, be less rigid, and settle. They tended to favor the strikers and aim at Athey, but they also castigated the union. They were for public intervention.

Major owners began to ask management questions, and fairly direct ones, about the cost of the strike. Directors, becoming uneasy in their position, began to call Athey. The union, in the person of Scanlon, its vice-president, tried to pressure him through a director.

Clayton, too, felt increasing pressure from Scanlon and other union officials as well as from the employees. And, of course, Hunt was continuously urged by his superiors to hurry a settlement.

As these tensions mounted and encircled the negotiators, they had a tempering effect on them. The professionals knew this and used it to their advantage. But they were worried, too, that things might get out of hand—a back-to-work movement, violence on the picket line, public intervention.

While it may not have appeared to be so to the public, these men had the toughness and the courage to stand, and they successfully brought a reasonable settlement out of an extremely difficult situation.

The responsibility for the strike, with its severe tensions and mounting pressures, had an exhausting effect on the negotiators. Hunt knew that a worn-out negotiator is not a good one. He makes mistakes. That is why he used Thanksgiving weekend as an excuse to rest the teams, even though he was under hard criticism for not speeding up the meetings to a round-the-clock pace—a very questionable procedure.

Frequently, inexperienced, or "soft," negotiators will nervously fall into a give-all settlement when subjected to the harassment of pressures. This is no settlement, but capitulation, and benefits no one.

The Change in Athey

Noticeable during the course of the strike was the change in Athey. He lost some of his adamancy, but neither his strength nor his convictions. Why?

As events unfolded, he came to realize that to continue a strict and rigid stand could lead eventually to economic hardship for the company, its employees and customers, the community, and himself.

He was pragmatic and flexible enough to see this, and although it was very difficult for him to give up the "old way," he eventually realized that he must. At the very last minute, with dragging reluctance, he decided to permit the reinstatement of Murray, a decision that will rankle inside him for some time to come.

Athey as well as the others who figured in bringing about the strike, had to recognize the depth of his responsibility toward those affected by it. He was a kind man, and in his own way always had regard and concern for all who work for the firm. And as the strike deepened, he became more pliable.

At the end he agreed to what it took to settle. With the resilience characteristic of a successful executive, he decided how he would go about making a recovery from the strike and planning the future course for the firm within the framework of this new relationship.

His behavior did not change basically; it was only modified.

15

The Inclusive Society

MUCH of what is contained in this chapter has been said or implied before, but the purpose here is to summarize and project what leadership skills will be required to manage successfully in this age of dissent and social upheaval. For that is what we are experiencing now and will continue to undergo in the foreseeable future.

Similar to the eighteenth century, ours is an age of scientific as well as social inquiry, of questioning, of examining the validity of traditions and customs, while restless disapproval is rocking our institutions. Although poverty is still with us, we have never been more affluent. We are well educated and well informed. We seem to be growing more independent-minded than ever. These are some of the contributing factors which are pressing against the inertia of institutional status quo. Not only are we, in this country, subject to these pressures, but so are other nations that enjoy less abundance.

What these pressures are forcing are changes in organizational structures and leadership skills to satisfy the shifting wants of members. Institutional lag—delay in adapting to changes in group and individual outlooks—is the principal cause of so much of the active dissent we see around us now. Also, independent, informed individuals and groups are discontented with and unwilling to submit to patriarchal, exclusive leadership with an institutional structure to match.

The general demand is for a more inclusive society, whether within our broad political and religious organizations, a university, or a corporation. Never, since we first declared independence, has the drive for our traditional right to have a say in decisions affecting our lives been so strong.

Perhaps too slowly, but instinctively we are turning to meet the insistent challenge from a society restive for change.

The New Design

Institutional structures need more resilience—they must develop the adaptability to respond to new demands and provide more opportunity for member contribution to decision making. Present forms are so segmented, specialized, and run by decree that individual and group initiative and innovative spirit are neutralized. Energies that flow from these qualities are lost, and are replaced by dispirited listlessness. Individual effort is sometimes so confined and routine that the effect is monotonic. This runs counter to man's natural desire to contribute to group effort in a meaningful way. Antagonisms develop and take the form of trying to "beat the system." Active dissent serves as an outlet when these antagonisms are allowed to fester for too long.

As we know, excessive confinement to an underprivileged position is the cause of minority outbreaks. For too long our social standards have contained minority groups at the lowest level of organizations, political, economic, and social. For years the law and the courts were of little help. Traditional blindness ignored these conditions, and the explosive situation among us now is the cost we have to bear. While our efforts admittedly have been insufficient, an encouraging conscious movement to correct these inequalities is well under way.

Our institutions are still structured so that the command echelon decides what to do, when it is to be done, and by whom. There is too little conferring with those affected, and too little explaining why the action has been taken. Decisions are made by individuals and high staff committees, based on the concept that only those in general positions are equipped by experience and station to make top decisions. To some extent this is true, but it is false to view those at lower levels as lacking the ability to know what is good for them. This is in contrast to the ideas of such men as Thomas Jefferson, who contended two centuries ago that the public has the common sense to judge its own welfare.

Whether that was so was debated heatedly at the time, but in our society of well-informed citizens the opposite concept is hard to defend. In fact, the demand for inclusion in deciding institutional affairs is so strong that it is making itself felt through active dissent and overwhelming resistance.

When Nixon instituted his wage-price freeze, the announcement was made by the president following a series of tightly closed meetings. The anger this spurred among union leaders was ominous. The state of Texas threatened to revolt. Prior to the freeze no one had been consulted. Strenuous efforts for appeasement had to be made by the top, and repeated assurance was publicly given that any decision about what to do beyond the 90-day freeze would be made only after consulting earnestly with major interests. Major interests were spelled out to be: labor, industry, agriculture, state and local governments, and that forgotten man, the consumer. Surely, intelligent government leaders had reasons for secrecy. Perhaps they feared that a leak of information before the announcement could not be risked—initial resistance would be too strong—reasoning that the program might be destroyed before it could be tried.

Whatever the reasons were, the calculation fell woefully short in estimating the strength of the anger expressed by those who felt they had a right to be consulted. Clear hindsight questions the soundness of the judgment. At any rate, it drives home how forceful the demand for inclusion is. Fundamental corrections in organization are in order. Primarily, the organization structure has to be redesigned so that more decision latitude is delegated to lower levels within the organization. Along with this, more information about organizational affairs, habitually guarded as top secret, should be forwarded as decision latitude is enlarged. Lower levels have to be brought into higher levels of decisions. Each level from the top, being given more, delegates latitude proportionately. Information relevant to the decision making has to follow the same pattern so that intelligent decisions based on fact can be made.

It follows, too, that lower levels should be trained to decide and, within reason, should be allowed the freedom to make mistakes. This demands firm self-discipline at higher echelons. Very important is careful selection of those to whom authority is delegated to be sure they qualify to exercise authority well.

In the business world, sound techniques such as planning for immediate and long-range objectives, management information systems, and budgetary control for appraising results are well known but are not yet widely practiced. And in the present state of technique development, practitioners seem to be enthralled more by the systems themselves than by what their purpose is. But the trend is in the right direction, and, with improvements, these techniques will aid measurably in creating a more inclusive organization environment. They can and should be applied in any organization that is striving to improve its inclusive structure.

The techniques may be known, but what isn't well understood is the demand for inclusiveness and the power of the discontent with the old way.

Not only does inclusiveness apply up and down the organization, but across as well. Lateral limits ought to be expanded to include more varied activities and to reduce the number of narrow segments into which individuals and groups are tightly boxed. The number of vertical and lateral divisions of authority areas should be reduced. Experience has shown that having fewer and wider areas of latitude allows capable individuals to use more talent, be more effective and satisfied—and the cost is less.

As an illustration, the top executive would allow a well-trained, competent subordinate officer to make decisions involving larger sums of money than previous restraints permitted. In turn, this officer turns more authority over money decisions to his immediate group. Also, the subordinate officer is deliberately included in high-level councils involving general decisions, particularly those related to his own area of responsibility. Involvement in top-level actions would restrict his time to attend to his immediate responsibilities, and force him to release more authority to his staff, if he is to be successful.

Laterally, individuals and groups are instructed to seek the counsel of others, when their actions may have an impact on their areas. If an engineer wants to make a change in a product design, he ought to consult with those who make and sell the product before he does so. This may seem to be obvious, but it is not unusual to find that problems arise because the action wasn't well coordinated.

Lateral inclusion is not limited to the immediate confines of the institution, but also reaches those outside who have an interest in its daily and long-term actions. If the top command is considering an action that will have an impact on the community in which the organization is located, opinions of appropriate community leaders should be thoughtfully sought. If, for example, the intention is to enlarge operations, which will bring more jobs and money to the local economy, the assumption can be easily made that everyone will be happy about it. Suppose, however, no discussion with community leaders is held and the project is optimistically launched. Imagine the dismay in executive quarters when an angry citizen group comes forward and threatens legal action because of the esthetic eyesore and pollution the expansion would bring to the community.

The inclusive structure is not easy to operate. It requires more tact, diplomacy, and tolerance than command by edict, but it is more sound in terms of meeting member and community needs. More importantly, it is necessary for successful survival because the trends of the times demand this form.

Some top leaders are very skillful with inclusion, but many only pay it lip service without really understanding how to manage this kind of environment. How well the top is operating inclusively can be determined obviously by the amount of active dissent scored against the organization, as well as by the more concealed discontent revealed through anonymous surveys.

Tolerance

Leadership today must be more tolerant than in the past. Open, fair-minded disagreement can no longer be censured as disloyalty. Within reason, the right to disagree should be encouraged and treated with respect. Inquiry and debate are characteristic of the times, and executives will fare better if they hone their debating and speaking skills and not come off the losers—as surely will happen if they continue to attempt to throttle an open forum.

Some of us seem to forget that debating is an old American custom, one which our forebears followed with candid vigor. Apparently, those of us in the older and higher ranks have been so preoccupied with technological competence that we have left these skills underdeveloped.

The youth of today don't want to accept decrees, preferring to examine and argue the point. This is healthy. To paraphrase Voltaire, we may disagree with what they say but should defend and encourage their right to say it. Expressions of dissatisfaction should not be seen as disloyal or insubordinate but as the functioning of vigorous minds.

Viewing decrees as unacceptable isn't confined to the student generation; many among the older of us as well have been caught up in the spirit of inquiry and debate and are now expressing our discontent more openly. Rather than simply opposing the questioning of dissenters with imperious irritation, we too should question whether it is justified and act accordingly, or give a skillful rebuttal if we disagree.

Tolerance is an attitude necessary in leaders during this period in which nonconformity is the mode. Rigid insistence on conformance to hair and clothing styles of the fifties is unrealistic, and can only result in ridicule. More than a few top executives have had to beat a hasty retreat from requiring adherence to past fashions, particularly where women are involved. Even the military services—with the exception of the marines, who, as usual, stand steadfast—have sensibly flexed with the times and set less restrictive standards of dress.

Allowing more individuality in sartorial elegance is only a superficial bow to tolerance, however. The concept has to be extended to norms of behavior. Ideas and actions that do not conform exactly to institutional traditions should be tolerated. Those of us who are older should look back and recall whether we ever rebelled against the rules of our parents. Most individuals— except the least imaginative—at some time of life have wandered, however temporarily, from the orthodox path.

Reasonable conformance to rules is necessary to the order of an institution, but rigid demands stifle ideas, the valuable along with the wild. To insist that others follow a completely prescribed manner, method, or procedure is asking for more than conformance. It locks up freedom of expression and runs against the natural grain of human behavior. Independent-minded individuals and groups today simply will not stand for this automatic approach; they will rebel either through active dissent or by leaving the institution, no matter what kind it is.

Each of us develops his own orthodox pattern of behavior through the years, and we automatically react in a defensive way against suggestions for changing that pattern. We should discipline ourselves to question this reaction, and to keep an open mind. A short time ago a subordinate came to my office to discuss the application of an established technique to a management study we were undertaking. Three times he tried to insert a suggestion as I droned the standard approach to him. The thought suddenly struck me that he hadn't had his say. When I stopped talking, he opened with an idea to adapt the procedure to a special situation. My impulse was to reject it. This alerted me. Together we looked at the idea more carefully and found it to be a simple and sound solution.

This leads one to wonder how many times every day executive orthodoxy excommunicates a fresh and constructive idea.

Lessons such as this have led us to adopt a policy of subjecting the management techniques we have developed to periodic rigorous criticism, because, in this fast-changing world, what is progressive today may be obsolete next week.

Consent

The best leader is the one who wins the consent of those he represents by acting in such a way that they believe he places the organization's and their best interests first. Clearly, that is his single-minded purpose. While he is not always right in his decisions, his objectives are sound. For this reason, members are more forgiving toward errors.

Rule by edict has become obsolete, and so has authority willfully imposed. Widespread, active resistance attests to that. But, as we have seen, authority there must be, to keep order in institutional houses. The difference lies in how to exercise it in a contemporary world full of questioning attitudes.

Authority should be exercised with constraint. Firm decisions have to be made. Institutional groups want their leaders to be decisive, but not arrogant. Decisiveness wins consent.

In addition, consent in its truest sense involves something more. Today, consent is won not only by virtue of the correctness of a decision, but also by the decision maker's seeking approval from those interested before, not after, the judgment is made. What we really seem to want in our institutions is Jeffersonian democracy, by which a people, enlightened by education—which must be kept free—can, under democratic and republican institutions, govern themselves better than by any other system.

Communications

Communications today often underestimate the sophistication of the publics at which they are aimed. It is the communicators, not the listeners, who are naive. Too much emphasis is placed on repetition and not enough on quality. Believability is suspect.

The Madison Avenue advertising formulas that have worked so well in the past seem often to miss the target now. Huckstering products as all-purpose curatives leaves informed receivers cold; gimmicks, except for good-humored fun poking, are equally unconvincing.

Attempts have been made to transfer product-advertising techniques to the area of public relations for projecting a sweet image of an institution and its top command. Often these attempts come through as superficial, and, therefore, unbelievable. To try and present a pale-faced, narrow-shouldered politician as a man of the soil or as a rugged outdoorsman raises considerable chortling. The defense is that the technique has worked before, so why not now? The answer is that attitudes, behavior, and levels of sophistication are different from what they used to be.

To summarize what has been said before: Attitudes and opinions need to be repeatedly and accurately plumbed to keep a sensitive gauge on the direction of wants and behavior. This can be accomplished with the aid of advanced techniques developed by behavioral scientists. Response should be based on current wants, not those that have disappeared. Behavioral scientists can also provide counsel for predicting how a particular response will be received.

Whatever the communication intends to project should be basically honest. If a product is a good one, what need is there to tout it as the greatest thing since the invention of the wheel? In fact, where a straight presentation would be accepted, such hoopla may result in more wonder than persuasion. And if the product is bad, no amount of advertising can turn a lemon into an orange. This is as true in internal communications as it is in advertising. Integrity will help to increase believability and dispel discontent.

Communications should be inclusive. Habitual executive proneness to "tell" can be reflected in such communications as the statement "This pernicious coffee habit must cease," which only forces the brew underground. Seriously, just as it applies in executive actions, so should communications not dictate—try to shove ideas and actions on others or tell them what is good for their well-being. Communications should be straightforward and carry a sincere tone of respect for the intelligence and integrity of those at whom the message is beamed, and, where practical, a constructive response ought to be encouraged. How to word these is a technical matter; the tone is the essential element.

Leadership Development

For leading in an inclusive society, more range and a different emphasis on skills are needed in our executive development processes. Much attention has been directed toward executive development in recent years, and while considerable progress has been made, the practice is still far from being as satisfactory as it should and will be.

To the present educational development process should be added skills in foreign languages for use in an international world. Skills are needed in the behavioral sciences—psychology, sociology, and economics—for increasing our ability to apply the advances in these fields to the management of others. Political science is another field from which useful knowledge can be gleaned. The intention here would be not to produce professional specialists, but to learn how to use professional skills in these fields as consultants, to help create the inclusive environment we are instinctively seeking.

The experience of upcoming leaders should be expanded outside the institution as well as internally, to provide a broader understanding of how other organizations work. Many of our current problems rise from too much institutional provincialism. When we concern ourselves with organizations beyond our own, our attitudes toward them are developed from measurement against our own institutional standards. This is a fundamental reason for the traditional suspicion between business and government. Suspicion also exists between other institutions—religious groups, political parties, geographical areas of the country, and entire nations.

Tomorrow's leaders will come to top responsibilities badly equipped, if their views are parochial and the world around them is megalopolitan. Because he lacks sufficient breadth, such a leader will not be acceptable, and will only cause discontent to rise.

Development patterns should be consciously designed to remove executives from departmental confines and place them in other functions. A few organizations do this well, but most do not, or only pay lip service to it. In the field of executive development there is still much talk and only moderate action compared to what there should be.

Executive development ought to urge participation in community and government affairs, for purposes of civic contribution as well as the development of breadth. Rising executives, in whatever field, should be encouraged to associate with their counterparts in organizations different from their own for exposure to other points of view and ways of life.

Wherever possible, development should include international experience. Without some type of overseas experience, the leader of tomorrow will be seriously handicapped. For example, Russian suspicion is to a large extent due to leadership provincialism. Leaders judge the West on hearsay, having little or no actual experience beyond the Kremlin walls. More international face-to-face engagement at all levels is paramount if we are to live peaceably together. It is helpful to read about the Chinese, Japanese, Russians, Egyptians, French, Spanish, and others, but only by sitting down with them or living among them will we develop any true understanding.

In today's technical age the speed of communications and transportation far surpasses the speed of our mutual understanding. The emphasis in leadership development has to be modified so that less attention is given to technical competence and more to the range of human affairs.

Selection of potential leaders needs to be—and is coming to be —more sophisticated and systematic. Often it has been said that a leader, because it is his nature to do so, will rise to the top naturally. This he may do, but he will arrive not so well equipped in range as he should, and both he and the institution will suffer a period of trial and error as he learns his job. Surely this is inefficient and wasteful. Leadership training should begin with the selection process, using psychological assessment to identify potential so that intelligent development planning can be made. Conscious selection and development in broadening phases for planned succession will provide the strength and quality of leadership equal to the demands of the inclusive society.

Top executives will be more planning-oriented, moving ahead on a thought-out, not an expedient, basis. More sophisticated techniques—computers and operations-research predicting on a mathematical basis—will be more commonly and effectively adapted. The plans approach will not eliminate problems, but by anticipating them and not waiting for the roof to fall in, their number will be reduced.

Present forms of organization are too stultifying, demanding a restrictive conformance that is out of place in this era. Some are so rigid that they seem to be no more than a series of interconnected cages piled in pyramid shape, with a main door that opens in the morning to receive the daily inmates and closes behind them in the late afternoon. The stifling and loss of talent is incalculable, and the organization is a wasteland. Leaders will have to establish a more open environment—one that will allow individual expression and freedom of participation.

Because training and development will be planned and experience built in deliberately, tomorrow's leadership will be ready to take over at a younger age. With youth in an open environment will come bold and imaginative innovation.

To bring all this to fruition, the first phase must begin at the top. Attitudinal habits at the command level will have to undergo changes. The patriarchal view will have to give way to a more Jeffersonian attitude, and the deliberate move to a more open organization. The old dog must either learn new tricks—many can and do—or be supplanted by someone who will.

Once the change has begun at the apex, it will follow downward throughout the rest of the organization and the inclusive environment will actively develop. But it must start at the top, because the top commands. These changes will come. They have to, if for no other reason than that they are forced into being by active dissent against an exclusive system. That is the hard way. Why wait? The most favorable time to begin is today.

The young protest about the ills of the world, but the world is not the sorry mess they believe it to be. The future holds untold adventure and the promise of fruitful progress, not only in space, but in a more productive and satisfactory life within our institutions.

While they may protest, our biggest asset for the future, as always, is the next generation. With their urge to express nonconformance, they baffle their parents, raised when conformance was the rule. But underneath this pose lies awareness of our problems, education, intelligence, and strength. Experience will hone and temper their capabilities into expert leadership skills capable of meeting the problems of the coming years.

Index

DATE DUE